EVIL *at*
LAKE SEMINOLE

The Shocking True Story
Surrounding the Disappearance
of Mike Williams

EVIL *at*
LAKE SEMINOLE

*The Shocking True Story
Surrounding the Disappearance
of Mike Williams*

STEVEN B. EPSTEIN

Black Lyon Publishing, LLC

Reviewers are saying …

"As few true crime books do today, Steve Epstein's EVIL AT LAKE SEMINOLE captures the humanity of victim Mike Williams, while laying out a solid case with journalistic acuity and grace. Epstein takes readers deeply into the facts, offering a thrilling and, at times, heartbreaking journey. All at once sympathetic and riveting. A new voice in true crime, Epstein is a must-read for fans of the genre."

—M. William Phelps, *New York Times* bestselling author of 41 books including WHERE MONSTERS HIDE, DANGEROUS GROUND, and several history titles; and the creator and executive producer of Investigation Discovery's TO CATCH A KILLER and many other television series.

Our books may be ordered through your local bookstore or by visiting the publisher:

www.BlackLyonPublishing.com

Black Lyon Publishing, LLC
PO Box 567
Baker City, OR 97814

ISBN: 978-1-934912-91-1
Library of Congress Control Number: 2020935477

Published and printed in the United States of America.

Black Lyon True Crime

More praise for this book!

"Steve Epstein's EVIL AT LAKE SEMINOLE is the unputdownable story of the investigation into Mike Williams' disappearance while he was duck hunting on Florida's 37,000-acre reservoir. I was initially frightened by the forbidding alligators and ultimately terrified by the cold-blooded human beings at the heart of the story. This is a well-reported, gripping thriller about a case that baffled a family, a community, and law enforcement for nearly 20 years."
—Rebecca Morris, New York Times bestselling true crime author of
BOY MISSING: The Search for Kyron Horman,
IF I CAN'T HAVE YOU: Susan Powell, Her Mysterious
Disappearance and the Murder of Her Children, and A KILLING IN
AMISH COUNTRY: Sex, Betrayal and a Cold-Blooded Murder

"A fascinating and riveting read. In EVIL AT LAKE SEMINOLE, Epstein takes you on an incredible excursion through the amazing developments in a 17-year quest for justice. You won't want to set it down until you reach the improbable conclusion."
—Diane Fanning, author of 26 books including
DEATH ON THE RIVER, MOMMY'S LITTLE GIRL,
and WRITTEN IN BLOOD

"Steve Epstein takes readers on an intense, harrowing journey to witness the EVIL AT LAKE SEMINOLE. Frighteningly unforgettable! A very exciting read I thoroughly enjoyed."
—Dan Zupansky, host of "True Murder: The Most Shocking
Killers"and author of TROPHY KILL: The "Shall We Dance" Murder

"Steve Epstein takes you on a wild ride as he leads you through a 17-year murder investigation that has more twists and turns than an upside down rollercoaster. In his second true crime book, Epstein once again pairs in-depth research and eloquent prose with a fascinating story that promises to keep you turning the pages until the shocking conclusion."
—Amanda Lamb, author of nine books including
LOVE LIES, EVIL NEXT DOOR, and DEADLY DOSE

"Steve Epstein lays out every relevant detail of this story, from Mike Williams' humble beginnings and how they shaped him into the man he became to the long-awaited resolution of the confounding 17-year mystery surrounding his disappearance. Epstein effectively describes what happened along the way until the truth finally boiled over, all while giving praise to the one individual who kept pursuing justice in spite of the massive toll it took on her. I was locked into the story with every flip of the page."
—Tony Holt, founder and former host of the Sun Crime State
podcast and reporter for the Arkansas Democrat-Gazette

For Benjamin, Madeline, Enzo, Tucker, and Thomas—
Dream big. Go chase. With everything you have.

Preface

I had time to kill. My 14-year-old son, Thomas, had just completed his first high school football game—an away game. It would be at least 45 minutes before his team bus would make it across town to his school, and for him to emerge from the locker room. How would I occupy my time?

By that late August evening, my first book, *Murder on Birchleaf Drive: The True Story of the Michelle Young Murder Case*, had been out less than three months. I already had several book signings under my belt—a brand new experience. I enjoyed interacting with readers and seeing their expressions as I read from the book.

At a few of those events, I was asked a question I wasn't prepared to answer: Was I working on another book? Frankly, I was elated to have published *one* book and to be talking with real people—other than my mother—who had actually read it. I wasn't quite ready to entertain the thought of writing another. Yet deep inside, I believed I could warm up to the idea *if* another story grabbed ahold of me the way the Michelle Young tragedy had.

In putting together the website for *Murder on Birchleaf Drive*, I had been surprised to learn how many different weekly podcasts focus on true crime. Dozens. I had listened to a few in the weeks before that fateful August evening—open to being inspired. But nothing remotely interested me. As I waited for Thomas following his game, I randomly selected another episode and began to listen.

As I sat in my SUV in the Broughton High School parking lot, I found myself transfixed by what I was hearing—a story completely unlike anything I had read or heard. A duck hunter had vanished without a trace, suicide note, or logical explanation. For nearly 20 years. The story was gripping—filled with mystery, intrigue, and suspense.

"Darn," I thought to myself as I detected my son in my peripheral vision slowly approaching my vehicle. I still had nearly ten minutes left in the podcast. As we drove home and made small talk—me complimenting him on his good play—my mind was elsewhere. I didn't yet know how the story ended and desperately needed to find out.

I was nearly in panic-mode when we pulled into the garage at my home—dying to learn what happened. As Thomas grabbed his backpack from the backseat, I decided to buy some time. "I'll be in in just a minute," I told him, pressing "play" on my iPhone. Finally, I learned the shocking details that would bring the story to a close.

When I awoke the next morning, I was as certain as I had ever been about anything important in my life. Another story had indeed grabbed ahold of me, one even more mesmerizing than the one I had just written about. A mere 12 hours earlier, I didn't know anything about Mike Williams and had never heard of Lake Seminole. Yet here I was now, ready to fully immerse myself once again in the dark beauty of true crime.

Within three weeks, I had completed what would ultimately become Chapter 10, deciding to write what I considered to be the most haunting chapter first. (Spoiler alert: don't even consider jumping ahead to learn that chapter's title. You're not ready.) My body was literally tingling as the final words appeared—almost magically—on my laptop screen. I shared the chapter with my wife Aletia that same evening, eager to learn whether she believed the story to be as powerful as I did. She did. There was no turning back. I was all in.

Yes, there was plenty of research still to be conducted. Thousands of pages of documents and court records to review. Dozens of interviews to undertake. Even a trip to Tallahassee, Florida to see various sites for myself and meet with people at the heart of this story. All of that would come in time. In the meantime, I was off to the races, words flowing from my brain through my fingers like water from a firehose—my laptop molding and shaping the story like a clay sculpture, day after day, week after week, month after month.

The pages that follow represent a true labor of love. A love of writing and storytelling. A love of bringing someone back to life whose family had tragically lost him far too soon. And a love of making deep connections with complete strangers—the way only an author can. It is my privilege to share this story with you. So strap on your seatbelt and prepare yourself for an intense, harrowing ride.

When you finish reading the last page—but not before—if you want to explore this case in even more depth, please visit the website I've built just for you: www.EvilatLakeSeminole. com. There you will find everything you could possibly want to know about the characters and events described in the next 350 pages. Enjoy.

Part 1
Missing

1

Duck Hunting

Lake Seminole is a 37,500-acre reservoir straddling the Florida-Georgia line just south of the southeastern corner of Alabama. It was created in the 1950s by the construction of the Jim Woodruff Lock and Dam, which intercepts the flow of the Chattahoochee River on the west, Spring Creek in the middle, and Flint River on the east. Not only does the dam fill a massive area with water, it also generates hydroelectric power for the entire region.

From just beyond the dam, the Apalachicola River curlicues its way south across the Florida Panhandle for 100 miles or so before emptying into the Gulf of Mexico at the City of Apalachicola, a charming seaside tourist spot with enchanting beaches, bay-front restaurants, and cozy inns perfect for romantic getaways.

Like the nickname adopted by nearby Florida State University, the reservoir was named after the Seminole Indian tribe. Its marshy waters stretch over miles of abandoned fields, as well as farmland, swampy floors, and forsaken fruit orchards. Surrounding the lake's 376 miles of shoreline are communities whose culture is permeated by the Deep South—lazy days, slow, southern drawls, and menus filled with biscuits and gravy, deep-fried foods, and sweet iced tea.

Since its opening to the public in 1957, Lake Seminole has

become a fishing and hunting mecca, attracting outdoorsmen by the droves. World-renowned among anglers for largemouth bass fishing in the spring and summer, the lake is equally popular for duck and goose hunting during late autumn and winter. Waterfowl are particularly attracted to the marshy coves near the shoreline, where hunters have been floating out decoys and camouflaging themselves in duck blinds for decades.

Jerry Michael Williams, a 31-year-old real estate appraiser from Tallahassee, was an avid outdoorsman, seizing every opportunity his jam-packed schedule permitted to go deep-sea fishing or duck hunting. He found hiding in a duck blind just before sunrise soothing to his soul—a pleasant diversion from his long hours at work. Lake Seminole was one of his favorite places to hunt. He had been making the hour-long pilgrimage to its southwestern shore—just north of Sneads, Florida—since he was a teenager, proudly bagging hundreds of ducks since his first visit.

It was well before dawn when Mike left home on Saturday, December 16, 2000, his small hunting boat—filled with duck-hunting supplies and gear—fastened to the trailer.

That late fall day just happened to be the eve of his sixth wedding anniversary. He and his wife Denise had been sweethearts at Tallahassee's North Florida Christian School since their freshman year. Now more than 15 years later, they were the proud parents of a 19-month-old daughter named Anslee. Both mother and daughter were fast asleep as Mike began his journey northwest toward Sneads.

He was expected home around noon. When he hadn't returned by 2:00 p.m., Denise called her father Warren Merrell, who lived nearby with her mom. She explained that she and Mike had plans to leave early that afternoon for the Gibson Inn at Apalachicola Bay for their anniversary celebration. Mike had arranged for Denise's sister Deanna to care for Anslee during their overnight trip. As the drive to the seaside hotel would take nearly two hours, their dinner reservations were already in jeopardy.

Denise told her dad Mike had gone to the lake by himself, which was a little unusual, as he typically hunted with a friend. She told him she had called Mike's cell phone several times, to no avail, and didn't understand why he hadn't gotten home yet or at least called—especially with their out-of-town anniversary celebration mapped out so meticulously.

"Something doesn't seem right," she said. She asked her father if he wouldn't mind heading to the lake to investigate.

Denise also called Damon Jasper, a younger friend of Mike's, who had recently graduated from Florida State. Jasper had gone duck hunting with her husband at Lake Seminole just the prior weekend. He detected the anxiety in Denise's voice as she told him Mike should have already been home to get ready for their trip.

Within 30 minutes, Denise's dad and Jasper were at Mike and Denise's home, trying their best to assure her everything would be okay. They speculated that Mike's boat had probably broken down somewhere on the lake—preventing him from making it back to shore. Recognizing they were in a race against darkness, they hopped in Warren's car and began their journey.

It was about 3:30 p.m. Eastern Time—2:30 p.m. in Sneads—as the pair arrived in the small town near the lake's southwestern corner. Warren and Jasper drove along River Road at the edge of the hunting and fishing oasis. They first checked out the concrete boat ramps closest to where Jasper and Mike had been the weekend before, but didn't see his truck anywhere. After widening their search, they finally spotted Mike's green and tan 1994 Ford Bronco tucked away in a grassy area near a dirt ramp just off the road. The boat trailer hitched to the back was empty.

Neither Mike nor his boat was anywhere in sight. Something was definitely wrong.

At 3:00 p.m. Central Time, Warren called the dispatch center for the Florida Fish and Wildlife Conservation Commission, or FWC, the agency charged with maintaining law and order at the lake. He told the dispatchers Mike had left Tallahassee early that morning to go duck hunting—alone—and was now missing.

FWC officers showed up within ten minutes and met with

Warren and Jasper at a nearby check station. Mike was an avid duck hunter who had been coming to Lake Seminole for about 15 years, they said, and was hunting by himself that morning when he apparently vanished. They told the officers where they found his truck and expressed their concern he might be in trouble in his boat, still on the lake.

Based on the location of his truck, the officers surmised that Mike probably launched his boat from the dirt ramp just a few yards from his parking spot.

With sunset now only a few hours away, the officers quickly initiated what ultimately would evolve into a massive, multi-agency search-and-rescue operation over ten acres.

The cove where searchers concentrated their efforts was called Stump Field by the locals, a fitting nickname for a stretch of water where hundreds of dead trees and stumps poked through the surface or lurked menacingly just below. The submerged tree stumps created invisible hazards that often tormented even skilled boaters.

Directly across the shoreline from where Mike's Bronco was found—to the east—was a grassy, weed-filled island. About 165 yards of water separated the island from the shoreline where Mike's truck was parked. Stump Field ended about a half mile south of the dirt ramp, where a patch of land filled with trees jutted into the water.

The lakebed at Stump Field was covered in hydrilla—rapidly growing, dense green plants whose stems could extend as long as 25 feet. The hydrilla formed a thick carpet just below the water's surface, extending all the way down to the lakebed. The plants were capable of entangling living and inanimate objects in their pesky grasp and lengthy reach, making swimming in the area a virtual impossibility.

Giant green lily pads blanketed the water's surface toward the shoreline, creating visual appeal and charm. The lush vegetation attracted a wide variety of aquatic creatures, fish and fowl alike. The large bounty of creatures, not surprisingly, attracted predators apart from hunters like Mike. In particular, alligators. During the summer and fall, the lakebed and shores at Stump Field were filled with them.

••••

Nick Williams, Mike's older brother, spent nearly every Saturday with their mom, often taking her around town on her errands. December 16, 2000, was no exception. That morning, they got lost in some last-minute Christmas shopping—Cheryl Williams was eager to find just a few more presents for her only grandchild.

At one store, she eyed a shiny red toy wagon she believed Anslee would enjoy pulling behind her. Cheryl borrowed Nick's cell phone to check with Denise just to make sure her daughter-in-law would approve. The wagon sounded like a good gift, Denise assured her mother-in-law. Cheryl sought out Mike's thoughts too, but Denise reminded her that he had gone hunting at Lake Seminole that morning. He was due back about noon, she said.

When they got back to her home following lunch and a quick stop at the grocery store, Cheryl told Nick she was heading out for an afternoon stroll, a routine she began shortly after her husband Jerry passed away two years before. She walked down the hill about two miles to Lake Iamonia—one of the places Mike had learned to hunt as a youngster—then circled back toward home.

When she walked through the door at about 3:00 p.m., Nick was extremely distraught, tears rolling down his cheeks.

"What's wrong?" his mother asked, puzzled by his change in demeanor.

"Denise just called," he told her. "Mike's missing."

"What do you mean he's missing?" she asked quizzically.

Denise had told him, Nick explained, that Mike hadn't returned home from his hunting trip at Lake Seminole. She was so worried, he said, she called her father, who was already on his way to the lake to investigate. Nick decided to jump in his car and head there himself.

••••

As the search-and-rescue operation began, the FWC officers on site adopted a seemingly reasonable working hypothesis: Mike's boat had likely collided with an underwater stump he couldn't see in the pre-dawn hours and the jostling of the boat caused him to fall overboard—a fairly common occurrence at Stump Field. But that didn't explain why the missing duck hunter was unable to climb back into his boat or swim to safety along the shoreline.

Officers and other searchers quickly put boats on the water and shouted out for the missing hunter, hoping to hear or see something. Anything. Not only was night approaching, bad weather was on the way, too.

By 4:45 p.m., a torrential rainstorm at the leading edge of a cold front had blown in, making it impossible to continue the search. Powerful winds gusted more than 50 miles per hour. A helicopter that had been readied to search from the sky was called off due to the weather flareup. Making matters worse, a tornado watch had been issued lasting several hours—a portent of the three tornadoes that actually touched down not far from Stump Field.

The squall line didn't clear until nearly 9:00 p.m., when the search finally resumed. Darkness was now the enemy, as was the cold weather blown in by the storm. The air temperature at the southern tip of Lake Seminole had fallen into the 30s and water temperatures were down in the 50s.

Nonetheless, an FWC helicopter was able to rise at long last into the pitch-black sky, shining a spotlight onto the waters and banks of Stump Field as a slew of Fish and Wildlife officers, Jackson County Sheriff's deputies, and volunteers searched for Mike. A thermal-imaging device was on board the helicopter, capable of detecting heat emitted by human bodies on the ground or in the water.

The radar did home in on the searchers, but revealed no sign of Mike. By then, several of his friends and relatives had joined the search—including Mike's brother, Nick. Denise stayed at home with Anslee, receiving reports from her father every so often.

More people arrived as the distressing news spread, including Mike's best friend since the ninth grade, Brian Winchester, and his father Marcus—both of whom were financial planners and life insurance agents. Though the official search was suspended at midnight until daybreak, Brian and his dad remained in their boat, trolling and scanning the water into the early morning hours, guided by the headlights on their foreheads.

At about 2:30 a.m., Marcus spotted something against the tall reeds along the western shoreline, no more than 75 yards south of the dirt ramp near Mike's Bronco. As the father and son edged closer, the first significant question about Mike's disappearance had its answer. They spotted his 13-foot Gheenoe—a canoe-shaped motorboat—sitting upright, behind some stumps protruding above the water. Yet no sign of Mike. Their calls for him were met with eerie silence.

When the FWC morning crew arrived a few hours later, Marcus and Brian led Officer David Arnette to the boat. The wildlife officer had to fish through two inches of rainwater pooled inside to inventory its contents: 39 decoys, an anchor, two life jackets, a paddle, an aluminum push pole, a plastic ammunition box, and a 12-gauge, three-inch Beretta over-under shotgun, still zipped up in its case, lying next to the driver's seat.

The throttle on the five-horsepower Go Devil motor was flipped to the "on" position—nearly full throttle. The fuel tank was filled almost to capacity, a sign the boat couldn't have been in the water long before whatever unfortunate mishap took place.

Oddly, the helicopter pilot actually spotted Mike's boat the night before, but assumed—incorrectly—it was one of the search boats and brought it to no one's attention.

Brian told Officer Arnette that he and Mike had gone duck hunting together on numerous occasions, and Mike would typically wear chest-high waders—long, loose-fitting rubber boots that joined together above the waist and were held up by straps around the shoulders, similar in appearance to bib overalls. Hunters and fishermen like them wore waders to keep dry while standing in streams and shallow marshes.

Mike typically sat or squatted in the boat while firing his shotgun, Brian added, and occasionally stood to get off a good shot.

Damon Jasper told Arnette that he and Mike had been duck hunting at Lake Seminole the prior weekend—using Mike's boat—and confirmed Mike had stood in the boat while firing his gun.

These accounts supported the working theory Mike's boat had hit a stump that morning—rocking it while Mike was standing—causing him to fall overboard. What was unknown, however, was whether he had been wearing his waders.

No waders turned up after a thorough search of Mike's Bronco—just Mike's wallet and driver's license. Putting the puzzle pieces together, if what Brian had said about his friend typically wearing his waders was true, and Mike had been jostled in the darkness by an underwater stump and fallen overboard, the waders would have quickly filled with water—like large buckets—pulling him underneath the surface before he had a chance to extract his legs and swim to safety.

"We're afraid he's probably down there wrapped in hydrilla, in heavy winter clothing," lamented a wildlife officer in an interview published by the *Floridian*, the local Jackson County newspaper. "The hydrilla no doubt doubled his dilemma. As it's wrapping around you, there's a panic factor and if you swallow a little bit of water, that makes it worse. The water temperature is pretty cold, so there's a physical shock to the system as well."

The collective hope of those gathered on and by the lake that Mike would be found alive began fading rapidly. Though their efforts were publicly billed as a search-and-rescue operation, most everyone at the lakefront had already begun to grapple with the bitter, morbid reality: if they were to somehow find Mike, the likelihood of him still being alive was somewhere between slim and none.

••••

Sunday, December 17, 2000, was Mike Williams' sixth wedding anniversary. But rather than spending the day celebrating with his wife as planned, the successful real-estate appraiser and devoted father was missing, his disappearance utterly confounding.

Throughout the day, a trickle of friends, family members, coworkers, former classmates, and fellow church parishioners would grow into a small army dedicated to finding even the smallest clue that could explain what might have happened. As Sunday stretched into Monday, Tuesday, and then Wednesday, both the size of the army, and the level of angst and trepidation among its members, mounted steadily. No one was ready to accept the reality that Mike was gone forever.

One clue that turned up the first morning was a neoprene hunting sock discovered on the lake's surface not far from the dirt landing near Mike's truck. A wildlife officer called Cheryl Williams at home to find out what kind of socks Mike wore with his hunting boots. Though Mike's mom told him she wasn't sure because it had been so long since her son had lived at home, she was certain he would have been wearing the latest and greatest gear to keep his feet warm. If that was neoprene, she said, then that made perfect sense.

••••

The search was made significantly more difficult by the frigid temperatures—at least by Florida standards. During the two weeks after Mike's disappearance, daytime averages were around 55 degrees with overnight lows below freezing—tumbling to a bone-chilling 19 degrees the morning of December 20. Water temperatures descended into the mid-40s.

It got so cold that FWC officers had to begin several mornings chopping through ice some 20 feet out into the lake just to get their boats launched. Divers were unable to stay beneath the surface for long out of fear they would develop hypothermia.

Near the FWC tent that had become the makeshift headquarters for the massive operation, a fire blazed from a 55-gallon drum. It became the place where shivering searchers would congregate after spending time out on the water. Volunteers saw to it that all those laboring tirelessly to find Mike had proper sustenance, bringing in a steady stream of food each day for lunch and dinner.

As time wore on, wildlife officers and sheriff's deputies eventually lined off a grid pattern throughout Stump Field, fastening white ropes to the dead trees and stumps poking through the surface. A half dozen boats searched the water, each concentrating on a single square at a time. From each boat, searchers probed the lakebed every few inches with 14-16-foot-long PVC poles—a process the officers referred to as "poling."

Some of the poles had drag hooks attached so searchers could try to grab at anything ensnared in the hydrilla and pull it to the surface. Others had cameras hooked on, opening a window to the soda cans, fishhooks, and other small items stuck in the hydrilla and resting on the lake bottom. But despite the meticulous search, still no sign of Mike emerged.

One theory was that Mike's body hadn't yet surfaced because it was tangled up within some hydrilla. Polers were told to pay attention to anything they came across that felt like a spongy mass—which might be a portion of Mike's dead body. Anytime an officer or volunteer felt something questionable, the spot was marked for further investigation by underwater divers.

Meanwhile, well-trained search-and-rescue cadaver dogs patrolled the shoreline, hunting for any scent that might lead to clues of Mike's whereabouts. Other dogs accompanied officers in boats, alerting several different times near a stump not far from the western shoreline. Yet the lakebed was clearly visible in the shallow water there—and again, no sign of Mike.

The search was hampered by the unwieldy conditions within the lake. The hydrilla was so thick and tangled it made it nearly impossible for divers to see much of anything, even with the aid of underwater cameras. Enhanced-depth sonar recorders called bottom finders didn't prove any more helpful.

Worse still, searchers were knocked overboard several times by low branches hanging from trees in the middle of the lake. Others were tossed into the chilly water from the lurch of their hulls bumping into submerged stumps—further fueling the conjecture that the same thing had happened to Mike.

What searchers had no trouble finding, though, were alligators. They spotted eight the very first night and many others as the hunt for Mike wore on—particularly from the elevated perch of the helicopter.

The gators, some as long as 12 feet, lurked in the hydrilla and were seen sunbathing along the shoreline. Their nests littered the small island just to the east of where Mike's boat was found. One of the reports describing the search efforts noted personnel were "routinely entertained at night by the sounds and eyes of numerous alligators inhabiting the area."

••••

The afternoon of December 18 offered a brief glimmer of hope. A volunteer poked something with his PVC pole that seemed unusual. But when a diver went down to get a better look, the suspicious object turned out to be nothing more than a spongy, dense patch of hydrilla. It was so cold that afternoon—30 degrees with a wind chill of about 20—the diver's underwater breathing apparatus froze just as he resurfaced.

Excitement swelled yet again on December 19, when one of the bottom finders signaled an unusually dense object on the lake bottom. Divers investigated the spot the following day. But spirits were dashed again when they resurfaced. The suspicious object was nothing more than a thick log.

On the morning of December 30, another ray of hope emerged. A camouflage-patterned bucket hat seemingly appeared out of nowhere—hung up in some hydrilla near the island across the shoreline from where Mike's truck was found. FWC Officer Alton Ranew plucked it out of the water—shocked it hadn't been detected before then—and brought it to the FWC tent for closer inspection.

The hat appeared almost new—it wasn't slimy or covered

in sediment from the lake—nothing at all to suggest it had been in the water for two weeks. Brian Winchester showed up at the tent later that morning and told Ranew the hat looked very familiar.

The next day, Brian was back in the tent with a framed 5x7 photo to show Ranew. In the picture, Mike appeared to be wearing what the very same hat. Brian recounted how Mike had bought the hat over the Thanksgiving weekend when the two had gone to Arkansas together on a hunting trip.

Thus, by year-end, searchers had recovered Mike's vehicle, boat trailer, Gheenoe motorboat, duck-hunting supplies, a shotgun, and now Mike's bucket hat. But still, they were no closer to solving the nettlesome mystery of what had happened to Mike.

On January 8, investigators discovered three different pieces of soft tissue at the end of a concrete culvert a quarter mile north of the dirt ramp. They wondered whether the remains were Mike's. But when the Medical Examiner's Office took a closer look, it was determined that the small pieces of flesh more likely belonged to a deer, pig, or large dog.

••••

Fish and Wildlife officers felt certain that Mike's body, once it filled with gases as it decomposed, would eventually float to the surface—as had occurred with each of the 80 people who had drowned at Lake Seminole prior to December 2000. They assured Mike's family and friends his body would inevitably be recovered. But as the days turned into weeks, no body surfaced.

Mike's best friend Brian made the trek to Lake Seminole nearly every day, becoming more and more distraught as time marched on. Yet each time searchers found a promising clue, he froze up, unable to deal with the prospect of having to see Mike's body being pulled out of the water. On more than one occasion, he asked Mike's coworker Brett Ketcham to drive him down the road for a cup of coffee while a new discovery was explored. "I just don't want to be here when they find

Mike," he explained. Brian was so gripped by emotion he wept openly, leading Ketcham—who barely knew him—to embrace him for comfort.

Though Denise herself never made the hour-long journey to Lake Seminole to join in the search, her father Warren was there every day, sunup to sundown, as determined to find Mike as anyone. Warren provided his daughter daily briefings on the frenetic activity at the lake. He had posters made with Mike's picture—the word "missing" scrawled across the top—which were fastened to trees and telephone poles for miles along the shoreline and throughout Sneads, where many hunters and fisherman lived or stopped for bites to eat on their way to and from the lake. Yet Warren's weeks-long devotion to finding Mike didn't lead to a single promising clue.

••••

By late January, Mike's mother Cheryl had grown so frustrated by the lack of answers from the FWC, she retained a private search firm from Alabama named Montgomery County Search and Rescue Inc., or MCSAR for short.

On January 26, MCSAR deployed a sophisticated K-9 unit and underwater dive team. The company had three well-trained German Shepherd cadaver dogs thoroughly search the area from late January through February 11. The dogs alerted in several, disparate locations, leading the head of the team to conclude "that the alerts and indications of my dogs were consistent with human remains."

MCSAR's dive team leader reached an even more blood-curdling conclusion, hypothesizing that, based on the abundant hydrilla in the search area—and the presence of numerous alligators—"the alligators have dismembered and stored [Mike's] remains in a location that we would not be able to find. Possibly a den or maybe under a log near the den." That, he believed, explained why the cadaver dogs had alerted, even though no human remains had been found.

Yet in the FWC's February 23, 2001 report, the agency stated that after 735 hours of searching—400 by boat, 285 by land,

and 50 by air from December 16 through February 10—it was unable to determine what had happened to Mike. And those figures didn't include the thousands of hours contributed by volunteer searchers.

In the last paragraph of its report, the FWC stated: "Nothing in [the] investigative search and rescue efforts has produced any definitive evidence of a boating accident or a fatality as of this date. Mr. Williams is still missing."

••••

On February 11, 2001, hundreds of Mike's friends, family members, coworkers, fellow church parishioners—as well as officers and deputies who had searched so tirelessly for nearly two months in inhospitable conditions—gathered at Thomasville Road Baptist Church in Tallahassee for a memorial service arranged by Denise's family. A large swath of Mike's high school graduating class was there, including Brian Winchester.

As a montage of images of Mike flashed across a large screen, showing the progression of his life from childhood to marriage and fatherhood, even the burly wildlife officers—most of whom had never met him—began to weep. A profound sense of anguish and sadness filled the sanctuary: for a life cut short in its prime, a daughter left to grow up without the love and guidance of her father, and a wife suddenly widowed at age 30.

Denise was an emotional wreck. When the service ended, she had to be helped out of the church, unable to put one foot in front of the other without assistance.

Even though the event wasn't officially advertised as a funeral, very few in attendance had any delusions Mike would someday turn up alive. By then, the theory that he had accidentally fallen overboard, drowned in his waders, and been picked apart and stored in a hidden lair by alligators, seemed as likely as any.

2

Jerry Michael Williams

Despite having served as the capital of the State of Florida since territorial days—even before Florida achieved statehood in 1845—the City of Tallahassee hasn't evolved into a major metropolis like several of its Sunshine State counterparts, most notably Miami, Tampa, Orlando, and Jacksonville, all of which boast professional sports franchises and major industries. The city's tallest building—the State Capitol—is a most unattractive, white 25-story concrete structure completed in 1977. The downtown cityscape hardly qualifies as a skyline.

Located at the eastern edge of Florida's Panhandle, Tallahassee is roughly centered between the Georgia state line to the north and Gulf of Mexico to the south, about 30 minutes by car in either direction. As of the 2000 census, the city had about 150,000 residents, with a diverse population only about 60 percent white.

Apart from the ubiquity of state government buildings and agencies, the most prominent institution that calls Tallahassee home is Florida State University, widely regarded as among the nation's best public schools. Not only does Florida State occupy more land than any other enterprise in the city—sprawling across more than 1,600 acres—it is also its second largest employer, behind only the State of Florida.

Tallahassee has long been known as a high-crime city. Indeed, the crime rate in Leon County, to which Tallahassee serves as the county seat, has consistently been among the highest in all of Florida, often topping the list. The city's public schools have a less-than-stellar reputation as well, driving a significant percentage of households to send their children to private schools—even those of fairly modest means. Many lower-income families dissatisfied with their public school options sacrifice other modern conveniences to free up enough cash to afford a private education for their sons and daughters.

Jerry and Cheryl Williams made precisely that choice when they purchased a 2.3-acre lot on Jeffrey Road in 1973 in the small town of Bradfordville, just beyond the northern edge of the city, about 12 miles from the Georgia border. To Cheryl, it was more important for her two boys—William Nick Williams, born November 2, 1966, and Jerry Michael Williams, born October 16, 1969—to receive a solid education than to live in a large house with fancy fixtures and furnishings. She considered it equally important to have a large, wooded yard for Nick and Mike to play in and explore. So rather than building a traditional home on their Jeffrey Road lot, she and her husband decided to purchase a doublewide house trailer and raise their boys there.

The mobile home also served as headquarters for Cheryl's business—an in-home daycare and after-school program for area families. She had started looking after neighborhood kids when Nick was only 18 months old. On any given day, a half dozen to a dozen babies, toddlers, and preschoolers were dropped off early in the morning to spend their day in her care—with elementary school kids joining the crowd in the afternoons and for the summer. As the children grew up, they formed attachments to "Ms. Cheryl" that long outlived their time in her care. Many of her "kids" continued to visit her during their high school and college years—some well beyond.

Jerry, known by family and friends as J.J.—short for Jerry Jerome—was a bus driver for Greyhound. During Mike's early years, his dad was often sent on routes far and wide, sometimes two to three weeks at a time. Later on he secured a daily route to his hometown of Dothan, Alabama, which departed Tallahassee in the late afternoon and returned home about 2:00

a.m. Between J.J. and Cheryl, their income was barely enough to send the boys to North Florida Christian School, or NFC, some ten miles to the south.

NFC—originally known as Tallahassee Christian School—was founded in 1966 by a Baptist pastor to provide a refuge to white parents seeking to evade orders to integrate Leon County's public schools. At the time, it was known as a "segregation academy," one of many private schools that had sprung up across the South in the wake of the Supreme Court's landmark *Brown v. Board of Education* decision declaring segregated public schools unconstitutional.

The NFC campus on Meridian Road housed an elementary school, middle school, and high school. Though it ultimately accepted students of all races, when Mike Williams enrolled in kindergarten in 1975, the student population was entirely Caucasian. When he graduated high school 13 years later, only one of his classmates was African-American.

Though religion—of the Baptist variety—was an important part of NFC's mission and curriculum, Cheryl and J.J.'s decision to send their boys there had nothing to do with its spiritual emphasis. They were certainly strong believers in God and the notion that God had a plan for them. But they didn't regularly attend church or participate in organized religion. They sent their kids to NFC solely because of its excellent academic reputation—and because it was the best they could afford.

••••

As a young boy, Mike had blue eyes and blonde hair, just like his mom, who nearly every day gathered hers into girlish pigtails—a trademark she refused to abandon through the decades, even as her hair gradually turned from blonde to gray. For his part, Mike's hair had darkened to brown by the time he began middle school.

In his early years, Mike was an "accident going somewhere to happen," Cheryl would tell her friends, always in a hurry, trying to do four to five things at once. By age six, he had learned to hunt with a bow and arrow in their densely wooded backyard and enjoyed shooting at creatures of all kinds. But he also was afraid of the dark—and wouldn't sleep alone until age 13.

Mike loved animals and begged his mom and dad for a horse when he was in elementary school. Cheryl was able to convince him that such a large animal wasn't the best fit for their family, but was willing, she told him, to entertain the thought of another pet. Since they already had two cats—JoJo and Penny—they settled on a dog, a black Lab named Ginger, whom Mike adored.

One of the games Mike loved to play with his dog was "take my hat." Ginger would run after him, knock him to the ground, and grab at his hat with her chompers until she wrangled it off. Apparently, the Lab didn't realize this was just a game. Whenever friends or relatives showed up in the backyard wearing hats, she would do precisely the same thing to them. It happened so often that Cheryl and J.J. had to warn backyard guests to remove caps before stepping foot into Ginger's domain.

••••

Though Jerry Williams wasn't home much during Mike's formative years, he was a quiet force in his sons' lives nonetheless, earning their respect with very few words. He instilled in them two critical life's lessons: First, he made clear that he didn't like a liar. Honesty, he would tell them, was a true mark of character. Second, he expected them to work and pull their own weight—without relying on others to do for them. Mike took both lessons to heart and tried to live up to them throughout his life.

J.J. had promised his boys he would build them a tree-house on their new property. Though it took him more than a year to assemble it—in part because he had a bad fall during the construction, injuring his back—the outdoor hideaway was a masterpiece, standing 25-30 feet above ground, replete with a rope ladder and a trap door. Not only did Mike and Nick regularly congregate there, so too did the older children for whom Cheryl cared during the workweek.

A tire swing hung from a large oak near the treehouse and took the boys and Cheryl's kids back and forth over Ginger's dog pen like a pendulum. When one of Cheryl's kids had a shoe fall off right into the pen, Ginger devoured it as if it had been dropped into her pen solely for her enjoyment.

J.J. and Cheryl eventually scraped together enough money to build an in-ground swimming pool. They put the finishing touches on it in November 1980, just after Mike turned 11. The chill in the air that late fall day didn't deter Mike from taking the inaugural plunge off the diving board—throwing himself into nearly ten feet of freezing water with reckless abandon.

"No, Mama, the water's not cold," he said, teeth chattering, stretching his dad's first maxim just a bit. By the following summer, he and his older brother were swimming and playing in the pool constantly. Between the pool, the treehouse, and dozens of acres of woods behind their home, J.J. and Cheryl had created an expansive outdoor wonderland that would fill their sons' time with adventure and fun throughout their childhood.

••••

Because many of the children for whom Cheryl cared were around Mike's age, he quickly formed friendships with several. He would usually arrive home from NFC before the neighborhood public school kids, sometimes setting up shop in the branches of a tall tree in the front yard waiting for the others to arrive. Ever the prankster, Mike would conceal himself in the foliage while surreptitiously dropping items in front of the other kids as they approached the front door—causing quite the fright for them, and abundant amusement for himself.

Mike formed an especially close friendship with two public school boys—Jason Fykes and Cliff Fitzgerald. The "Three

Musketeers," as they called themselves, would venture off into the woods for hours with bows and arrows, BB guns, or their bikes and fishing poles. Sometimes they even made the two-mile trek down to Lake Iamonia to fish. The trio played war in the woods with other children in Cheryl's care, building forts and having a truly grand time. Being kids, they sometimes pushed a bit beyond Cheryl's strict boundaries, ultimately suffering her consequences.

Mike's mom put the Three Musketeers to work during the summer when her next-door neighbors would leave for weeks at a time. Instead of doing all the chores herself, she got the boys to help feed their dozens of chickens, collect the hens' eggs, and harvest peas and squash from the extensive backyard garden.

They had their chores, for sure. But Cheryl also gave them ample time to play in the woods and at the lake, to huddle in the tree house, frolic in the pool, or play football games in the front yard. Summer for the boisterous boys would fly by in the blink of an eye.

••••

From an early age, Mike expressed an interest in hunting—even though neither his dad nor his brother hunted. Cheryl asked Howard Drew, a federal correctional officer whose daughter Rachel was in her daycare, to teach Mike the basics.

Drew, or "Mr. Howard" as Mike called him, first took Mike to a hunter's safety course when he was 15. J.J. joined them too, witnessing his son pass with flying colors. After that, Drew started taking his eager pupil on actual hunting trips.

Mike found hunting a bit challenging at first. Once while hunting deer with Drew, he climbed a sycamore tree with his shotgun in tow. When he eyed a buck grazing nearby, he shook so badly the tree's spiky seed balls began falling to the ground. The buck became so startled it bolted before Mike could fire a single shot. Yet despite his initial display of nerves, Drew found Mike to be a good student and easy learner who quickly picked up both the science and art of hunting.

Drew bemoaned years later that he "made the mistake" of taking Mike duck hunting, "and he just went crazy. I told him duck hunters weren't very sane because they always went out in freezing cold weather … and sat in a boat. At least deer hunting, you could sit in a stand." He was hoping Mike would loathe the experience. But precisely the opposite happened: Mike fell in love with duck hunting, which quickly became not just his favorite hobby, but his passion.

••••

Mike was very social, quite gregarious, and easily made friends at NFC. Though he was smart, he enjoyed the outdoors a bit too much for his own good, often letting his studies slide. That prevented him from being a straight-A student. He made as many Bs and Cs as As.

By the eighth grade, he had become good friends with a girl named Denise Pate, who lived across the street with her parents. Her grandparents actually lived next door to Mike and his family. Unlike the Williams boys, Denise went to public school. Though they ran in different circles, she and Mike really hit it off. Mike would find himself at Denise's house nearly every afternoon, listening to country music, talking about school, and occasionally even doing a little homework.

Before long, their friendship had blossomed into a full-blown eighth-grade romance. They "dated" for about nine months. But another woman eventually came between them—Mike's mother, who did little to hide her disapproval. She preferred her son to date private-school girls, concluding that public-school girls weren't good enough for her child.

Recognizing she was driving a wedge between Mike and his mom, Denise decided to pull the plug on their romance and go back to simply being Mike's friend. Fully aware of her reason for ending their relationship, Mike, an eternal optimist, told her, "Don't worry, I promise one day my mama is going to love you."

Denise quickly moved on to another boyfriend and Mike

to a girl named Kathy Aldredge, who had attended NFC with him since the fifth grade. Her parents owned a printing business in town named the Copy Shop. Unlike Denise, Kathy, a private-school girl, earned Cheryl's seal of approval. But Mike continued to hang out with his old flame after school, despite their new romances.

Some four months after their teenage breakup, Mike arrived at Denise's house one day finding her in tears. Her boyfriend had just broken up with her, she told him, giant teardrops rolling down her youthful cheeks. Mike tried his best to console her.

The next day, Denise was called into the central office at her school. The ladies who greeted her asked if it was her birthday. Puzzled, Denise looked over to a table, spotting a dozen long-stemmed, red roses towering over a vase.

She pulled the card from the envelope nestled in the arrangement, instantly recognizing the handwriting. The text included the lyrics to the song, *I Guess It Never Hurts to Hurt Sometimes* by the Oak Ridge Boys—one of her and Mike's favorites while they were dating. The card was signed, "Love you always, Mike."

About an hour after she got home from school that day, Mike came running down the street, screaming, "Did you get them? Did you get them?"

"Where in the world did you get the money to buy them?" Denise asked. Mike told her not to worry, that the money hadn't come from his mom, but rather from his own savings.

Long after her own marriage to her high school sweetheart, Mike's incredibly thoughtful gesture was still burned in Denise's memory. As she recalled, "He was one of the most genuine, nicest people that I have ever met."

••••

Toward the end of his freshman year of high school, Mike fell head over heels again. For yet another Denise. Denise Merrell, a whip-smart, pencil-thin, blonde-haired girl, first entered NFC as a ninth-grader following her own private-school journey through Holy Comforter Episcopal School. She was the second of four girls—the four "Ds: Deanna, Denise, Deborah, and Darla," all two years apart in school. They lived in a modest home about two miles from the State Capitol.

Denise's father, Warren, was an engineer for the Florida Department of Transportation. Her mom, Johnnie, had her hands full raising four girls, running the house like an Army drill sergeant. Warren pretty much left it to his wife be the chief disciplinarian and scheduler, also ceding to her the task of getting the girls to and from school and their activities. For a few extra bucks, Johnnie even shuttled a few neighborhood kids to school, requiring them to stand outside—even in the bitter cold—until she and the girls emerged through the side door each morning.

Like Mike's family, the Merrells also were of modest means—with two more mouths to feed than the Williamses. Yet they, too, scraped together the necessary funds to send their girls to private school, with all four transferring to NFC in 1984.

To Johnnie and Warren, outward appearances mattered. A lot. Consequently, when the Merrell girls left for school each morning, they were immaculately dressed and well groomed. There was no other option.

They also were very religious, attending services at Parkway Baptist Church, where Warren served as a deacon. They attended church twice on Sundays and on Wednesday evenings as well. It wasn't unusual for all six members of the family to linger in the narthex until the very last moment before the start of the main Sunday service, the family then strolling down the aisle together to their customary spot in the front pew—directly in front of the minister. They considered themselves a righteous, upstanding family, and wanted others to draw the same conclusion.

Denise would later confide in Cheryl she knew Mike was the one for her the first time her eyes gazed upon him. She and Mike dated steadily throughout high school. Mike's new gal was a leader in the Civinettes service club—supplying food to the needy and visiting nursing homes—was on the cheerleading team and, in her senior year, served as student council secretary and was a finalist for homecoming queen. Not surprisingly, she was voted by her classmates as "best dressed."

Denise's choice of clothes inspired Mike's own sense of fashion. He began pitching fits when Cheryl would buy him clothes from Sears or Kmart—insisting he wouldn't wear them. He would tell Cheryl he only wanted to wear Polo shirts and other brand-named clothing, doing his level best to emulate the characters on *Miami Vice*. By the time he graduated high school, Mike easily could have competed for "best dressed" himself.

Cheryl's first impression of Denise Merrell was that she was "beautiful, friendly, and crazy about Mike." She believed her son's new girlfriend came from a nice family and soon loved Denise as the daughter she never had. Unlike Denise Pate who lived across the street, Denise Merrell, Cheryl decided, *was* good enough for her son.

Cheryl was so keen on her son's new girlfriend, she bought her a beautiful bouquet of flowers for her birthday that March, the start of a tradition that would continue from Denise's teens until her early thirties.

The new gal in Mike's life would sometimes remark to Cheryl how much she enjoyed coming over to her home, especially because the Williams family kept Doritos in the cupboard. Denise confided in her that her family, trying to scrimp and save every way they could, would only spring for store-brand products.

For his part, during his afternoon visits with Denise Pate, Mike would mention how crazy he was about the new Denise in his life, and all the things *he* would do for *her*. His former gal would quiz him, asking what nice things his new girlfriend would do *for him* in return—questions Mike had difficulty answering and would often deflect. The old Denise didn't approve of the new Denise. As a result, the friendship between Mike and his first love began to wane.

••••

Active in student politics throughout high school, Mike served ably as student council president of his 70-member senior class, was president of the Key Club, and was voted "best personality." His classmates considered him a great leader.

He also was a standout athlete for the NFC Eagles, playing cornerback for the football team—Denise cheering him on from the sidelines—though almost losing his eligibility when he earned a D in one of his courses. During the spring, he ran track and field, a member of both the 440-yard and mile relay teams.

Though Mike dreamed of playing college football, by his senior year he was forced to confront the reality that his 5'10," 165-pound frame disqualified him from serious consideration. He blamed his mom—all of 5'2"—for his diminutive stature, telling her, "Mama, it's your fault I can't play college football." Had his height come from his dad, he might have had a fighting chance. Jerry Williams stood an impressive 6'2."

In addition to juggling sports and extracurricular activities—not to mention his courtship of Denise—Mike also worked several jobs, as he knew he would need to pay his own way through college. He worked in the evenings following football and track practices and on weekends. His jobs included shelving cans at the Food Lion, rolling coins at the bank, working in a Circle K convenience store, and roofing houses during the summer.

••••

Someone else who came into Mike's life during the ninth grade was Brian Winchester. Like Denise, Brian had attended private school at Holy Comforter before transitioning to NFC for high school. He and Denise had been friends during middle school and had actually known each other since attending preschool together at Parkway Baptist Church—first meeting at the tender age of three.

Like Mike, Brian lived in Bradfordville. His family's home was more luxurious and spacious than Mike's, however, just footsteps away from Lake McBride and some of the priciest homes in the Tallahassee area.

Brian, the epitome of tall, dark and handsome, could stop his female classmates dead in their tracks just by flashing his killer smile. When he did, he revealed his most prominent facial feature—a set of low-hanging, razor-sharp canine teeth which easily could have given Dracula a run for his money.

A full year younger than Mike, Brian was one of the youngest students in the ninth grade. He too was in the Key Club, but didn't participate in school sports.

By the end of the ninth grade, Mike and Brian had become best friends. Yet the two had very different personalities. Mike operated with tremendous self-discipline and restraint for a teenager. Brian, on the other hand, lived on—or just beyond—the edge, sometimes requiring his parents to bail him out of tough situations.

Brian's dad, Marcus, owned Winchester Financial Group, a financial planning firm and life insurance agency with deep connections to Tallahassee's upper crust. Unlike Mike's and Denise's parents, Marcus and Patricia Winchester didn't break a financial sweat sending their children to private school.

Brian sported the finest department-store attire and traveled with his family on exotic vacations. The Winchesters owned a ski boat and invited Mike to go waterskiing with them on several occasions. Marcus also chaperoned Brian and Mike on numerous duck hunting trips and quickly grew very fond of his son's best friend.

During the 11th grade, Brian latched onto a pretty cheerleader himself—Kathy Aldredge, the girl who happened to be Mike's romantic interest between the two Denises. Before long, Brian and Kathy and Mike and Denise had become a fearsome foursome. By the time they graduated from NFC in 1988, the four were inseparable.

Their paths to college would diverge just a bit, however. Denise, Brian, and Kathy all enrolled at Florida State. Though Mike wanted to go there as well, his grades weren't quite good enough to get in. He spent his freshman year at Florida A&M University, or FAMU—also in Tallahassee—where he received a small track scholarship, living at home to minimize his expenses.

During his college days, Mike would come home after classes to clean up before heading to work. He would first grab a quick bite in the kitchen—often fish sticks with ketchup and French fries—and then head to his room for a shower. He would later reemerge in the playroom in clean clothes and plop down on a chair.

The children for whom his mom was caring would usually be napping all around him. As they began waking up one by one, Mike would yell out—with a wry smile—"Hey Mama, this one needs a spanking. He won't stay asleep!" The offending child would immediately close his or her eyes and pretend to go back to sleep.

••••

While Mike was a freshman at FAMU, Denise abruptly ended their relationship with hardly any explanation at all. He was devastated, moping around in his bathrobe for months acting like his life was over, unable to muster the will even to go hunting.

His despair suddenly lifted, however, when a stunningly attractive blonde named Shellie Scheider came into his life. Shellie was crazy about Mike. His friends and family found her to be incredibly sweet, thoughtful, and caring. She would drop by Ms. Cheryl's daycare and play with her "kids"—something Denise Merrell rarely did. Shellie also was more attentive to Mike and quick to give gifts, such as the blue, stonewashed jean jacket—with a Quicksilver patch across the back—he often wore.

But Mike's heart just wasn't in that relationship—there was only one girl for him. And when Denise Merrell found out about Shellie, she made it known she was ready to resume her romance with Mike. After only a couple of months, he dropped Shellie like a hot potato. For his only true love.

Mike's grades as a freshman at FAMU were good enough to earn him admission to Florida State as a transfer student the following fall, where he joined Denise, Brian, and Kathy. Each of the four friends commuted to college from home to reduce costs—even Brian and Kathy despite their families' financial good fortune. At Florida State, Mike majored in political science and urban planning and Denise in accounting.

During one of his night courses in urban planning, a fellow student told Mike about a great place to work in town—Ketcham Appraisal Group, a small family-owned real-estate appraisal firm that operated out of a stately two-story brick home on Thomasville Road that had been converted into office space. From that location, Clay Ketcham operated Ketcham Appraisal and his wife Patti, a realtor, would eventually run Ketcham Realty.

Clay shared the ins and outs of the appraisal business with Mike as he worked part-time while finishing his Florida State coursework. Between his FAMU track scholarship, savings, and earnings from Ketcham Appraisal, Mike managed to graduate without a single penny of debt.

Mike wasn't like most other college students. He had little interest in keg parties, dive bars, or college nightlife—not really a drinker at all. When his new boss Clay Ketcham toasted his 21st birthday with champagne, Mike merely pretended to sip from his glass. He was about as straightlaced as they came, rarely saying a bad word.

Even his voice matched his personality—soft, gentle, and soothing. He was humble and kind, always finding good in other people even when most others didn't. He also was religious, attending church with Denise's family every Sunday at Parkway Baptist Church until its implosion in the early 1990s, when the Merrells joined Thomasville Road Baptist Church.

But Mike did have a handful of vices. For one, he enjoyed chewing tobacco—especially while hunting and sometimes while at work. Punctuality was not his strong suit. Rachel Drew, Howard Drew's daughter, who became like a little sister to Mike—some eight years his junior—would fondly tell others, "Mike was never on time for anything. He wasn't even on time for his own birth."

He was also neglectful about keeping his truck filled with gas—much to the consternation of his father. Mike would run out of gas, walk to the nearest home, and call J.J. to rescue him. Because the nearest gas station in those days was often ten miles or farther from their Bradfordville home, it would take a huge chunk out of his dad's day to bail Mike out of his predicament. The two would argue and bicker about his lack of responsibility.

Once when Mike called on J.J.'s day off—telling him he'd run out of gas yet again—his peeved father asked him, "What do *you* want to do about that?"

Mike told J.J. he expected *him* to come put gas in his pickup truck so he could drive home. But he didn't get the response he usually did.

"Sorry about your truck," J.J. replied. The next thing Mike heard was a dial tone.

Cheryl, however, wasn't about to let her husband desert their child, no matter his age—or irresponsibility. Against his druthers, J.J. and Rachel piled into his truck. When they arrived at the location where Mike was stranded, it was actually Mike's "little sister" who gave him the tongue-lashing.

"You should have to walk home," Rachel scolded him, as only a ten year old could. Mike sheepishly got into his dad's truck, seemingly having learned his lesson about keeping his fuel tank filled. For the next couple of weeks, the precocious preteen would needle him, asking, "Are you sure you have gas in your truck?"

Mike also wouldn't have won any awards for tidiness or organization. His truck was in a constant state of disarray, littered with clothes, bookbags, shoes, hunting gear—making it nearly impossible for him to find most anything. He kept his rubber waders wedged between the outside of the cab and bed of the truck, boots upside down—his ingenious method of drying them following hunting and fishing expeditions.

"What's the point of leaving them there if they're just going to get rained on?" Rachel would quiz him. But Mike didn't seem to care. If the urge to go duck hunting struck, he wanted to be ready to take off on the spur of the moment without having to remember where he had left his waders.

Even though he ultimately made good money as an appraiser, Mike could also be tight with money. When he filled his vehicle with gas, rather than dropping a coin into the soda machine to quench his thirst, he would sneak around to the side of the building and drink water from the garden hose—the price of which he found significantly more manageable.

Just a few months before he vanished—also while at a gas station—another patron accidentally drove into the driver's side door of his Ford Bronco. When Mike found out how expensive the repairs would be, he decided to live with the broken door, climbing across the passenger seat every time he had to enter or exit the vehicle. Even though he submitted an insurance claim, he decided to put those proceeds to better use: to buy a fancy Beretta shotgun for hunting, the very one found in his empty boat the morning of December 17, 2000.

••••

Mike graduated from Florida State in 1992 and immediately went to work full time with Clay Ketcham as a residential and commercial real-estate appraiser. By then, Clay had become both a mentor and father figure. Mike's boss considered him "the hardest working man I ever saw." He was especially impressed with Mike's character, describing him as "straight as an arrow." He also marveled at Mike's incredible energy, work ethic, and stamina. No matter how much work Clay threw his way, Mike got it done, and done well.

Denise also got her Florida State degree in 1992, ultimately passing all four parts of the CPA exam. She landed an accounting job with the State of Florida's Board of Administration—where she worked on the state's retirement system. There was little doubt she was a smart young lady.

Denise would ultimately become a regular at Ketcham Appraisal office gatherings and trips. When times were good, Clay treated his employees—and their significant others and children—to mini vacations to places like Universal Studios and Disney World in Orlando and to Panama City at the Gulf. Clay and Patti found Denise to be shy, reserved, and somewhat aloof—not the easiest person to connect with or warm up to.

Brian and Kathy had jobs waiting for them after college, each going to work in their family's business. Brian joined his father's financial planning firm and Kathy her parents' printing company. Brian eventually handled investments and financial planning for Mike and for Denise's father and sisters. He also sold life insurance to several of his NFC and Florida State classmates—including Mike.

As adults charting their own professional lives, Mike, Denise, Brian, and Kathy were ready to conquer the world—or at least their hometown of Tallahassee. And it wouldn't be long before wedding bells would ring and they would be forming families of their own.

3

Till Death Do Us Part

When it came time to pop the big question, as was his habit with Denise, Mike went all out. He plunked down a huge pile of hard-earned money for a two-karat diamond engagement ring—from Tiffany's of course. The future bride and groom settled on December 17, 1994, as their wedding date, almost ten years from the first time they held hands as high school freshmen. As they planned and prepared for the big day, the Williamses and Merrells got to know each other much better. The two families couldn't have been any happier about the impending nuptials.

Sadly, however, tragedy struck the Williams family at 2:00 a.m. the very morning Mike and Denise were to tie the knot—a mere hours after the rehearsal dinner ended. Mike's dad awoke suddenly with what felt like 20 elephants on his chest. Just 56 years old, he was in the throes of a severe heart attack. Mike and Denise rushed to his hospital bedside later that morning, offering to postpone the wedding. But J.J. would have none of that, insisting from his hospital bed that his son and future daughter-in-law hold their ceremony without him.

The last several years had been no picnic for Jerry Williams. Greyhound had locked out its drivers in March 1990, when Mike was just a sophomore at Florida State. Though the bus drivers initially believed they would be back at work in no time, the lockout ended up lasting four and a half years. During that time, J.J. picked up work for a charter bus company in his native Alabama. But that position didn't pay nearly as much as his Greyhound job, making it all the more difficult for him and Cheryl to make ends meet. The lockout had finally ended just before his son's wedding. And then boom, a heart attack.

So when the families and friends of Mike and Denise gathered at Thomasville Road Baptist Church to witness their joinder in holy matrimony, Mike's brother Nick stood in for their father as best man. Kathy—now married to Brian—served as a bridesmaid and Brian as a groomsman, reversing the roles Denise and Mike had played at their wedding just seven months before.

Rachel Drew, now a senior in high school, was also a bridesmaid. But she had been tasked with an even more important responsibility: getting the groom to the church on time—no easy task, considering her "big brother" was a nervous wreck.

"Are you sure you want to go through with this today?" Rachel asked, wondering if it made more sense to wait until J.J. was well again. Even more worrisome, it had rained steadily that morning, which even at 17 she knew was a bad omen.

"I'm marrying her *today*," Mike insisted. "Let's go."

The church sanctuary was resplendent with gorgeous floral arrangements and filled nearly to capacity. Mike fidgeted nervously with his two-flower boutonniere, his brother Nick and his groomsmen standing by his side. His hair cropped short, parted neatly to the side, the groom looked most debonair in his black tuxedo.

His groomsmen, including Brian, sported matching tuxedos, while Denise's bridesmaids, including Kathy, donned elegant, dark-green gowns. Another bridesmaid was Denise's good friend and NFC classmate Shannon Norris, who years later would be better known as Fox News journalist Shannon Bream.

As the wedding march rang out from the massive church organ, Warren Merrell proudly linked arms with his daughter and slowly walked her toward her groom, her hands wrapped around a beautiful, multi-flower bouquet. Denise turned heads in her gorgeous white, V-neck embroidered gown with a lengthy train trailing behind her. An elegant veil extended down from her lush blonde hair and large pearl earrings dangled from her ears. Her radiant smile exuded sheer happiness.

When the handsome young couple kissed after agreeing to love and honor one another "until death do us part," not a single guest could have imagined anything other than a "happily ever after."

After a small reception in the fellowship hall with cake, cookies, and punch—typical Baptist post-nuptial fare—Mike and Denise ventured off for their honeymoon cruise to Cozumel, Mexico, a wedding gift from her parents.

While the newlyweds were away, Jerry Williams had successful open heart surgery. He was back behind the wheel of a Greyhound bus within six months. Though he quickly returned to good health, his heart attack would serve as an ominous harbinger of even more significant health troubles looming on the horizon.

••••

The couple quickly settled into a comfortable rhythm as husband and wife—Mike working as an appraiser and Denise as an accountant. They would dine together at home nearly every evening. Most nights, however, Mike would return to the office and stay until late, already a workaholic in his mid-20s.

On the weekends, he would often awake before dawn to go hunting or fishing with friends—more often than not, with his best friend Brian. When his mom would fuss at him about burning the candle at both ends, Mike would glibly reply, "Mama, sleep is a waste of time." And he actually believed that.

The marriage couldn't have begun on more solid footing. According to Mike's friends and coworkers, he worshiped the ground his wife walked on—putting her on a pedestal like a fairy princess. He loved her deeply. "Denise said 'jump,'"

Mike's friend Scott Dungey would later say, and, "Mike wanted to know how high." He would do anything for her. The feeling was mutual.

"She loved him like a woman would love a life partner, a soulmate," recalled Denise's friend and coworker Becky Maas.

The young couple enjoyed their time together, both at home and out on the town, often turning heads with their good looks. Denise was a striking blonde, albeit bleached, with a good figure and great smile. Mike bore an uncanny resemblance to Dabo Swinney, then an assistant football coach at the University of Alabama—years later, the head coach of the national champion Clemson Tigers.

Residing so close to their old stomping grounds at Florida State, Mike and Denise lived and breathed Seminole football each fall, donning their garnet and gold attire to attend games when they could, watching on TV when they couldn't. They would go to movies together and, with a healthy income between them, were blessed to be able to dine frequently at their favorite haunts. Life was good. Almost too good.

••••

As adults, Mike and Denise's relationship with Brian and Kathy grew stronger still. The Winchesters were frequent guests in the Williamses' home, and vice versa. The foursome went on weekend trips and would go out to movies, local nightclubs, and restaurants together. They even took a ski trip to Colorado. The four were more inseparable than they had been in college.

While Mike was charting his career as a property appraiser, Brian was content working in his father's shadow as a financial planner and insurance agent, becoming more and more skilled at handling other people's investments. Though he hadn't been an athlete at NFC like Mike, Brian continued to hone his waterskiing skills both at Florida State and as an adult, ultimately winning multiple national championships in slalom skiing. Brian also competed in hunting and fishing tournaments, was an avid bicyclist, and had developed considerable expertise training hunting dogs, in particular Labrador retrievers.

Unlike Mike, Brian didn't have to kill himself with work in order to make ends meet. Marcus Winchester provided generously for his son and daughter-in-law, freeing up some of Brian's time to pursue his passions. Brian would use those hours to plan his next big hunting excursion, shop for the latest in hunting gear, or plan fun vacations. Mike was a tad jealous his best friend wasn't forced to slave away like he was.

Shortly after Mike and Denise's wedding, Brian suggested that his friend increase his life insurance beyond the $100,000 policy he had sold Mike shortly after their college graduation. That's what married men did, he told Mike. Thus, on February 2, 1995, Mike upped his Kansas City Life policy to $250,000, listing Denise as the 80% beneficiary and his parents as 20% beneficiaries.

••••

By the summer of 1998, Kathy and Brian were expecting their first child. Mike and Denise were thrilled for their friends. And very soon, for themselves as well. That September, they learned Denise was pregnant. They were on cloud nine.

Their joyful news should have been a cause for celebration for the entire Williams family. Unfortunately, it was overshadowed by a horrible accident. In early September, Cheryl and J.J. were attending a fish fry at the home of another Greyhound bus driver. Their host had just received a motorcycle as a gift.

Though J.J. hadn't been on a motorcycle for some 20 years, the sight of the shiny chrome body and handlebars proved too great a temptation. He hopped on the bike to give it a whirl around the block. A mere minutes later, after the motorcycle had landed on top of him, he was in an ambulance on the way to the hospital with a broken collarbone, broken ribs, and bumps and bruises all over his body.

The next morning, the doctors discovered he also had a detached retina—and was minutes away from losing his vision. They performed emergency eye surgery with J.J. in his hospital bed, afraid to move him to the O.R. He had to remain flat on his back for another three days. While lying prone unable to move, things got worse yet again—he developed pneumonia.

J.J. was finally discharged on Labor Day. Just before leaving, however, he and Cheryl noticed how swollen his stomach had become. He also was having significant trouble breathing. When his oxygen-saturation level was measured, it was an alarmingly low 50 percent. But his doctors sent him home nonetheless, with a canister of oxygen and a pep talk that everything would soon return to normal and that he'd be back to work in six weeks.

Sadly, Jerry Williams didn't live another six days. It turned out the motorcycle crash had caused a stress ulcer—he had been bleeding internally for days without detection. The blood had been pouring into his stomach, which is why it had become so swollen. He passed out the Friday after Labor Day and was rushed back to the hospital. The same hospital, on the same day, Mike and Denise were learning the exciting news about her pregnancy. By then, J.J. was in a different room, hooked up to monitors and machines, unconscious. He died the very next day, just 60 years old.

Instead of celebrating the news of the impending start of a new generation of Williamses, the entire family was now mourning the loss of its patriarch. What should have been a very happy time turned into a gut-wrenching, tumultuous grind. Nick and Mike found themselves burying their father, right in the prime of his life. And at the age of 54, their mom Cheryl was now a widow, her soulmate gone forever.

What kept her going was knowing she would soon be able to share her love with a grandchild. Cheryl clung to that thought each and every day. In the meantime, she poured herself into her work—her "kids" needed her. And now, more than ever, she needed them.

Something else that helped distract Cheryl from her grief was a gift from Mike and Denise—a chocolate Lab she named Hershey. Thanks to the puppy's affection and loyalty, Cheryl was able to lumber through the most difficult stretch of her life, counting the days until she would be a grandmother.

••••

The year 1999 would evolve into a very special one indeed, not only for Mike and Denise, but for their best friends Brian and Kathy as well. It began with all four sets of eyes glued to the TV screen on January 4 as the Florida State Seminoles took on the Tennessee Volunteers in the Fiesta Bowl in Tempe, Arizona—the inaugural BCS National Championship Game. That Denise and Kathy were each several months pregnant didn't stop them from hooting and hollering alongside their husbands with each big play. The game ended in disappointment, however, with the Noles losing a close one, 23-16.

Stafford Teal Winchester entered the world on February 25, 1999. Mike and Denise—now nearly seven months pregnant herself—were there to celebrate his arrival and among the first to hold him.

As for Mike and Denise, a Hollywood movie studio couldn't have penned a better script for the arrival of Anslee Merrell Williams on May 8, 1999—the evening before Mother's Day. She wasn't even a full day old when a WCTV camera crew stumbled upon the new parents while roaming the Tallahassee Memorial Hospital hallways in search of a heart-warming story for the evening news. Mother's Day balloons by the window provided a perfect backdrop to frame the footage.

The interview of the brand-new mom and dad aired for all of Tallahassee to see. Mike held a sleeping Anslee in the crook of his left arm, his adoring eyes cast down toward her from under the garnet brim of his Florida State cap. The baby girl had a full head of dark hair with a pink bow wrapped around a wisp hanging over her forehead. Like many new dads, Mike was in awe of his wife's strength through the delivery and the power of love that swept over him once Anslee arrived. "It was unbelievable," he said. "I have a whole new respect for my wife and women in general for what they go through to bring a new child—a new life—into the world."

"We're just totally overwhelmed," Denise added, beaming with pride. "She was due Tuesday and she would have made me wait a whole 'nother year for Mother's Day." Instead, the new parents got to take their beautiful baby girl home on Mother's Day, and to celebrate with all their friends and family.

When Cheryl held Anslee for the first time and gazed into her eyes, she couldn't help but notice that she was the spitting image of Mike just after he was born. Not only that, the new grandmother couldn't mistake her husband's likeness in the newborn's face. "It was like God had given me Jerry back," she would tell her friends. Having just gone through the most arduous period of her entire life, Anslee's birth gave Cheryl reason to be happy and hopeful again.

••••

Mike and Denise began adjusting to their new routine as parents. Because Denise was suffering from post-partum depression, her husband would come home several times a day from his nearby office to check on her and the baby, typically taking a break to make dinner, read to Anslee, and get her to bed. He would then go back to the office to complete his day's work.

Denise eventually returned to her Board of Administration job, though only part-time, leaving Anslee with her mom during the few hours she worked each day.

When she wasn't working, Denise would frequently call Mike with what she considered urgent requests. She'd ask him to leave the office to bring food home when she was hungry. If her car needed gas, she would drive to a station near Mike's office and sit in her car next to the pump—waiting for her husband to meet her there. Denise thought it was Mike who should get his hands dirty doing such tasks, not her.

When his wife made these requests, Mike would drop everything, head out the office door for however long it took to fulfill needs, and would then return to work. His coworkers became so accustomed to hearing the rush of his footsteps down the stairs from his second-floor office, they routinely turned to each other with knowing looks after the first step or two. "Denise must need something," they'd often say.

"We all said we wanted to be married to Mike Williams," Clay Ketcham would later tell a reporter. "I mean, we all need a Mike Williams in our lives."

Mike loved being a dad. He adored his baby girl, the light of his life. He enjoyed feeding her, playing with her, and bringing her to his mom's for homey visits. He was as devoted to his daughter as he was to his work. She often was right there beside him during late-night and weekend shifts. Denise would get time to herself and he'd tend to his stack of paperwork while gently rocking their daughter in her car seat with the ball of his foot.

On some weekend afternoons, Mike would swing by Scott Dungey's house and join him in his backyard pool, the two dads splashing playfully in the water with Anslee and Dungey's son Logan, about a year her senior. Despite his grueling work schedule, Mike Williams was fully present in his child's life—as very few fathers were.

••••

With a growing family, and Mike's work going well, the new parents decided they were ready for a bigger home. On August 31, 1999, they purchased a two-story, three-bedroom brick home on Centennial Oaks Circle in an upscale subdivision named Midyette Plantation on the east side of town. Their lot backed up to one of Tallahassee's most picturesque streets, Miccosukee Road, a narrow two-lane avenue lined for miles with moss-draped oak trees that leaned into the street to form a stunning canopy. The young couple's new home was 25 minutes from Mike's mom and 15 minutes from Denise's folks.

Though their new place was on a large wooded lot similar to Mike's boyhood home—more than an acre—the resemblance ended there. Mike and Denise Williams' daughter wouldn't grow up in a doublewide trailer cramped for space. She would be raised instead in a well-appointed house featuring modern appliances and top-of-the-line furnishings and fixtures. With over 3,000 square feet of living space, there was more than enough room for everyone.

Mike and Denise especially enjoyed decorating their spacious master bedroom, which became somewhat of a shrine. Giant-sized framed photos from their wedding—their second happiest day—covered their walls. It was a comfort to Mike waking up to those pictures each and every day.

On October 16, 1999, Mike celebrated his 30th birthday, surrounded by friends and family—and his five-month-old pride and joy. The soft-spoken appraiser loved everything about his life. He had a beautiful wife, an amazing baby girl, a new home, a loving mother and brother, supportive in-laws, great friends, and a solid job that allowed him to earn a good living and provide for his family. He was even able to sneak in duck hunting many weekend mornings—his greatest passion apart from his family.

It was around that time Scott Dungey introduced Mike to deep-sea fishing, which became yet another love. They would often fish on Dungey's boat, the Cuda B. Mike was ultimately able to invest in a sharp-looking 17-foot fishing boat of his own. His favorite place to go deep-sea fishing with Dungey was at a secluded spot on the Gulf of Mexico—Alligator Point.

Mike had grown into a man of unparalleled character. Not an enemy in the world. Completely devoted to his mom, wife, and daughter. Fiercely loyal friend and brother. Honest to a fault. Kind and generous to all—someone who would literally give the shirt off his back to a complete stranger. "There was not a finer man on earth than Mike," Dungey would later remark, observing that "Denise found a gem."

"He was just a good-hearted man," Howard Drew, his hunting mentor, added.

Though Mike's eyes would light up every time he talked about—even thought about—hunting, he often organized hunting excursions intended for others as much as himself. He would lease a nearby farm and invite numerous friends and coworkers for a dove hunt. During the hunt itself, he would walk up to each one of his guests to make sure they had plenty of water, that their equipment was working properly, and that they were having a good time. If nothing else, Mike Williams was a pleaser—and nothing gave him more joy than pleasing those he loved and respected the most.

••••

The year 2000 couldn't have begun in more storybook fashion for Mike, Denise, Brian, and Kathy. Once again, the foursome gathered in front of the TV on January 4 to root on their beloved Seminoles as they played for the national championship—this time at the Sugar Bowl in New Orleans. Not only did the Noles defeat the Virginia Tech Hokies quite comfortably—winning 46-29—the victory left the team with a perfect 12-0 season. The champagne flowed freely not only in the Florida State locker room, but at 5017 Centennial Oaks Circle as well.

Not lost in those bubbly moments was the memory of the recent death of Mike's father and the grim reality of the huge impact it had on the family left behind. With a daughter of his own and a mother struggling to fill the financial void from the loss of her husband's income, Mike began contemplating his own mortality.

As an avid hunter and fisherman—growing a bit more daring with each passing year—he worried a horrible accident might suddenly leave his family in a financial lurch. After all, an unforeseen tragedy had left his own mother a widow—and in considerable financial straits—at just 54 years old.

The $250,000 life insurance policy Brian had sold Mike in February 1995 wouldn't be nearly enough to take care of Denise and Anslee should something happen to him. He was now earning around $200,000 a year. With Denise still working only part-time, their existing coverage was barely more than a year of their combined earnings. Mike decided he needed more.

In late March 2000, Mike sat across from a local insurance agent named Jack Stansel, telling him how his own father had died with hardly any life insurance in place to protect his mother. He didn't want the same thing happening to his wife, he said, especially now that they had a child. He told Stansel he was meeting with him over Denise's objections, as she didn't think they needed to spend his hard-earned money on life insurance. As they talked, Mike completed a Cotton States application for a $500,000 policy, naming Denise as the sole beneficiary.

When he told Brian about his acquisition of additional insurance, his best friend was dumbfounded—about two things: first, why Mike had gone to a competitor to purchase a life insurance policy. And second, why he hadn't gotten more.

Clay Ketcham also weighed in, suggesting that Mike "load up" on insurance. Mike shared with him details about the cost of various levels of coverage Brian had proposed, all the way up to $1 million. Clay's response was that, in view of Mike's risky behaviors as a hunter and fisherman, how much he adored his wife and daughter, and what had happened to his own father, $1 million made perfect sense. "Besides," he added, "you'll never be able to get it any cheaper."

Following that pep talk from his boss, Mike agreed to replace his Cotton States policy with an additional $1 million policy from Kansas City Life—written up by Brian—bringing his total with that company to $1.25 million. His plan was to stop paying premiums on the Cotton States policy and let it lapse. Mike's April 15, 2000, Kansas City Life application listed Denise as the primary beneficiary and her mom and dad as contingent beneficiaries.

••••

May 8, 2000, was a perfectly glorious Tallahassee spring day, allowing Mike and Denise to set up in their backyard for Anslee's first birthday party. The center of attention sat in her Graco highchair—five colored, helium-filled balloons floating above her—as she curiously inspected the cake set before her, her fingers covered with globs of vanilla icing.

All of Denise's family members were there, as were Cheryl and Nick, Brian, Kathy, and Stafford—as well as Clay and

Patti Ketcham, who marveled over Anslee's uncanny resemblance to the baby pictures they had seen of Mike. Much to the delight of all the partygoers, the toddler took her first steps that very day—with a crowd of spectators cheering her on.

••••

By the fall of 2000, the luster of Florida State's national championship victory had become a faint, distant memory. Mike found himself working grueling 15-hour days on top of all of his responsibilities at home—often remaining at the office until 1:00 or 2:00 a.m. He had a nagging fear a recession could be just around the corner and wanted to make all the money he could while the work was there.

Mike knew all too well what it felt like growing up in a family that struggled to make ends meet. He wanted just the opposite for his young family, and was willing to work himself to the bone if that's what it took.

For her part, Denise still hadn't returned to work full-time, complaining of continuing post-partum depression. Mike actually confided in a female coworker that he and Denise hadn't had sex since Anslee's birth, wondering how post-partum depression could last so long. His coworker speculated to Mike that Denise might have been enjoying some action "on the side." Though he hoped that wasn't the case, he really wasn't sure.

Mike and his mom spoke by phone most every day, often after 10:00 p.m. while he was working self-imposed night shifts. He would lament the difficulty of his long hours combined with the responsibilities of parenthood. Not to mention Denise's constant requests to fulfill her every need and address her every passing whim.

His running regimen of 25 to 30 miles a week was now down to a three-mile run once or twice a week. Occasionally he got in a game of racquetball, the only other physical exercise he could squeeze into his hectic days.

By then Mike was serving as a mentor to Damon Jasper, the Florida State student he had taken under his wings at Ketcham Appraisal. "Don't ever think having a kid is going to fix a marriage," he cautioned Jasper. For the first time in his life, Mike started drinking to cope with his stress.

While returning from a site visit with Clay Ketcham one day, Mike confided in his boss about the stresses and strains in his marriage. He and Denise had an agreement neither would spend more than $50 without the other's approval, he said. Yet he had just reviewed a Visa statement revealing that Denise had taken out a $3,000 cash advance without his knowledge.

Mike told his boss that Denise explained away the withdrawal as something she had to do to pay for a large quantity of marijuana she used to make herself pot brownies, raising questions in his mind about her veracity and her fitness as a parent.

Even worse, he told Clay, while he was at an appraisal course in New Orleans—a trip his boss had offered to pay for Denise attending as well—without his knowledge or approval Denise had apparently left Anslee with her mom and gone to Orlando with Brian and Kathy. He told Clay he found out the three had gone to a seedy establishment named Club Firestone, a dive reputed to be a haven for hard-core drug addicts. He felt certain, he said, Denise had gone there for the drugs.

His wife had been raised in such a strict environment, Mike explained, she was "kicking up her heels" as an adult, experimenting with things she never would have dreamed of doing in Johnnie and Warren Merrell's rigid household. "But I can't have this going on with Anslee," Mike said, gravely concerned. "I'm going to get this in front of a judge and get custody of Anslee because she's an unfit mother."

Trying his best to hide his shock and horror at what his protégée was telling him, Clay attempted to reassure Mike that things probably weren't as bad as he feared. Furthermore, his boss said, it would take quite a lot for him to wrest custody of his daughter away from Denise. He was gradually able to talk Mike down from the ledge.

But Clay was quite shaken by their conversation. Mike had never before confided in him about any troubles with Denise—certainly nothing as serious as her being a hardcore drug user. He was so unnerved he shared his concerns with his wife later that evening, unsure of how he could help his young friend. As they talked, though, he and Patti convinced themselves Mike's revelations didn't amount to anything more serious than growing pains in a young marriage—which they believed would probably subside over time.

••••

Mike was also involved in two hunting mishaps that year—serious mishaps. The first occurred during the winter at Lake Miccosukee, about 30 minutes east of Tallahassee, where Mike was duck hunting with Brian. The water level was so low that day, the lakebed was mostly dry. Mike slipped and fell into a "gator hole," which started sucking him into the mud like quicksand. He had a split second to decide what to do: either hang onto his gun or drop it and reach for a nearby tree trunk. Fortunately, he made the right decision and was able to grab the tree and hang on for dear life until Brian was able to pull him to safety.

Mike was so upset about losing his shotgun that he devised an elaborate plan to retrieve it. He ordered a pair of snowshoes from Cabela's, a retailer for outdoorsmen. After they came in the mail, Mike trudged back to the same spot and used the flat, racket-like footwear for extra traction as he fished through the mud in the hole that had swallowed his gun. He finally found it and pulled it to safety—thrilled his experiment had worked and that his trusty weapon was now back in his possession.

The second mishap occurred over the Thanksgiving holiday, when Mike and Brian drove together to Arkansas in Brian's Suburban, his best friend's champion hunting dog, Maggie, in tow. Not only were the two men part of a duck-hunting group, Brian's pooch was set to compete in a dog-hunting trial. During their lengthy ride, Mike confided in his best friend about the escalating difficulties in his life and strains in his relationship with Denise. He didn't understand why she still hadn't gone back to work full-time. She also seemed more distant, less interested in him as a man, he said, acknowledging they hadn't had sex even a single time since Anslee's birth.

While the two were duck hunting in Brian's boat, Mike accidentally fell overboard. Had Brian not reacted so quickly—pulling him out of the frigid water in barely an instant—he easily could have drowned.

Yet Mike didn't escape the incident unscathed. He came down with pneumonia. By the time the men returned to Tallahassee, he was too weak to gather his hunting gear from Brian's truck. As he gingerly walked inside his Centennial Oaks home in the pitch black, he told Brian he would collect his things later. Mike was so ill, he missed an entire week of work for the first time in his life.

Despite these two unfortunate accidents and the mounting challenges in his marriage, as he looked forward to 2001, Mike chose to focus on the silver linings in his life, rather than the dark clouds. He was experiencing pure, unconditional love as only a new parent could, his daughter Anslee the love of his life. He planned to either become a partner at Ketcham Appraisal or to establish his own appraising business, just one exam remaining to complete the Appraisal Institute's MAI designation, the highest certification in his field. He was scheduled to sit for that exam the following February.

Mike also envisioned himself running for local office once he was more well known in the community—hoping to land a seat on either the city council or county commission. He was already a member of the Tallahassee Rotary Club and had made lots of connections that might help him with a political campaign. His long-term goal was to be able to retire as a millionaire by his 50th birthday—and he was well on his way to achieving it. Mike Williams' refreshing optimism and hope sprang eternal.

••••

As he did every Thursday evening, on December 14, 2000, Nick Williams pulled down the long gravel driveway of his childhood home on Jeffrey Road to pick up his mom. It was

Friends night at Mike's house—their weekly ritual. They drove across town, entering Mike's upscale neighborhood at about 7:30 p.m. Cheryl and Nick marveled at the beautiful Christmas lights and decorations adorning the nearby homes.

Only Denise and Anslee were home when they walked through the front door. Mike had gone to pick up some pizza, Denise said, telling her guests her older sister Deanna had just taken their official Christmas portrait. As they took off their coats, Cheryl and Nick took in the splendor of all the decorations, eying a massive pile of presents under the tree in the living room. Cheryl recognized many of them—her gifts for Anslee.

"Grand Mama!" Anslee squealed in delight as she spotted Cheryl approaching. The toddler waddled up to her and wrapped her tiny arms around her grandmother's leg, causing Cheryl to smile ear to ear. She was never happier than when she was in Anslee's presence.

When Mike finally returned home, he warmly greeted his mom and older brother, setting the pizza box on the kitchen counter. The group settled onto the couch in the living room near the TV, feasting on the pizza while waiting for *Friends* to air.

Mike shared with Cheryl and Nick his adventure earlier that week having Anslee's picture taken with Santa at Northwood Mall. She screamed and cried, Mike told them, terrified by the overweight man in the big red suit and bushy white beard. It became clear very quickly the toddler wouldn't be sitting on his lap posing for a picture. Instead, Mike was forced to squat on Santa's left knee, his arms wrapped tightly around his toddler to prevent her from wriggling free and fleeing. Though Santa wore a jolly wide smile for the photo, the 19 month old couldn't have looked any more miserable.

On that same mall trip, Mike bought Denise a pair of expensive gold earrings. But he carefully avoided talking about that gift—for obvious reasons—as the group chatted in the living room. And just to be sure it remained a surprise, he entrusted Kathy with the jewelry—all of his Christmas presents for Denise in fact. Brian's wife had even agreed to wrap them.

His plan was to surreptitiously place them under the tree on Christmas Eve.

The subject of gifts did come up, though, as the family members made small talk before *Friends* came on. Mike and Denise fussed at Cheryl for going overboard with her Christmas gifts for Anslee.

"She's my only grandchild and I'm allowed to spoil her if I want to," the 56-year-old matriarch protested.

Without missing a beat, Mike interjected, "Mama, are you ready to be a grandma *again*?"

Confused, Cheryl glanced toward her eldest child—still a bachelor—and deadpanned, "Nick, are you pregnant and not telling me?"

"No, Ms. Williams," Denise said with a serious expression, redirecting her mother-in-law's attention. "It's us. We're going to start trying to have another baby in the next month or two." Cheryl was stunned. She had assumed from what Mike had been telling her that he and his wife were no longer in the baby-making business—but was immensely pleased her assumption was incorrect.

Mike and Denise also discussed their anniversary plans for the weekend ahead. They would be leaving for the Gibson Inn—a historic hotel at Apalachicola Bay—that Saturday afternoon, they said, as soon as Mike returned from an early morning duck-hunting trip. They told Cheryl and Nick that Mike would be heading to Lake Seminole with Brian very early Saturday morning while Denise and Anslee slept in.

He would begin that Saturday on a quiet lake engaged in the activity he loved most and end it at a romantic seaside resort with the woman he loved most. How could his day be any more perfect than that? Mike asked.

While they watched *Friends*, Anslee played exuberantly with her plastic Halloween Jack-o'-lantern—pacifier protruding from her lips. She darted gleefully from one adult to the next, thrilled to be in her grandmother's and uncle's company. Her playful giggles filled the room, adding silliness and warmth to the family gathering.

When the TV show ended, Cheryl and Nick walked to the

front door, grabbing their coats on the way. Mike walked out with them, holding his daughter in his arms. There was a noticeable chill in the air as the group stood on the porch saying their goodbyes. Mike and Anslee gave Cheryl a big hug and smiled and waved as she and Nick walked down the steps toward Nick's car.

As they pulled away from his home that evening, Jerry Michael Williams' mother and brother didn't have the slightest inkling they would never see him again.

4

Grieving Widow

Clay and Patti Ketcham's home phone began ringing around 8:00 Sunday morning, December 17, 2000. They had slept in after hosting a graduation party for their daughter Lindsay, who snagged her diploma at Florida State earlier that Saturday.

Patti finally grabbed the phone, listening as one of Denise's sisters asked if she could pass the phone to her husband. Rubbing his eyes, Clay sat up and took the receiver. Denise's sister explained that Mike hadn't returned from an early-morning hunting trip the prior day. Within seconds, she was saying "goodbye" and beginning to hang up.

"Whoa, whoa!" Clay responded, making sure to keep her on the line. "What are you saying? Give me some details. Mike is supposed to be at the Gibson Inn celebrating his anniversary."

Mike had gone hunting at Lake Seminole Saturday morning, Denise's sister told Clay, and never made it home. A search was underway to find him, she said.

Instinctively, Clay and Patti threw on some clothes and headed out the door. By 10:00 a.m., they were just north of Sneads, there to see for themselves what was going on.

One of the first people they encountered was Brian Winchester. He appeared ashen, shaky on his feet. Utterly distraught. He told the couple he and his father had discovered Mike's empty boat on the water about 2:30 that morning. There was already talk Mike had drowned, he said despondently.

With the search operation beginning to gear up for the day, Clay and Patti jumped right in, doing anything they could to help find Mike. At dusk, thoroughly exhausted, they got back into their car and headed home—gripped by sadness and desperation. The situation looked very bleak. They drove straight to Mike and Denise's Centennial Oaks home, wondering why Denise hadn't been out there with them looking for her husband.

Denise's mom Johnnie greeted them at the front door. As Clay and Patti walked inside, covered in mud from their day-long efforts at the lake, they were startled to observe a scene that looked more like a Norman Rockwell Christmas painting than a vigil for a missing husband and father.

All of Denise's sisters were there, as were boyfriends and a fiancé, everyone sharply dressed in Christmas attire. Cookies and punch were neatly displayed on the dining room table. The atmosphere was almost casual, the discussion focusing as much on the upcoming holiday as Mike's disappearance. Considering the circumstances, Clay and Patti found the gathering surreal.

Johnnie explained their collective absence from Lake Seminole, telling the Ketchams someone needed to stay back in Tallahassee just in case Mike was found and was being treated in a nearby hospital. "We would need to know where to go, wouldn't we?" she remarked, somewhat defensively.

Hearing new guests arrive, Denise slowly came down the stairs. She looked dreadful. Eyeing Clay, she approached him, wrapped her arms around him, and buried her head in his chest, sobbing. She had apparently been crying all day, the only member of the group whose reaction to Mike's shocking disappearance the Ketchams considered within the realm of normal.

Denise sat on the steps, head in her hands, weeping uncontrollably. As Clay and Patti stood at the foot of the staircase, trying to console her, Patti spotted a suitcase on the floor near the bottom step, a painful reminder of the anniversary trip that would never occur. Her heart ached for Mike's wife as she hugged her tightly.

After commiserating with Denise for a while, Clay and Patti drove over to Cheryl's home on Jeffrey Road. The juxtaposition between the two households couldn't have been more pronounced.

The mood gripping Cheryl's doublewide—where Mike's family and friends had gathered—was extremely somber, excruciating anguish tormenting virtually everyone. Tears streamed down several faces. Cheryl welcomed Mike's boss and his wife with warm hugs and appreciation for their efforts at the lake, which she immediately discerned from their muddy shoes and outerwear.

There was no discussion in Cheryl's home about the holiday ahead. Rather, they were speculating back and forth about what could have happened to Mike. Cheryl told everyone her son was a strong hunter and had terrific survival skills—perhaps he had made it to an island, she suggested, and would soon be found. Though she was very tearful, Mike's mom was hopeful nonetheless. Her hope gave Clay and Patti hope as well.

····

By Christmas Eve, Cheryl had finally worked up the courage to have a look around the lake herself. She had heard that the wildlife officers' working theory was that Mike had fallen overboard and been eaten by alligators—a theory Brian Winchester had been echoing. Yet her son had told her almost as long as he had been duck hunting that alligators don't feed during the cold, winter months. What she was hearing didn't make any sense.

Cheryl fidgeted in the passenger seat and chatted nervously as Nick drove his now familiar route to Sneads. The fretful, yet hopeful, mother had never been to Lake Seminole before.

When they arrived, Howard Drew was outside the FWC tent, tending to the fire in the 55-gallon drum. That had been his role pretty much since the start of the search. After Drew gave them an update, Cheryl walked down to the lake's edge—alone. The 56-year-old widow peered across Stump Field, searching for answers to her many questions. She then closed her eyes.

As she prayed in silence—just a few feet from the dirt ramp where most thought Mike had probably put his boat in—a powerful sensation came over the spiritual woman. She believed it was God communicating with her.

"Cheryl," she sensed him saying. "Mike is not in Lake Seminole. He did not drown. He did not get eaten by alligators. You need to find him and bring him home."

As she and Nick walked back to his car at the end of the day—after she had thanked every official and volunteer for their efforts to find her son—Cheryl was more determined than ever to discover what had happened to Mike and to find him. Alive.

Though she would return to Stump Field several times over the ensuing months—even after the official search concluded in February—it wasn't because she believed Mike's body would be pulled up from the lake. Rather, she kept coming back with hopes of finding clues to where her son really was.

••••

Denise kept a very low profile the days and weeks after Mike went missing, barely venturing out. She didn't make a single trip to the lake to witness for herself the massive search operation or to thank the countless officers, friends, former classmates, coworkers, and church parishioners who had tirelessly devoted themselves to the task of finding her husband.

Nor, for that matter, did she send notes or cards to thank anyone for their efforts. She attributed her reclusiveness to her need to care for Anslee. But in reality, in the weeks following Mike's disappearance, Denise ceded virtually all childcare responsibilities to her mother, sisters, and friends—including Kathy. One or more of them would sleep over her home each evening, get up with Anslee in the morning, and make sure all of her needs were addressed throughout the day. For the most part, Denise quarantined herself in the master bedroom, coming out for meals, but little else.

Because Ketcham Appraisal paid Mike based solely on a percentage of his invoices—rather than a straight salary—dozens of invoices for appraisals that had been completed before his disappearance were still in the pipeline for payment. Since Mike was missing and presumed dead by most everyone, Clay had Mike's checks made out to Denise as clients paid their bills. During the next ten months, the checks she received would total more than $20,000.

In late December, Denise took Anslee with her to Ketcham Appraisal's office to pick up the first check. The toddler instantly recognized the surroundings where she had spent so much time. "Daddy's house," she blurted out. Her words were so heartbreaking to Clay and Patti, they decided then and there that Patti would deliver all future checks to Denise's home—to protect Anslee from yet another reminder her father was gone.

Each time Patti went to the Centennial Oaks property to return Mike's belongings or deliver another check, she became closer and closer to Denise, the two reminiscing and grieving together. Often Johnnie or one of Denise's sisters would be there when Patti arrived, helping with Anslee and providing emotional support. Occasionally, Patti was able to get Denise out of the house for lunch.

In late January, Patti found Denise at home all alone, fighting the flu. Her family had taken Anslee to avoid getting sick themselves. Patti, not so worried about the germs, sat and talked with Denise for hours—the first opportunity she'd had since Mike's disappearance to go on at length about the deeper issues now facing Denise. Her host was particularly somber as they discussed her plight, sobbing uncontrollably at times.

Seemingly out of nowhere, Patti raised a subject she had been meaning to bring up, but hadn't wanted to discuss with Denise's family members present. "You need to have a memorial service for Mike," she suggested. "We're not going to find him. He's not alive." This was the first time anyone had suggested such an idea to Denise. They proceeded to discuss the pros and cons of holding a service.

"What if they find him and he's alive?" Denise asked, seemingly resistant to Patti's suggestion.

"Then you'll deal with that then and it will be a joyous occasion," Patti replied.

But when Denise raised the idea with Cheryl later that week, Mike's mom quickly shot her down.

"You don't have a funeral if you don't have a body," her mother-in-law responded, annoyed Denise had already given up on finding Mike alive. They didn't discuss the topic again.

In early February, however, Denise's father dropped by to visit with Cheryl and Nick—his very first time in Cheryl's mobile home. Without seeking Cheryl's input, Warren bluntly informed her that his family *would* be holding a memorial service for Mike at their church. "It's time for our daughter to move on," he said. He asked Cheryl and Nick to participate in the service if they could, but told them he and Johnnie would understand if they couldn't.

Though Cheryl and Nick ultimately agreed to participate in the service at Thomasville Road Baptist Church, they didn't conceal their displeasure that such an event was occurring. Cheryl put her personal feelings aside, however, rounding up baby and school pictures of Mike for the slide show chronicling key moments in his life. She even took to the floor to share poignant memories from Mike's childhood.

Howard Drew offered some of his fondest memories of Mike as did Denise's sister, Deanna.

Brian Winchester and Clay Ketcham recorded audio messages in advance that were played during the service, neither believing he could hold his composure together in front of the somber gathering.

But when the minister told the packed gallery Mike was in heaven, Cheryl became perturbed. God was telling her Mike was still alive. She thought it was most presumptuous for this man of the cloth to be preaching a different message.

Her irritation only grew as she listened to the final hymn, *This One's With Me,* about the gates of heaven opening to a new entrant, Jesus saying:

> "Father, this one's with me,
> Part of the family,
> One of the reasons I died on Calvary,
> Father, welcome him in,
> I paid the price for him,
> Father, Oh Father, this one's with me."

Cheryl wasn't ready to accept that the gates of heaven had opened for her son, who she believed was still very much alive—on earth. And she was peeved that Denise and her family had already written him off for dead.

By the time the service was over, the uncomfortable divide between the Merrell and Williams families was evident for all to see. The two clans sat in different sections of the sanctuary, rather than together, refusing to greet one another as the crowd dispersed.

Following the service, family and friends gathered at Mike and Denise's house, but Denise was too distraught to join her guests downstairs. Cheryl waited patiently for her daughter-in-law to make an appearance, hoping to introduce her to her father—then in his 80s—who had made the trip from Jacksonville. But Denise never came downstairs, resulting in Cheryl and her dad leaving without saying a single word to her.

••••

Warren Merrell wasn't the only father figure looking out for Denise in the months after Mike vanished. Marcus Winchester, who devoted his career to helping people plan for the future—and tragedy—sprang into action as well. Fully aware his son Brian had sold Mike two different life insurance policies through their firm for a total of $1.25 million, he considered it his professional obligation to get that money into Denise's hands as quickly as possible.

Denise apparently hadn't informed Marcus—or other friends or family members—that Ketcham Appraisal had been delivering Mike's paychecks to her on a regular basis. To the outside world, she acted and spoke as if she were on the brink of financial ruin. She even had Mike's friend Scott Dungey help her sell her husband's deep-sea fishing boat, his prized possession.

Marcus had checked with his counterpart at Kansas City Life to determine when the life insurance proceeds could be paid out short of Mike's body being recovered and a death certificate being issued.

Without an official death certificate, Marcus was told, the life insurance company couldn't make any payments. But in exceptional circumstances, he learned, the probate court could declare a person dead even without a body. Marcus was advised to consult a lawyer to explore that legal avenue.

Marcus called Curtis Hunter—the probate lawyer to whom he most often referred clients—and informed him about Denise's situation, hopeful Hunter could figure out how to get Kansas City Life to release the $1.25 million to Denise, as Mike's sole beneficiary.

After doing some research, Hunter explained to Marcus that, under Florida law, a missing person couldn't be declared dead until five years after his or her disappearance. But an exception in the statute existed, he said, through which Denise could petition the probate court for a "presumptive death certificate." The petition would need to establish that Mike had been exposed to a "specific peril" so likely to have resulted in his death it could be presumed it did. The probate lawyer set up an early March meeting with Marcus, Brian, Denise, and her father Warren to discuss the situation further.

When the group met together in a conference room at Hunter's office, the attorney voiced his skepticism that sufficient evidence existed to convince a probate judge that the statutory standard had been met. There was certainly a specific peril he could cite—Mike falling overboard from his boat at Lake Seminole and being eaten by alligators. But with no actual evidence that had occurred, Hunter said he was concerned a judge would deny the petition. Denise sat quietly through the meeting—her head resting on the table—Brian and her father doing the talking for her.

Hunter told them they would need to prove that Mike wouldn't have staged the scene at Lake Seminole and just skipped town, leaving his existing life behind and starting over somewhere else. That sort of thing happened more often than most people realized, the lawyer said. Indeed, apart from the "Mike was eaten by alligators" hypothesis, the "Mike staged his own death to begin a new life" theory was the second leading candidate to explain his still mysterious disappearance.

Hunter asked Denise to prepare a written statement explaining why Mike would never have left his family behind — including details confirming the strength of their marriage and his bond with Anslee. In the meantime, Hunter said, he would work on gathering and reviewing the official reports from the various searches at Lake Seminole. His hope, he said, was that one of the reports would contain language that could persuade the probate judge that the only logical reason why Mike's body hadn't been found was because it had been fully consumed by alligators.

••••

Denise's probate lawyer had been hard at work on her case for about three months when he received word of a miraculous development: a pair of waders had been found at Lake Seminole, literally appearing out of nowhere.

Joe Sheffield had fished in Lake Seminole's calm waters since he was six — not long after the reservoir opened to the public. On the morning of June 21, 2001, he was sitting in his boat at Stump Field, patiently waiting for a speckled perch to nibble at his line. Out of the corner of his eye, he glimpsed a large brown object floating just beneath the surface. He motored over to get a better look.

When he pulled his find onto the side of his boat, Sheffield realized it was a pair of hunting waders. He found them to be slimy — covered in some sediment and algae — as if they had been in the water for an extended period of time. Oddly enough, the shoulder straps were pulled down near the pant legs. When he unzipped a fanny pack still strapped around the waist area, the fisherman found 13 steel shot shells stored inside.

"Oh my God," Sheffield thought to himself. As a resident of Sneads, he was fully aware of the massive search for Mike the prior winter. He eased the waders back into the water and motored back to the boat landing where his vehicle was parked. The fisherman called FWC Officer Alton Ranew, who lived just minutes away.

Ranew told him to stay put and not to lose sight of the waders. The wildlife officer contacted others at the FWC and Jackson County Sheriff's Office, then met up with Sheffield at the lake. He was joined there by Sergeant Jeff Johnson with the Sheriff's Office—one of the divers involved in the initial search—the two jumping into an FWC boat and following Sheffield in his.

The waders were still floating where Sheffield had left them, about 30 yards from the small island across the water to the east of where Mike's Bronco had been found. That spot just happened to be the deepest area in the search grid—a "hole" thoroughly searched by officers and volunteers on numerous occasions a mere months before. Indeed, a white PVC pole was sticking out of the water right beside the waders, signaling something suspicious had actually been detected there during the winter search—though obviously nothing of significance had been found.

Johnson and Ranew carefully fished the waders from the lake, making sure to retain whatever water was filling the boots, just in case it contained any human remains.

The officers took the waders to Ranew's nearby home, meeting up there with FWC Officer David Arnette. Arnette carefully strained the water from the boots through a filter into a five-gallon bucket—yielding no obvious evidence of any human remains.

The officers' assessment of the waders differed greatly from Sheffield's. In their opinion, they showed no evidence of having been submerged in lake water for six months. To them, they appeared to be in pristine condition. There were also no tears or punctures—not the slightest indication that whoever had been inside them had any interaction with alligators.

FWC officers met with Brian Winchester in Tallahassee the next day, displaying the waders to see what he thought. Brian told the Fish and Wildlife officials the waders appeared similar to a pair he and Mike had purchased during their Arkansas hunting trip over Thanksgiving, though he couldn't positively identify them as those very waders. Brian made it clear he thought it entirely plausible that they had been in the lake all that time even though no one had found them during the massive search.

After the officers left, Brian called Scott Dungey, letting him know Mike's waders had apparently been found in the lake. He asked Dungey to arrange for a diver friend of his to search the lakebed in the spot where they had been found.

On June 23, Dungey and a friend named Kip Bembry drove up to Lake Seminole. On the way, they picked up Lamar English, a cave diver from Havana, Florida, a Tallahassee suburb. English had agreed to perform an underwater search.

After launching their boat and arriving at the hole where the waders were discovered, English dropped down into the warm water with a scuba tank strapped to his back. Amazingly, he resurfaced within five minutes holding a small yellow flashlight he found buried in the silt at the lake bottom.

Shockingly, when Dungey turned the flashlight on, a bright light emerged, confirming it was still in perfect working order. Investigators soon learned that Mike had grabbed a similar flashlight from his mom's home about six weeks before he vanished.

English went back down to search for more, this time resurfacing with an even more important treasure—a lightweight camouflage hunting jacket, which he had pulled out of a dense patch of hydrilla. Its sleeves were inside out, suggesting someone had struggled to wriggle free of the garment while underwater.

The jacket was otherwise undamaged and in good condition—no holes or tears from alligator teeth. Nor was any algae or sediment visible on the jacket. The brass buttons showed no discoloration indicating an extended submersion. It also had no odor of any kind.

Even more remarkable was what was inside one of the pockets—a temporary Arkansas hunting license printed on flimsy, unlaminated computer paper, in remarkably good condition and still readable. The name and signature on the license? It was none other than Jerry Michael Williams.

English also made two significant observations while underwater. First, the hydrilla in which the jacket had been lodged was torn, in a manner that looked unnatural. Second, next to that patch of hydrilla, sitting on the lakebed, was a hardened pile of excrement. Alligator feces.

These discoveries put all three men in the camp of friends and officials gravitating toward the "Mike was eaten by alligators" theory.

••••

Just six days later—now armed with these additional pieces of evidence—Curtis Hunter filed a petition for a presumptive death certificate in the Leon County Circuit Court's Probate Division.

The first line of the June 29 court filing made clear Denise harbored no illusion her high-school sweetheart turned husband would ever step foot in their Centennial Oaks home again. In her mind, the man with whom she had shared so many milestones was no longer alive.

The petition began, "COMES NOW the Petitioner, Denise Merrell Williams, the surviving spouse of Jerry Michael Williams, presumed to be dead." On December 16, 2000, it continued, "the decedent" had left home at 4:30 a.m. "to go duck hunting by himself on Lake Seminole" and was "last seen at approximately 5:30 a.m. eastern time on a backwater section of Lake Seminole by fellow hunters."

For the latter point, Hunter cited the report of the Alabama search-and-rescue company Cheryl hired in late January—even though the company had no first-hand knowledge of that fact.

Mike had been scheduled to return home by 1:00 that afternoon, the petition said, "in order to leave at 2:00 p.m. to take his wife to the Gibson Inn in Apalachicola, Florida to celebrate their sixth wedding anniversary." It recounted the massive search operation designed to locate Mike, or his body, attaching the reports of several agencies that had been involved.

The petition cited the discovery of the waders, Mike's hunting jacket, and the flashlight as further evidence that he had drowned and been eaten by alligators. Hunter also indicated he had been in touch with attorneys for Kansas City Life, who had "acquiesced to the entry of an order presuming the death of Jerry Michael Williams on December 16, 2000."

Based on the circumstantial evidence, the petition closed, "the only reasonable inference is that the decedent met his death on December 16, 2000, as a result of an accident on the waters of Lake Seminole." Denise, as petitioner, requested "that this court enter an order presuming the death of Jerry Michael Williams on December 16, 2000." She signed the petition "under penalty of perjury," stating that "the facts alleged are true, to the best of my knowledge and belief."

Hunter also supported the petition with an affidavit signed by Denise, which focused on the strength of her marriage to Mike, which she described as a "loving, caring relationship." Denise stated Mike's family "meant the world to him," not just her and Anslee, "but his mother and my family as well." Mike had made babysitting arrangements with her sister weeks before December 16, 2000, she said, but waited until December 15 to tell her—"as a surprise"—they were going to the Gibson Inn to celebrate their anniversary.

Her affidavit also stated she and Mike were planning to have two more children—spaced three years apart—and intended to start trying for a second child within a month or two of December 2000. She indicated how much Mike loved being a father and how devoted he was to Anslee. "There is no doubt in my mind," she said, "or anyone who knew Mike that he would never leave me or Anslee."

"Everyone who knew him or came in contact with him liked him," the affidavit continued. "He was a genuinely nice person … adored and respected by the people that worked with him." He was planning to become a partner at Ketcham Appraisal very soon, she added, and was one exam away from achieving the highest certification in the appraisal industry. "Mike loved his job," she said, "and the prospects for his career and our future."

Denise mentioned a cruise she and Mike had been planning to take to Hawaii in March 2001 to celebrate both him getting that exam behind him and her birthday on March 7. They were also planning to take a work trip to Jamaica together later in 2001, she said. She closed with these words: "Mike had everything going for him and a family who loved him and whom he loved. I am totally confident that the only reason he did not come home Saturday, December 16, 2000, is because he died in a tragic accident."

The very same day the petition was filed, Denise and Hunter appeared before Circuit Judge John Crusoe in a hearing room at the Leon County Courthouse. No one else was present in the room.

In just a few minutes' time—without requiring any additional evidence—the judge scribbled his signature on an order Hunter had prepared for him. The order concluded that Denise had met the statutory requirements to have Mike declared dead even though five years hadn't elapsed since his disappearance. The death certificate Judge Crusoe signed later that day described Mike's cause of death as "Accidental drowning while duck hunting on Lk Seminole."

With Mike's death certificate in hand, not only was Denise able to collect on Mike's life insurance, she was also able to start receiving his Social Security survivor's benefits. If there had been any concerns about money before, they existed no longer.

All of this transpired without anyone breathing a word to Cheryl or Nick Williams. Oddly, it was Brian who informed Mike's mom of these events. In early July, while searching for his hunting dog Maggie near Lake Iamonia, he bumped into Cheryl part way through her daily walk. He rolled his truck window down and asked if she had seen his dog. "No," she told him.

"Aren't you surprised the judge declared Mike dead so quickly?" he asked, apparently not realizing Cheryl had no idea what he was talking about.

But she pretended to know exactly what he was getting at, responding, "Not with all the evidence that just popped up out of nowhere" — referring to the waders, hunting jacket, flashlight, and hunting license she learned had been found at the lake.

"What do you mean?" Brian asked.

"That stuff was planted, Brian," she answered.

"No, it was a miracle from God," he said with a smirk, driving off, tires squealing.

Not only had Mike's mom been kept in the dark about Denise's successful petition to have Mike declared dead, she was also unaware of three key facts recited in the petition and in Denise's affidavit, which would have been screaming red flags had she been shown the documents.

First, whereas the petition stated Mike went duck hunting at Lake Seminole "by himself," both he and Denise told Cheryl and Nick the Thursday evening they watched *Friends* together that Mike was going to Lake Seminole *with Brian*. When she heard that FWC officers believed Mike had gone to the lake alone, Cheryl believed they were mistaken.

She went to visit Denise the Sunday afternoon after Mike disappeared to ask her daughter-in-law about that inconsistency. Denise told her Mike had indeed gone to the lake alone, explaining he had awakened her at 3:00 a.m. that morning to tell her Brian had called to cancel. Rather than abandoning his duck hunting trip altogether, she said, her husband told her he was pressing forward with his plans to go to Lake Seminole *alone*, but would be back by noon for their anniversary trip.

Cheryl would later learn that Brian told Nick the very same thing during the first evening of the search, telling him — in view of what happened — how horrible he felt about canceling on him at the last minute. Brian said he called Mike at 1:00 a.m., only hours before their scheduled departure, to let Mike know he had to go to Kathy's family Christmas party in Cairo,

Georgia, and even offered him an invitation to tag along with them instead of going to Lake Seminole.

Yet something about those explanations nagged at Mike's mom. They sounded a little too convenient. Too coordinated as well. As if Denise and Brian were somehow in cahoots. She would have loved to have been able to share those details with Judge Crusoe before he granted Denise's petition to have Mike declared dead, but never had the chance.

Second, Denise's affidavit stated Mike first told her about his plan to take her to the Gibson Inn "the day before he went hunting as a surprise." Yet Cheryl and Nick were aware of that plan a day earlier—while they all watched *Friends* together— because both Mike and Denise told them about their anniversary plans in great detail. The trip to the Gibson Inn was no surprise at all.

Third, Denise's petition stated that Kansas City Life Insurance Company was the "only party with an interest in this Petition who could object to this petition being filed." But that also wasn't true. For starters, Cheryl and Nick obviously had an interest in whether Mike was declared dead. Moreover, Mike also had an insurance policy with Cotton States—for $500,000—which he had obtained just before taking out the $1 million Kansas City Life policy. Yet there was no reference to Cotton States in Denise's petition whatsoever.

By the time Cheryl learned about the contentions in Denise's petition, it was far too late for her—or for Cotton States, for that matter—to challenge them. In the eyes of the law, Mike was already dead.

••••

In the months following Mike's disappearance, as the divide between the Merrell and Williams families grew wider, Cheryl and Nick found their time with Anslee restricted to once a week—ninety minutes every Monday at 6:30 p.m. in Denise's Centennial Oaks home. Denise was always part of the visits, keeping a watchful eye on her mother-in-law and brother-in-law to make sure they didn't fill her daughter's head with topics she considered off limits—such as what had happened to her father.

The tension between them was palpable. Cheryl, well aware Denise had told Anslee her daddy was in heaven, would tell Denise that wasn't true, that Mike hadn't been eaten by alligators. Denise would treat her mother-in-law as if she were certifiably insane. Cheryl and Nick felt more disrespected and marginalized with each passing visit. But they continued to abide by Denise's strict limitations and rules, recognizing that, as Anslee's exclusive gatekeeper, she could cut them off from the child any time she pleased.

At the same time, unbeknownst to Denise, Cheryl had been sending handwritten letters to the *Tallahassee Democrat*, begging the local newspaper to run a story about Mike's disappearance to draw attention to the search to find him. Though none of those requests led to an actual article being published, a reporter who was writing a story about missing persons of local interest came across them as he was conducting his research.

The reporter contacted Cheryl about the possibility of including Mike in the story. She readily agreed, encouraged the article would heighten public awareness which might help investigators solve the mystery surrounding her son's disappearance. She had Nick run Mike's high school yearbook picture over to the newsroom to include in the story. Finally, she thought, something good was happening.

The article—including Mike's picture—was published on Sunday, August 5, 2001. It included quotes from Cheryl stating that Mike would never have knowingly or willingly suddenly dropped everything and walked away from his existing life. But it also included the theory that "he may have fallen victim to alligators. While they don't normally feed during the cold weather, the night he disappeared was unseasonably warm. Deputies spotted eight to ten alligators in the area only a few hours after Williams vanished."

Several friends called to let Cheryl know they had seen the article and congratulated her for her persistence. But she also received a call of a very different nature. From Denise. She could sense from the tone of her voice that her daughter-in-law was livid. "You and Nick need to get over here right now," she demanded.

When they arrived at the Centennial Oaks property, Denise met them in her front yard, not even allowing them inside. She was furious. Without pausing to make small talk, she told them she had read the article in the *Democrat* and had seen Mike's photo.

"I don't *ever* want to see Mike's picture in the paper again," she said, seething with anger. "I don't *ever* want to know anything you're doing about Mike again. I have to get on with my life."

When she finally paused to take a breath, Cheryl retorted, "If that were Anslee in the lake, you would just leave her there?"

"I would believe the authorities," Denise shot back, noting everyone had concluded Mike had drowned and was not going to somehow turn up alive.

"If you persist in trying to get a criminal investigation going, *you will lose Anslee*," she threatened.

It was an ugly confrontation. Cheryl and Nick got back in the car without even being given the courtesy of seeing Anslee—unsure if they would ever see her again.

5

Life Goes On

Not long after the search at Lake Seminole began, Warren Merrell was allowed to drive Mike's Ford Bronco back to Tallahassee.

Authorities at the lake had no further need for the vehicle, as there was no thought at the time foul play had been involved in Mike's disappearance. Because Warren didn't want the vehicle stored at 5017 Centennial Oaks Circle—where it would serve as a painful reminder to his daughter and granddaughter about Mike's disappearance—he asked Marcus Winchester to keep it at his property near Lake McBride.

In early August 2001, Cheryl called Marcus seeking permission to swing by his home to take a look at the Bronco for herself.

"Now why on earth would you want to do that?" Marcus asked.

"Because I'm his mother and I haven't seen the truck since he disappeared," she replied, annoyed Marcus—no kin to Mike—would even intimate he had more right than she did to decide what happened with his truck.

A few weeks later—the afternoon of Labor Day—Denise arrived at Cheryl's front doorstep with a key to the truck, ready to accompany her and Nick to Marcus's home. When they arrived, the pair spotted Mike's Ford Bronco parked under the carport.

Nick took the key from Denise and opened the driver's side door. When he did, he and his mom immediately noticed a foul odor. The upholstery and floorboards were soaking wet and mildewed.

Nick began unloading the items in the truck and handing them to Cheryl: clothes, tennis shoes, boots, socks, caps, shirts, shorts, a jacket—all of which were drenched—for her to wring dry. Nick also found Mike's shotgun, still in its case, and handed it to Denise for safekeeping.

"Why is everything soaked?" Cheryl quizzed Marcus, suspecting something fishy had occurred in the eight-plus months the vehicle had been stored on his property. "Has someone sprayed the truck with water?"

"It's probably just condensation," Marcus answered, leaving both Cheryl and Nick bewildered and suspicious.

Though Cheryl had intended to wash Mike's clothes when she returned home, she and Nick thought better of it. Perhaps there was something in them, they thought, that might be a clue to his disappearance. They left his clothes sealed in garbage bags, hopeful law enforcement officers would later consider them important.

At about 5:00 p.m. the following Monday, as Nick and Cheryl were getting ready to head to Centennial Oaks for their weekly visit with Anslee—which Denise had allowed to continue despite their uncomfortable confrontation in early August—the phone rang. It was Denise. She told Cheryl she was bringing Anslee there. "I also want to pick up Mike's clothes," she said, almost under her breath. Her mother-in-law responded that she hadn't washed them yet and was keeping them bagged up at her place for the "investigation."

"I'll be there shortly," Denise said as the conversation ended. Yet neither she nor Anslee ever arrived. Instead, at about 7:30 p.m., Warren pulled down Cheryl's long gravel driveway, finding her pacing on her front porch. Cheryl was afraid something had happened to Denise and Anslee on the way.

"Where's Denise?" she asked, genuinely concerned. "Did she have a wreck?"

Warren, however, was in no mood for a conversation. He was seething. "She will never come here again!" he screamed. "I won't allow it. Every time you get around Denise, you and your big mouth upset her. I won't have it anymore! Do you understand?"

Not sure why he was so angry, Cheryl invited Warren inside to discuss his concerns with her and Nick. But when he got inside, Warren continued his tirade: "You're crazy! You need psychiatric help," he yelled, eyes bulging as if they might fly out of his head. "Your son is dead in the lake. I told you so. I told Denise he is in the lake and that is where he is."

"You can tell your wife and daughters what to think, but you cannot tell me what to think," Cheryl retorted, beginning to lose her cool herself.

"If you were a Christian and in the church, you would believe your son was in the lake," Warren told her.

"I am a Christian," Cheryl shot back, "and there is no proof he is in the lake. If you know my son is in the lake for 100 percent, then you put him there!"

Demanding that Cheryl hand over Mike's clothes, Warren told her angrily, "Under no circumstances are you to call Denise's house. You are no longer welcome in her home. And don't call Johnnie either. She hates you too."

The confrontation was even uglier than the one Denise had initiated with Cheryl in August.

As Nick handed Warren a garbage bag filled with Mike's clothes and boots, Cheryl told him he had better have the clothes available when the police came for them. As well as the waders and hunting jacket she understood were given to him after they were discovered in June.

"Now I guess you're going to accuse me of planting those, aren't you?" Warren snickered.

"The only person I even mentioned that to is Brian Winchester," Cheryl answered. "Now I know you and Brian are in cahoots."

"If and when you get an official investigation going, I'll turn them over," Warren said angrily, snatching the bag from Nick's hands—hoping never to see him or Cheryl again. As he drove back down the gravel driveway, he had no earthly idea that another bag filled with Mike's clothes remained in the mobile home, at the ready for the criminal investigation Mike's mom hoped would soon commence.

••••

Almost from the day Mike vanished, the relationship between Brian and Kathy Winchester had begun to unravel. Their marriage was already pretty rocky before Mike's disappearance, Kathy often sleeping in Stafford's room or on the couch during much of the year of 2000.

Kathy had been extremely distraught about Mike, crying incessantly. Though Brian spent most days at the lake searching for his best friend, when he arrived home each evening, he wanted to change the subject. Kathy just couldn't do that. They had knockdown-dragout screaming matches over her inability to move on. It became clear very quickly their marriage was over.

On September 11, 2001, while the Twin Towers were falling in New York City, Kathy was flitting from one room to the next in her and Brian's Minnow Creek Drive home, methodically collecting and packing her belongings. She and Stafford moved in with her parents that day.

Despite their open hostility toward one another before they separated, the two tried their best to remain civil for Stafford's sake. They agreed to share custody of him equally, their divorce ultimately becoming final in late March 2003. In January 2004, Kathy married Rocky Thomas, a coworker at The Copy Shop. They had two daughters together who would grow up as Stafford's half-sisters.

••••

Denise, suddenly a millionaire thanks to the life insurance proceeds, needed guidance on how to handle her newfound money. She initially turned to Marcus Winchester, who recommended that she invest most of it in the stock market. He suggested she also acquire some land, which he told her wouldn't bear nearly the same risk as the market.

Taking his advice to heart, Denise had Marcus place several hundred thousand dollars into a Vanguard mutual fund account, trusting him to manage it wisely. She also began looking for lakefront lots she thought might make good investments, first finding a great piece of property at Miller Landing on Lake Jackson for the price of $135,000. Patti Ketcham attended the closing with her that spring.

During the summer of 2002, Brian suggested Denise take a look at another expansive tract of land—on Lake McBride in Bradfordville—which was owned by the president of Florida State University and his wife. A sign indicated the vacant lot was for sale. Patti helped Denise with her due diligence, eventually preparing a bid for the nearly eight-acre parcel, for which Denise paid more than $275,000. Notably, the lot—on Duck Cove Road of all places—was just down the street from Brian's childhood residence, the place his mom and dad still called home.

••••

Valentine's Day 2003 turned out to be a very special day for Cheryl and Nick. For the first time since Mike's disappearance, Denise entrusted her daughter to their care overnight. Though she didn't come right out and tell them, it seemed Denise had a special date planned that evening.

Ten days later, Mike's presumed widow confided in Patti she had begun dating a high school friend of Mike's named Jimmy Martin—whose parents lived across the street on Centennial Oaks Circle. Mike and Martin had gone hunting together on several occasions. He was actually living across the street, with his parents, at the time Mike disappeared.

Cheryl considered Denise's romantic interest in Martin perplexing. During their high school days, she distinctly recalled Denise telling her how much she hated him. "Creepy" was how she would describe him to her future mother-in-law. Shockingly, though, Martin had now emerged as Denise's first post-Mike flame.

In late February, Cheryl and Nick kept Anslee again—until 11:00 p.m.—while Denise and Martin were on another date. That evening, Anslee asked her grandmother, "Grand Mama Cheryl, do you know my daddy's telephone number? My mommy lost it." All Cheryl could muster in response was, "Anslee, they don't have telephone numbers in heaven," heartbroken by the child's question.

Denise continued dating Martin through May, her new beau happily accompanying her to Anslee's fourth birthday party on May 8. Brian Winchester was also at the party, telling Cheryl he too had already begun dating, his divorce from Kathy having been finalized more than a month before.

By late May, however, the romance between Denise and Jimmy Martin was over. On June 2, Denise had Cheryl keep Anslee so she and a man named Chuck Bunker—a coworker at the State Board of Administration—could go to an Eagles concert together. Cheryl later learned, after a little sleuthing, that Bunker was actually her boss. And that he was a divorced 43-year-old father of a 16-year-old girl.

In late June, unbeknownst to Cheryl, Denise and Bunker went together to an accounting conference in Atlanta. On their second night in town, something very odd occurred while the two were walking—hand-in-hand—through the hotel lobby. They were suddenly confronted by another man: Brian Winchester.

"What are you doing here?" Denise asked, shocked to see him hundreds of miles from home.

"We need to talk," Brian said. He seemed inebriated—and angry—a crazed look in his eyes. The three went outside, near the hotel entrance, where Brian threatened to kill both Denise and Bunker, claiming he had a gun in his pocket. He demanded that Bunker leave at once. Not taking any chances the crazed lunatic would make good on his threats, Bunker gathered his belongings and headed back to Tallahassee, leaving Denise and Brian behind.

After Bunker left, Denise was somehow able to reason with Brian and calm him down. He left the next morning. Bunker then returned and spent the rest of the week with Denise.

But by late July, Denise's relationship with Bunker was over. She told Cheryl he began stalking her and writing her threatening letters, leading her to seek a restraining order—and to report him to his superiors at the Board of Administration. Cheryl was confused by the abrupt turn of events. But none the wiser about what had occurred at the Atlanta hotel—as neither Denise nor Brian ever shared with her any of those particular details.

••••

When it came time to enroll children in preschool for the 2003-2004 school year, Denise, Brian, and Kathy all made the same decision: Anslee and Stafford would attend North Florida Christian School, the same place their parents had graduated from in 1988. The threesome—once a fun-loving foursome—would frequently bump into each other as they dropped off and picked up their preschoolers.

Apparently, Denise and Brian had been bumping into each other a lot more than at the NFC campus. Cheryl began hearing about sightings of them together across town. Before long, they were showing up as a pair at her home to pick up Anslee in Brian's brand new truck after evening or overnight visits. Though they didn't come right out and tell her, it appeared to Cheryl the two were dating.

Cheryl also heard from friends that Brian would snap at Anslee at restaurants—where Denise, Brian, and their children were spotted eating together as if they were a family. Brian would scold Anslee as if she were his child, Cheryl was informed. Though she had become highly suspicious and distrustful of her son's best friend almost immediately after Mike disappeared, Brian's poor treatment of Anslee raised her animosity toward him to a whole new level.

A few months later, an unlikely informant provided Cheryl with some additional insights—her granddaughter. During an overnight visit, Anslee told her that she and Stafford had been sleeping in the same room together. And that Stafford's daddy had been staying "in Mommy's room."

"Wow!" thought Cheryl, her suspicions about Brian—and Denise—now off the charts. She didn't breathe a word to either Brian or Denise, keeping Anslee's little secret just between them. Rather, Cheryl began watching them even more closely. Like a hawk.

••••

In the fall of 2003, Denise turned to a Christian counselor, ostensibly to help her deal with grief over Mike's death. Almost overnight, Christianity began to assume center stage in her life. She devoured Christian books and videos such as Pastor Rick Warren's *The Purpose Driven Life: What am I Here For?*, trying her best to use his teachings to walk a new, spiritual journey.

By December 2003, she had become a regular Saturday morning visitor at the nearby federal women's prison, sharing the Gospel with inmates, hoping to bring them to Jesus. She told friends she felt a sense of meaning and purpose for the first time in her life. Warren and Johnnie Merrell couldn't have been prouder of their daughter's new direction—and renewed commitment to God.

At her counselor's urging, Denise also decided the time had come for her to visit Lake Seminole. The counselor questioned whether Denise would be able to fully grieve Mike's loss without seeing for herself where he had drowned.

As they became closer, Patti Ketcham would periodically tell Denise of her willingness to escort her to the lake if she ever wanted to go. On January 6, 2004, Denise called Patti, telling her she was ready.

The following day, the two met at Patti's office to begin the hour-long journey to Sneads. As the realtor got behind the wheel of her car in the parking lot, Denise asked her to promise she would never tell a soul they had gone to the lake. Patti agreed she wouldn't.

With a full hour ahead of them, and not sure how best to pass the time, Patti remarked—before even putting her car in gear — "I've looked at all the Miss Manners books I could find, and there's nothing in any of them about how to handle a situation like this. Do you want to talk about Mike? Do you want to talk about the search? Do you want to talk about mindless stuff?" Denise chose the latter.

When they turned off Interstate 10 in Sneads, onto the road leading to the lake, Denise finally said, "Okay, now tell me the story."

With that invitation, Patti began telling her about the massive search operation, pointing out landmarks, such as the restaurants in which FWC officers and volunteers would congregate for lunch and dinner.

She parked her car just off River Road, pointing Denise in the direction of Stump Field. Patti told her to take whatever time she needed, explaining she had brought a book to read and would stay in her car.

Denise opened the passenger door, picking up the long-stemmed red rose she had brought with her. She also retrieved a note from her purse she had apparently written for the occasion and began walking toward the shoreline.

Every so often, Patti would look up from her book, checking to make sure Denise was okay. Finally, after what seemed like 30 or 45 minutes, she spotted Denise slowly walking back. It was obvious she had been crying. She was no longer holding the flower or the note.

"Are you all right?" Patti asked.

"Yes," I'll be okay," Denise replied. They talked about Mike the entire ride back to Tallahassee, sharing funny stories, memories of happy times, and speculating how proud he would be of his big girl Anslee—now approaching her fifth birthday.

••••

Throughout Anslee's year in preschool, Cheryl had the good fortune of being entrusted with her care on a consistent basis—often overnight. Denise needed her help, as she was spending Saturday mornings at the women's prison with her

Christian ministry and was going out many Friday and Saturday evenings, presumably with Brian.

Whatever the reason, the doting grandmother really didn't care. She treasured her time with Anslee, and was grateful that time had increased substantially from the tense, supervised visits in Denise's home she and Nick had been limited to following Mike's disappearance—despite his widow's threat that she would never see Anslee again.

Meanwhile, Cheryl's first-born was finally set to tie the knot, Nick's wedding to his fiancée Jeanne set for September 25, 2004. Shortly after the invitations were sent, Cheryl received a call—from Denise. During their conversation, her daughter-in-law finally came clean. She and Brian were dating, Denise said—as if Cheryl didn't already know. She asked for Cheryl's permission to bring him to Nick's wedding as her date.

Though Denise agreed for Anslee to be a flower girl at the wedding, the five year old had other ideas, throwing a fit just as it came time for her to perform. Cheryl sprang into action, grabbing the child's hand and beginning to walk her down the aisle as a flower grandma. But when Anslee glanced toward her mother in the midst of her duties, the waterworks began.

Denise shot out of her chair, gathered her up, and abruptly left the outdoor ceremony before the minister could even say, "Dearly beloved."

••••

On January 8, 2005, Cheryl and Nick were out to lunch at Chili's—part of their normal Saturday routine—when Nick's cell phone rang. It was Denise. She asked when he and Cheryl would be back at her place. Nick told her they would be there around 2:00 p.m. His sister-in-law said she would be coming over then.

Cheryl's first thought after Nick hung up was that Denise was bringing Anslee over to celebrate her 61st birthday, which was the very next day. She hadn't seen her granddaughter since Halloween. Cheryl rushed Nick to get home, eagerly anticipating a visit with Anslee.

But when Denise knocked on the door shortly after 2:00 p.m., Cheryl's exuberance was dashed. The guest standing beside her daughter-in-law wasn't Anslee after all. It was Brian.

"Where's Anslee?" she asked, clearly puzzled.

"She's taking a nap," Denise replied, her tone signaling that another confrontation was about to begin.

Denise sat across from Cheryl at her kitchen table, Nick standing beside his mom. Brian waited by the front door, his back turned to the other three.

Denise began their conversation calmly, saying, "You know that Anslee and I love you, but Brian and I don't like the lies you're telling about us."

"What lies are you talking about?" Cheryl asked, not sure where Denise was headed.

"All the lies you're telling about me and Brian," she replied.

Now perturbed herself, Cheryl retorted, "I am not telling any lies. All I want to know is what happened to Mike and where he is and both of you know."

Deflecting Cheryl's accusation, Denise issued an ultimatum: "If you will just stop this investigation, you can see Anslee again." She was referring to an investigation the Florida Department of Law Enforcement, or FDLE, had started in February 2004—at Cheryl's persistent urging.

"Denise, I can't stop this investigation," her mother-in-law said. "I wouldn't if I could."

At that point, Brian barged over to the table, eyes bulging. "You shut your mouth and let her talk!" he yelled. Nick glared at him, telling him to leave if he was going to treat his mother that way.

"Denise, Mike is Mama's son and my brother," Nick said to his sister-in-law, "and we just want to know what you and Brian did to him."

"Let's get out of here Denise," Brian angrily spouted. "We're not getting anywhere." The couple stormed out of Cheryl's front door.

To Cheryl, what Denise and Brian did that afternoon was

akin to waving a red flag in front of an angry bull. The iron-willed mother wasn't about to be bullied into submission. Especially by the very people she believed knew precisely what had happened to her son.

This time, though—with Brian's encouragement and support—Denise would follow through on her threat. She would never entrust Anslee to her grandmother's care again. Cheryl's time with her precious granddaughter came to a screeching halt. Forever.

••••

Saturday, December 3, 2005, was a glorious day in Florida's capital city. Over 100 guests had gathered by a picturesque, moss-draped oak tree near a small pond just off Centennial Oaks Circle, the rows of white chairs neatly divided in the green grass, a wide aisle between them.

Brian Winchester, sharply dressed in a black tuxedo, stood by the oak tree, patiently awaiting the arrival of his bride. The minister of the Four Oaks Community Church stood just to his right, Brian's identically-dressed groomsmen to his left. The bridesmaids were arrayed on the opposite side of the minister, their beautiful matching dresses absorbing the afternoon sunshine. The setting couldn't have been more storybook.

The faint clip-clop cadence of a horse-drawn carriage grew stronger and more pronounced. All at once, the guests turned in unison as the carriage came to an abrupt halt, just behind the assembled audience. First to step out was Anslee Williams, a beautiful blonde-haired girl, elegantly dressed, now six and a half years old.

She stood and waited as her mother—the soon-to-be Denise Winchester—stepped down in a stunning white, embroidered bridal gown. Denise took her daughter's hand and began marching forward, Mike Williams' widow about to join his best friend in holy matrimony. Five years, nearly to the day, since his still unexplained disappearance.

The audience included many familiar faces: Denise's three sisters and her mom Johnnie and father Warren; Brian's dad

Marcus and mom Patricia; and many of Denise's and Brian's classmates and friends from NFC and Florida State.

Notably absent, however, were Cheryl and Nick Williams, no longer welcome among gatherings of Merrells or Winchesters. Indeed, barely anyone attending the wedding beside the bride and groom themselves had any significant connection with Jerry Michael Williams. It was almost as if the whole point of the ceremony was to erase all evidence he had ever existed.

Among many gathered that day, as well as in the larger Tallahassee community, the spectacle of Mike's best friend marrying his widow—and becoming the stepfather of his daughter—was unsettling, if not downright eerie. The union of the pair was sure to draw scrutiny from cold-case investigators, still trying to piece together what had happened to Mike at Lake Seminole.

As the service began, the minister revealed that Denise and Brian had been in pre-marital counseling sessions with him for nearly a year. "There's nothing between these two that I'm not aware of," he announced confidently. Upon hearing those words, Clay and Patti Ketcham, who had all but concluded foul play by the bride and groom—not hungry alligators—was likely responsible for Mike's disappearance, smirked in disbelief.

Gently elbowing his wife in the rib cage, Clay whispered, "Well, there might be one minor little detail he doesn't know."

6

Persistence, Perseverance, Pursuit

Cheryl Ann Spearman grew up in Jacksonville, Florida, the oldest of five children; she had a matched set of two sisters and two brothers. Her father James, a World War II veteran, supported the large family working at the Post Office, leaving her mom Myra to stay home to raise the children. Both brothers, Jimmy and Mike, would be sent off to fight America's war in Vietnam.

From an early age, there was little doubt Cheryl possessed a sharp mind and intense determination, often exceeding her own goals. She excelled in academics, setting her sights on attending college before beginning high school.

During vacations to visit her mother's parents in the Panhandle each summer, the Spearman family would drive through the heart of Tallahassee, where Cheryl got her first glimpse of Florida State. It was love at first sight. She never considered any other college, working her tail off in high school to ensure her admission—graduating in the top ten out of several hundred students.

With an academic scholarship in hand and her trademark pigtails, Cheryl set off for Florida State in September 1962, determined to become a high school teacher. She majored in English and French secondary education, residing in the scholarship dorm.

During her freshman year, Cheryl fell in love a second

time. With football. A sport for which she had shown zero interest growing up in Jacksonville. Throughout the fall, she was among the most passionate, rabid fans at Doak Campbell Stadium, on cloud nine with each win, but down in the dumps for days each time her beloved Seminoles lost. Her love for Florida State football would remain steadfast through the decades that followed.

Not surprisingly, Cheryl immersed herself in her studies. By her junior year, she was well on her way to becoming a high school teacher. Having never learned to drive, she would take a Greyhound bus back home for school breaks, returning to Tallahassee on a Greyhound as well. So it was that the 21-year-old Florida State student found herself at a Greyhound Bus terminal in April 1965, ready to return from spring break in Jacksonville.

There were five buses lined up ready to depart. Cheryl randomly selected one, taking a seat next to a gentleman about halfway toward the back. When the driver—a tall, dark, and handsome 25 year old who had just started with Greyhound—walked down the aisle to collect her ticket, he asked the man seated beside her, with a wry smile, "Why don't you drive the bus and I'll sit next to her?" Cheryl instantly felt a flutter in her heart.

As passengers would disembark at each stop, she gradually moved her seat closer and closer to the front. Toward the end of the trip, she was seated in the row directly behind the driver—but not saying a word. Without taking his eyes off the road, the driver finally broke the uncomfortable silence. "You better speak to me," he said, "or I might just fall asleep."

Cheryl obliged.

Her roommate was waiting when they pulled up to the Tallahassee bus terminal. But her car battery had died. She told Cheryl she didn't know how they would get back to campus. Overhearing their conversation, the bus driver offered them both a ride. When they got out of his car at the girls' apartment, he asked Cheryl for her telephone number. She scribbled it on a piece of paper and said goodnight, a twinkle in her eyes.

When her roommate asked why she had given her number to a bus driver, Cheryl glibly replied, "Because I'm going to marry him." It was love at first sight all over again. Though she began her senior year at Florida State that fall, she would never complete college or fulfill her goal of teaching high school. By January 1966, she was married to her soulmate—a Greyhound bus driver named Jerry Jerome Williams, or J.J. for short. By February, she was pregnant with Nick.

••••

From the moment she stood on the shoreline of Lake Seminole on Christmas Eve 2000—when God told her Mike hadn't drowned in the lake—Cheryl had been determined to find out what actually happened to her second child. Though some may have assumed from her slight stature and pigtails the grandmother was meek and timid, Cheryl Ann Williams possessed the tenacity of a bulldog, the grit of a mountain climber, and the perseverance of a marathon runner. Giving up on solving the mystery surrounding Mike's disappearance simply wasn't an option—no matter how many months, years, or decades it would take or how much money it might cost.

Early on, she began taking copious notes of everything she heard that seemed even remotely connected to Mike's disappearance and everything that didn't make sense. And there was a lot that made no sense to Cheryl. For starters, 80 people were known to have drowned in Lake Seminole. A body had eventually floated to the surface every single time—as FWC officers had assured her would happen with Mike. When his body never surfaced, pure logic dictated he hadn't drowned in the lake.

She refused to accept that the reason Mike's body never floated was because he had been eaten by alligators. From his earliest days hunting at nearby Lake Iamonia, her youngest son had repeatedly assured her that alligators become dormant in the colder, winter months. Since duck hunting is only permitted during those months, he had told her, she didn't need to worry about his safety. Why FWC personnel didn't understand that was deeply troubling to Cheryl. Especially because the myth that alligators had consumed him had prevented a criminal investigation from occurring when it really could have made a difference—when physical evidence vital to determining what had actually happened could have been preserved and analyzed.

Despite the lack of physical evidence, Cheryl clung to her fervent belief that a criminal investigation could still unearth the truth. By 2002, she had written the FDLE, requesting that just such an investigation be launched. In January 2003, she had her notes typed up and sent all 27 pages to the FDLE. Her notes concluded with an urgent plea: "I do not believe my son is in Lake Seminole. I don't want to believe that he walked off. I believe that Mike is dead because of something he found out about someone he knew. PLEASE HELP ME FIND MY SON. THANK YOU."

Her persistence finally paid off. On February 6, 2004, an FDLE investigator named John Stevens met with her at her Bradfordville home. "Ms. Williams, now's your chance," he said. "Tell me what you want me to know."

For nearly two hours, Cheryl did just that, regurgitating everything she knew in intricate detail—reciting dates and key events from memory—and telling the detective about her suspicions of Brian, Denise, Marcus, and Warren. Something was very fishy, she said, about Brian supposedly cancelling his duck hunting trip with Mike in the wee hours of the morning he vanished. She questioned Denise's odd behavior since her husband disappeared—none of which seemed consistent with that of a grieving widow. Most troubling of all, Cheryl told Stevens, were the millions of dollars in insurance Denise was able to claim from Mike's death.

For the first time in over three years, Cheryl felt heard. And hopeful. Stevens told her the FDLE would be joining with other agencies, including the Jackson County Sheriff's Office (JCSO), in launching an investigation. She would hear from them very soon, he assured her.

Less than two weeks later, Cheryl met with two more investigators: Ronnie Austin from the State Attorney's Office in Tallahassee and Derrick Wester from the JCSO. Before long,

Cheryl found herself in constant telephone communications with the two detectives, them sharing with her new leads and her pointing them in new directions.

To Austin and Wester, there was a whole lot that didn't make sense beyond what Cheryl had told them, including virtually all of the evidence discovered at Lake Seminole. To begin with, the "boat ramp" adjacent to where Mike's truck was found was no boat ramp at all—a narrow patch of mud amid the tall reeds on the western shoreline. If Mike had been alone, they wondered, why on earth would he have attempted to launch his boat in those difficult, muddy conditions rather than at the concrete ramp just a few hundred yards away— which he would have passed by on his way to the dirt ramp?

And if he had actually been duck hunting, why were all of the decoys still neatly packed in his boat, rather than spread out on the lake? Why was his gun still zipped up in its case?

Moreover, though the throttle to the Go Devil motor was found in the "on" position, nearly wide open, the gas tank was almost full. How could that be? Wester contacted the owner of Go Devil Motors. He told the detective that if the motor had been running and Mike had fallen out of the boat, it would have continued running until the gas in the tank had been fully consumed. He speculated someone had deliberately placed the throttle in the forward position when the engine wasn't running.

Finally, since Mike's lightweight, empty Gheenoe motorboat wasn't found until after a torrential rainstorm had blown through, the storm's westerly winds should have pushed the boat up against the eastern shoreline, not against the western shoreline where it was discovered. It also made no sense that the boat was found behind several tree stumps. The detectives couldn't conceive of how it drifted to that location on its own.

It made even less sense that additional items were found in the lake weeks and months after the intense full-on search had turned up nothing at all—from the camouflage hat found two weeks later to the waders, jacket, hunting license, and flashlight found six months later. To Austin and Wester's experienced eyes, those discoveries were glaring red flags. Rather than supporting the notion Mike had drowned, to them, the sudden appearance of those items strongly suggested the entire scene had been staged—gradually, over a period of months.

With decades of experience between them, the investigators quickly concluded Mike hadn't fallen overboard and drowned. Whoever had staged the scene, they believed, had intended to throw law enforcement off the scent of whatever vicious atrocity had actually transpired. Over three years later, with that scent now long gone, it was up to them to put the puzzle pieces together and figure out what really happened—and who was responsible.

The who seemed much more obvious than the what. Brian and Denise were now a romantic couple—barely three years after his best friend and her life-long sweetheart had presumably drowned. *He* was the one who had written the $1 million life insurance policy a mere months before Mike's disappearance on which *she* had collected. As quickly as they concluded Mike hadn't drowned, Austin and Wester were already zeroing in on his best friend and his widow.

••••

As it turned out, Kansas City Life (KCL) harbored its own suspicions, deciding to investigate further before forking over the $1.25 million in proceeds on Mike's two policies with the company.

Incredibly, the life insurer first received a "notice of death" on December 27, 2000—*eleven days* after Mike disappeared—right in the thick of the massive search to find him. The notice was apparently called in by Marcus Winchester, who explained Mike had drowned after falling out of his boat while duck hunting.

Eight days later, on January 4, 2001, Denise and Brian each signed a claim form seeking payment on the two KCL policies, she as the beneficiary and he as the witness. The blank for the cause of death was filled in as "Accidental Drowning." Brian later supplied KCL with newspaper clippings from the

Floridian newspaper in Jackson County, which were full of information about the search to find Mike.

The life insurer retained an investigatory firm out of Illinois to conduct interviews, obtain medical records, and help ferret out what happened. An investigator interviewed Denise by telephone on January 5, less than three weeks after Mike vanished.

"Although she seemed very tense and upset she was very cooperative and forthcoming in her answers," the investigator wrote. Denise described Mike as an avid duck hunter who had planned to go hunting alone on December 16 before coming home to leave with her on an anniversary trip to the Gibson Inn. She noted Mike would either hunt with a friend or—if no one was available—would go alone. He wanted to be on the lake "at his hunting spot by dawn" the morning he disappeared, Denise told him.

She recounted that when Mike hadn't returned home by 3:00 p.m., she became very concerned because it was not like him to be late without calling. She told the investigator that Mike would typically go hunting in a camouflage coat, pants, and chest-high waders. Denise indicated there "were no marital problems and no infidelity on the part of either. They had no money problems and no problems with the law."

Almost immediately after he ended his call with Denise, the insurance investigator's phone began ringing. This time, Brian was on the other end. "He wanted us to know he had been a longtime friend of the insured," he wrote, "and wanted to be of any help that he could." Brian told him, "With what he was wearing and the fact that his waders would rapidly fill with water if he went over, it is not at all likely that he could have swum or stayed above water." And also that, due to the size and shape of the boat, "the insured could have easily lost his balance, if he were standing, and fallen out of the boat had he hit a stump or a log." Brian also mentioned that the lake was filled with "a wide variety of wildlife" including "some very large alligators."

On January 11, Brian and Marcus met directly with KCL representatives while attending a national convention for the life insurer's agents. Marcus was hopeful the good will and clout Winchester Financial Group had built up over many years selling policies for KCL would accelerate the payout on Denise's claim.

During the meeting, Brian told KCL personnel that, for the type of boat Mike owned, the driver had to stand up to keep the throttle open and to steer. He also revealed that wildlife officers at the lake had informed him they had recently seen 14-foot alligators in the area. For that reason, Brian said, the cadaver dogs weren't even allowed in the water or on the shoreline. He assured KCL's representatives that no foul play had been involved in Mike's disappearance. And urged them to process Denise's claim quickly.

Meanwhile, KCL was completely unaware of the existence of another insurance policy on Mike's life—the one taken out by Mike in March 2000 with Cotton States for $500,000. Curiously, Denise hadn't made a claim on that policy at the time she was pursuing the KCL policies. Even more perplexing, she actually sent a premium check for $398.30 to Cotton States on April 16—four months *after* Mike's disappearance—without offering the slightest hint her husband was missing.

Finally, on September 19, 2001—months after Judge Crusoe signed the presumptive death certificate—Denise submitted a claim to Cotton States, certifying that Mike had died in a hunting accident. Oddly, on that claim form, in the blank space asking her to list all other life insurance policies in force at the time of Mike's death, Denise listed only one of the two KCL policies: the $250,000 policy that had been in force since February 1995. Cotton States therefore had no reason to know Mike had taken out a $1 million policy with KCL the month after it had issued its $500,000 policy.

In April 2002, the Florida Department of Insurance (FDI) started its own investigation into these inconsistencies. By then, however, KCL had already paid Denise $1,327,024.30—eight-percent interest on top of its $1.25 million in coverage.

And Cotton States had paid her an additional $504,453.56. Despite the suspicious circumstances, Denise had recovered nearly $2 million in all. And before long, without any further evidence to go on, the FDI's investigation came to a screeching halt.

••••

On April 21, 2004, Cheryl was on her way back home from a long walk when she noticed an unfamiliar car driving down her long gravel driveway. When she arrived, she saw Kathy (Winchester) Thomas and her husband Rocky getting out of the car. Kathy apologized for not coming to see Cheryl sooner, telling her that Rocky's persistent urging—and her conscience—were responsible for their visit.

Kathy told Cheryl she had been tormented about things she had never shared with anyone about the day Mike vanished. With Rocky's help, she said, she had worked up the courage to finally come clean. She told Cheryl that Brian had no alibi—not until he showed up at her family's Christmas gathering in Cairo, Georgia after 4:00 p.m. that Saturday. He wasn't at home when she woke up that morning nor at any time until she and Stafford left for Georgia without him after 2:30 p.m.

She recounted that Brian had called her father Jimmy Aldredge the night before and arranged to go hunting together early that morning. But her dad had waited in vain for more than two hours at their designated meeting point—his son-in-law a no-show. Brian's father Marcus had actually called Jimmy later that day, telling him, "I hear Brian stood you up and slept in. He does that to me all the time." Yet the excuse Brian gave Kathy's father wasn't that he overslept. What Brian told Jimmy at 9:00 that morning was that he had to cancel because he couldn't find the keys to his boat.

The biggest bombshell Kathy dropped on Cheryl was her suspicion that Brian and Denise were having an affair *before* Mike disappeared. She wasn't positive, she said, but was aware of several troubling indications.

She also shared with Cheryl that Denise had admitted to her that Brian had followed her and Chuck Bunker to Atlanta and threatened them with a weapon. Chuck had actually written her a letter about the incident, Kathy said, in which he had mentioned some crazy, bizarre things he knew about both Denise and Brian. And warned her Brian was dangerous.

When it was finally her turn to speak, Cheryl told Kathy she had recently succeeded in getting the FDLE and other agencies to open a criminal investigation into Mike's disappearance. She provided telephone numbers for Ronnie Austin and Derrick Wester, pleading with Kathy and Rocky to contact them as soon as possible. Rocky assured Cheryl his wife would do just that. And she did, driving up to the Jackson County Sheriff's Office the following day, where she met with Wester and FDLE Agent Donnie Branch, who had recently replaced John Stevens on the investigation.

Kathy told the pair that she, Brian, Denise, and Mike had gone to Thomasville, Georgia to a Victorian Christmas event the evening before Mike disappeared. When they got back to Tallahassee, Denise and Mike went straight home. She and Brian, however, went out to Floyd's Music Store near the Florida State campus and stayed out late.

When she awoke the next morning, Kathy said, Brian was gone. She thought at the time he had probably gone hunting as he often did on Saturday mornings. But he was supposed to be back home in time to go to her family's Christmas gathering in Cairo. She waited for him as long as she could and then she and Stafford left in her car at about 2:45 p.m. Brian didn't show up in Cairo until after 4:00 p.m. She was very upset with him for not getting home in time to travel together and pressed him for the reason why he hadn't been home earlier. "I had a bad day on the lake," her husband told her, stating he had been hunting at Lake Miccosukee.

She also told the investigators Brian had gone to Lake Seminole every day to assist in the search for Mike. He appeared angry throughout that entire time period. He also instructed her not to speak with Denise until after the February 11 memorial service, which she found odd and troubling. Every time she asked Brian what he believed had happened to Mike, he responded that an alligator had likely eaten him. She told Wester and Branch she was fearful that if Brian discovered she was speaking with law enforcement, he would take Stafford and leave the area.

Kathy also provided the investigators a copy of the letter Chuck Bunker had sent her in August 2003. In his letter, Bunker wrote, "Denise and Brian have been leading a double life that few people are aware of. You need to be watchful of their behavior because they have been dishonest with you for the past two and a half years."

Bunker indicated he was aware of "shocking behavior" between the pair and claimed Denise had been "cheating on her husband with someone that she met in a class in Atlanta. So it was easy for her after her husband's death to start a bizarre affair with your then husband Brian." That relationship, he wrote, was "not a normal affair. It involved decadent sexual behavior with various people, strippers and other sordid acts."

Bunker shared with Kathy how Brian had confronted him and Denise in Atlanta and "held Denise captive for an entire night under a death threat to Denise, himself and one of Denise's friends." Brian told her he "had taken pictures and film of Denise performing in sexually explicit circumstances on different occasions over this two-and-a-half-year period and he threatened to send that information to you, Denise's parents and also post it on the Internet." He told Kathy he was providing this information so she could "understand how false both Denise and Brian have been with you and the type of atmosphere that your son could be exposed to."

Bunker implored Kathy "to pay close attention to Denise and your ex[-]husband" as they were "extremely meticulous, self-serving and scheming." He told her they were now "back together and who knows when the next blow up will occur. Hopefully no children will be around when this happens."

To Austin and Wester, Bunker's letter was jaw-dropping. Between what he had written and what Kathy told them, there was little doubt, the duo believed, that they were on the right track.

••••

Though in her heart Cheryl had never believed alligators had eaten her son, she reached out to a professor at Florida State to obtain an expert opinion to debunk that theory once and for all.

On May 29, 2004, Professor Matt Aresco, a "herpetologist" with the Department of Biological Science, wrote her that any official explanation attributing Mike's disappearance "to an attack by an alligator is highly unlikely." He told Cheryl alligators are "ectothermic, which means that they derive all of their body heat from their external environment." In northern Florida, as water temperatures begin cooling in November, he said, "the metabolic rate of alligators drop[s] with the water temperatures and they cease to feed. They do not begin feeding again until March or early April."

Professor Aresco noted that during the first eight days of December 2000 in northern Florida, air temperatures were below normal, five of those nights below freezing. That, he said, "would have caused alligators in Lake Seminole to become inactive. Although air temperatures rose sharply from December 9-16, that would not have been sufficient to cause alligators to become active and begin feeding." Therefore, "although attributing the disappearance of your son to an alligator attack may be a convenient explanation for the authorities," he wrote, "the scientific facts surrounding this case indicate that this explanation is virtually impossible."

Professor Aresco also explained how "extremely rare" it was for an alligator attack to result in a fatality, with only seven fatal attacks recorded in Florida the 47 years between 1948 and 1995. And in those rare cases of fatal attacks on adults, he pointed out, there was "always forensic evidence of the attack or remains found close to where the attack occurred, which was clearly not the case in your son's disappearance." The herpetologist closed his letter expressing his hope that the information he was providing "will help convince the appropriate authorities to re-examine the disappearance of your son and initiate an investigation to determine the actual cause."

Of course by then, Donnie Austin, Derrick Wester, and

Donnie Branch had already concluded that Mike's disappearance had nothing whatsoever to do with alligators—and everything to do with Mike's best friend and his widow.

••••

Since his very first conversation with Cheryl in February 2004, Derrick Wester had been pressing hard to interview Brian Winchester. On November 9, 2004, he and Donnie Branch finally got their chance, sitting down with Brian at the FDLE office in Tallahassee.

Brian told the pair he and Kathy had gone to a concert at Floyd's Music Store the night before Mike disappeared and that he had no plans to go hunting with Mike the next morning. Rather, he had intended to go hunting with his father-in-law in Jefferson County. But he ended up not going, he said, because he overslept.

Wester and Branch listened intently as Brian offered his rendition of the events of Saturday, December 16, 2000. According to Brian, he spent the *entire day* with Kathy, the two eventually traveling to Cairo, Georgia with their son Stafford—in one vehicle—for his wife's family's Christmas celebration. Recognizing the inconsistency between Brian's story and what Kathy had told them in April—which the investigators consciously decided not to reveal—they asked Brian, point blank, whether he had anything to do with Mike's disappearance. Brian denied any involvement, reiterating his belief that Mike had fallen out of his boat and drowned, and that his dead body had been consumed by alligators.

Brian admitted he and Denise had been involved in an active relationship since his divorce from Kathy became final in 2003. After the interview was complete, however, he called Wester to retract that statement, telling him he and Denise actually *hadn't* been in a physical relationship for approximately a year.

Before he left the FDLE office, Wester asked him if he would agree to submit to a polygraph exam. "Sure," Brian said. "I have nothing to hide."

"Good," said Wester. "We will expect you at the Jackson County Sheriff's Office on November 15 to take the test."

"I'll be there," Brian said, seemingly harboring no fear over the prospect of being hooked up to a truth-telling machine.

Three days later, however, an attorney friend of Marcus Winchester, Jeff Talley, called Wester. "Brian got a little ahead of himself," he said. "Upon my advice, he's decided not to take that polygraph exam after all." Talley also indicated that he now represented Denise. Wester asked if he could interview Talley's new client. The attorney responded he believed he could make that happen and would be back in touch.

As of his November 9 interview, not only was Brian unaware of what his ex-wife had told investigators during her April 2004 interview—or that she was cooperating with law enforcement at all—he also had no inkling of interviews Derrick Wester and Donnie Branch had conducted with two eyewitnesses who claimed to have seen Brian at Lake Seminole the morning of December 16, 2000.

On June 21, 2004, they interviewed a man named William Harold Mercer at his home in Cypress, just west of Sneads. Mercer told them that between 8:00 and 8:30 the morning Mike disappeared, he saw three vehicles parked at a dirt landing adjacent to River Road. One was a two-toned Ford Bronco, which was backing down the dirt landing so that the Gheenoe on the trailer could be lowered into the water. Mercer told them three men were talking together, one of them—presumably Mike—standing in the water dressed in hunting clothes and waders. Another man was standing on the bank, he said, talking to the man in the water.

Wester pulled out a photo lineup he had prepared for the occasion which contained the faces of six different men, all taken from driver license records. He asked his host if he recognized any of them. Mercer immediately pointed to the smiling face of Brian Winchester, telling the detective that was the man who had been standing on the bank talking to the man in the water.

The second eyewitness, John Joel Kirkland—a cousin of

FWC Officer Alton Ranew—was a passenger in his wife's vehicle riding down River Road just before dawn that morning. He noticed a man walking next to the road—at a brisk pace—toward the dirt landing near where Mike's truck was found.

As Kirkland rode by, the man turned in his direction. Wester showed him the same photo lineup he had shown Mercer. Sure enough, Kirkland picked out Brian immediately, telling the detective that was the man he saw walking along the road.

Thus, unless Kathy, Mercer, and Kirkland were all lying or mistaken, Brian wasn't at home the morning of December 16, 2000. Rather, he was at Lake Seminole—more than 50 miles away—with his best friend since the ninth grade, Mike Williams.

•••

On December 22, 2004, Jeff Talley made good on his promise, showing up at the Sheriff's Office with his new client, Denise Williams. Talley told Derrick Wester her only ground rule was that she wasn't willing to discuss anything about her personal life apart from what was going on around the time her husband Mike disappeared. With that proviso, Wester began his questioning.

Denise was unemotional throughout the entire hour they were together. Her answers were expressed in monotone, matter-of-fact statements. She told Wester she was unaware of any enemies Mike had or of anyone who might want to harm him, describing him as a "great guy." She denied any infidelity by him or by her.

Despite what Denise had told Cheryl about Mike supposedly waking her up in the early morning hours of December 16 to tell her Brian had called to cancel on him, Denise told Wester Mike didn't wake her up that morning or speak to her before leaving for his duck hunting trip.

Wester told Denise investigators had learned from Kathy that Brian was gone that entire morning and that she didn't know where he was. He also mentioned Kathy had told them she had called Denise to ask if she knew where Brian was. Denise stated she didn't remember any such call, but did recall that Brian was supposed to go hunting with Kathy's dad. "That's what I was told," she said, "and that's what I remember."

The JCSO investigator asked her why there was no mention of the Cotton States insurance policy in her petition to Judge Crusoe. She claimed the omission was her attorney Curtis Hunter's fault, as she was sure she had disclosed that policy to him. Hunter, however, would later deny having any knowledge of its existence.

Wester asked Denise to describe her life in the immediate aftermath of Mike's disappearance. Without even a hint of emotion, Denise replied she was "living a nightmare. It was like I was in a fog." She explained she kept mostly to herself, staying upstairs in her bedroom, while other family members tended to Anslee downstairs. She told the detective she wanted to go to Lake Seminole herself, but "people around me would be like 'no' and then other days I wouldn't want to go."

Denise told him her relationship with Brian began in *April or May of 2001*—a mere four to five months after her husband disappeared, and *two years* before Brian said their relationship had begun. They first got together, she said, when she and Brian were each in the midst of a crisis—Brian going through "some stuff" in his marriage and her "going through hell" after Mike's disappearance. "And that's when it happened," she added.

But by 2003, Denise explained, she was in a serious relationship with Chuck Bunker. "I was gonna marry him. It was so very serious," she told the detective.

She agreed with Bunker's recitation of the events in Atlanta— Brian holding them at either gunpoint or knifepoint, Bunker heading back to Tallahassee, Brian leaving the next day, and Bunker returning to Atlanta to stay with her. She told Wester she hadn't officially broken up with Brian before going to Atlanta with Bunker, which is why Brian had been so upset when he learned they were together.

Denise tried to steer the detective away from her relationship with Bunker, telling him it occurred nearly three years after Mike's death and wasn't relevant.

Ignoring Denise's attempt to establish a boundary, Wester confronted her with a statement he had obtained from Bunker in April, that Denise had apparently told him she couldn't leave Brian because he would have her arrested for insurance fraud if she did.

"I'm not surprised that Chuck said that, but that is not true," she said with a chuckle. "Chuck hates me. He hates Brian. I mean, I'm not surprised at all he said that. That's horrible. Unbelievable actually. But not really surprising coming from him. Insurance fraud? What would that even be?" She then retracted her earlier statement that Brian had held them at gunpoint or knifepoint in Atlanta, telling Wester that although Brian told them he had a gun, he really didn't.

Finally, the seasoned investigator drilled down on what Denise thought had really happened to Mike. She told him she fully believed the initial reports that her husband had drowned following a tragic accident. "That's what I had to believe. I had a daughter to raise. I didn't, I mean, and there's no way, if he was alive, he wouldn't be here with her. And there's no way that he is alive because he would be here with me and with her." She said it was "horrible not to have a place to go like a graveyard. It's horrible." But again, no emotion at all accompanied those words.

Denise then made some gratuitous, ugly comments about her mother-in-law, telling Wester that Cheryl "has been psycho from the beginning. And I feel sorry for her. I mean, she's lost her husband too. But she will not accept, she won't even accept her own husband's death." She told him Cheryl's relentless efforts to pursue an investigation were making it very difficult for her to raise Anslee—foreshadowing the confrontation in Cheryl's kitchen that would occur some 17 days later.

As Talley and Denise departed the Sheriff's Office, Wester shook his head in disbelief and amazement. In all his years in law enforcement, he had never experienced anything quite like that. As he would later tell his colleagues, Denise Williams was the coldest person he had ever met. And in view of the circumstances surrounding their discussion, he found that most illuminating indeed.

••••

By early 2005, Denise had cut off all communications with Cheryl. Yet despite her hostile stance toward her mother-in-law, her younger sister Deborah McCranie continued to send her son Parker to her home for daycare. Because of Parker, Cheryl continued to maintain regular contact not only with Deborah, but also with the eldest of the Merrell girls, Deanna Lamb, who would sometimes swing by Cheryl's home in the afternoon to pick up Parker as a favor to her younger sister.

Even though Denise had cut Cheryl out of her life and Anslee's, her older sister maintained a cordial relationship with Mike's mom. The two even talked about Mike and the possibility that foul play could have led to his demise. From their discussions, Cheryl sensed that Deanna was aware of information Derrick Wester and Ronnie Austin might find helpful and somehow persuaded Denise's sister to speak with the detectives. Deanna and her husband Cliff met with them at the Leon County Courthouse in Tallahassee on October 5, 2005.

What she shared with them wasn't merely helpful—it was shocking. Deanna told Wester and Austin that on December 16, 2000, she had been expecting Denise and Mike to drop Anslee off at her home on their way to the Gibson Inn. Instead, Denise called her in a panic when Mike hadn't come home when expected. She found that odd because Mike was often late, so much so that Denise often joked about it.

Deanna arrived at her sister and brother-in-law's home in Midyette Plantation between 2:00 and 3:00 p.m. She found no bags anywhere in the house suggesting that Denise and Mike were on the verge of heading out for a romantic, overnight trip. Nor did she see anything packed for Anslee, which she found equally strange, as the toddler would have needed all kinds of supplies for the 24-plus hours she was to be in Deanna's care.

"I think a lot of things don't add up," she told the investigators.

Austin and Wester would later learn that when Kathy came to the house the next day, she and Deanna together made a thorough search for any sign of packed bags or luggage—in both the house and in Denise's vehicle. They found nothing at all. Which made it all the more suspicious when Clay and Patti Ketcham spotted a suitcase at the bottom of the staircase when they came by Mike and Denise's home that Sunday evening.

Deanna then dropped another bombshell, expressing her doubts over whether Anslee was actually Mike's child. "It wouldn't shock me if I was told she wasn't," she said, speculating that Anslee could be Brian's offspring—though she quickly noted that her baby pictures and Mike's baby pictures appeared very similar.

Deanna also told the pair how deeply troubled she was by the discovery of the waders and the hunting jacket six months after Mike disappeared. Noting how shallow the lake was in that area, if Mike had gotten his waders off, she said, he easily could have gotten to a spot where he was able to stand. Something seemed very wrong, she told them.

"Do you think your sister Denise could have anything to do with Mike being killed?" Austin asked, finally honing in on the elephant-sized question filling the room.

"I don't think she could kill him," Deanna answered, somewhat tentatively. But she sensed her sister knew something about what had happened to Mike.

Austin asked whether Deanna thought Denise would have known something before or after her husband disappeared.

"I would hope after," she responded, but acknowledged she wasn't really sure. "The reason I'm sitting here is because a lot of times she doesn't act like my sister. I don't know. Um, I would hope after. But I don't, I don't know." Another stunning revelation.

Deanna told the detectives she and the entire Merrell family harbored an intense dislike for Brian Winchester. Austin asked why she personally felt that way, which led to yet another bombshell.

"Well, *I feel like he killed Mike* and I don't like him married to my sister. I'm scared for my niece. I don't want him anywhere near my niece and don't want him near my sister. He's conniving and manipulative." She told the investigators she had called Denise an idiot for agreeing to marry Brian and exposing all of her money to him. Deanna surmised that Brian was holding something over on her sister for Denise to even be considering marrying him. Yet Denise had pushed back, she said, telling her that her fiancé was a changed man because "he became a Christian."

Austin asked if Denise and Brian believed that their Christianity could absolve them of horrible sins.

"In their minds," Deanna replied. "I think they've built the community around them with the people in their church who are supporting them, um, but definitely, I, I can see in their minds saying, 'Well, everything before this day is, is fine,' uh, yeah, I could see them thinking that."

In sharp contrast to Denise's description, Deanna told Austin and Wester her sister's marriage with Mike was *not* a happy one. "I think he did know something was going on," she said. "I think he was trying to figure it out." She added, "At one point he had told me he was giving her six months to 'straighten up or I'm leaving.'" Though Mike didn't elaborate about what he meant, Deanna had assumed he had discovered Denise hadn't been faithful.

Since Mike's disappearance, Deanna confessed, she had come to believe Denise "may have had a different type of life that I didn't know anything about, that I can't comprehend, that I can't imagine because it's so foreign to me," a life which may have included drugs and other irresponsible behaviors.

Austin pressed her, asking whether she believed Denise was living a double life—acting one way in front of her family members, but a completely different way behind their backs. "I'd say yes," Deanna replied, "in light of everything that, you know, that I hear."

Austin and Wester left the courthouse that afternoon more convinced than ever they were on the right track. If Denise's own sister had been highly suspicious of her—and believed the man she was a few weeks away from marrying was the one who had actually killed Mike—that had to mean something. Something significant. They were getting closer. But they still needed more to make a convincing case. Without a body, a lot more.

••••

Just a week after meeting with Deanna Lamb, Ronnie Austin received an email from Kathy Thomas. She wanted him to know about an email exchange she had with Brian that very day.

"I know you are under a lot of pressure to blame me and Denise for it," Brian wrote, the "it" apparently referring to Mike's death. "We all—you, me, Denise, and Mike made a lot of bad decisions and committed a lot of sins but NONE of us ever committed murder. I do NOT know what happened or where Mike is but I know he would not want our kids to suffer and pay the price in this hunt for 'justice.'" He predicted many lives would be "devastated" if investigators ultimately tried to make a case against him. "I know how much they want you to believe that I am guilty of murder but it is NOT true."

Brian left little doubt he had learned of Kathy's statement that he was nowhere to be found the day of Mike's disappearance. And of eyewitness accounts of him being at Lake Seminole that morning. "Your memory and this recent 'eyewitness' are the deciding factors of their case," he wrote in his email. "You are the star witness. This terrifies me based on statements you have made to me in the past. I know you wish I were gone, but please think about Stafford and Anslee and if in your mind you are not 100% certain of facts, please say so. This is life and death serious. I have made a lot of bad choices but murder is not one of them."

••••

In October 2005, an ambitious investigative reporter named Jennifer Portman joined the staff of the *Tallahassee Dem-*

ocrat as a senior writer. The 35-year-old journalist arrived in Tallahassee with an impeccable pedigree, having obtained a Master's degree from the prestigious Medill School of Journalism at Northwestern University in Chicago before landing in Springfield, Missouri as city hall reporter and an editorial writer at the *Springfield News-Leader*.

Less than six months into her stint with the *Democrat*, Portman noticed a peculiar advertisement on page 15 of the newspaper's May 7, 2006, edition. Next to a photograph of Mike Williams, in large, boldfaced, uppercase lettering, the heading read, "MY SON IS MISSING. PLEASE HELP ME FIND HIM."

Underneath the heading were several dense paragraphs of text that began, "My name is Cheryl Ann Williams and I haven't seen my son, Mike, in over five years. Would you please take a moment to read this and help me find him?"

What followed read more like a Wikipedia page about the Mike Williams investigation than an ad for goods or services. It was chockfull of information and raised numerous troubling questions about the efforts to determine what had happened to the missing hunter and concluded with telephone numbers for Ronnie Austin, Derrick Wester, and Donnie Branch.

Though she knew nothing at all about Mike Williams or his disappearance, with her keen eye for a good story, Portman instantly recognized the potential for a blockbuster piece of investigative journalism. She learned from the newspaper's staff that Cheryl had plunked down $1,200 to pay for the ad space. As the daycare worker would later tell her as the two sat together on Cheryl's backyard patio, "you have to change a lot of diapers" to come up with $1,200 for a newspaper ad.

The more she dug into the story, the more riveted Portman became. About the crazy notion that alligators had consumed a full-grown man. About the nearly $2 million in life insurance proceeds paid out to Denise as Mike's beneficiary. And about her recent marriage to Brian Winchester. The journalist found it eerie—creepy even—that a man who had been Mike's best friend was now sleeping with his widow in the very bed Mike shared with her until his disappearance, and was now raising Mike's daughter Anslee as if she were his own child.

Portman pulled court records—including Denise's petition for a presumptive death certificate—and articles that appeared in the *Floridian* in Jackson County in the weeks following Mike's disappearance. She conducted numerous interviews, including with FWC Officer David Arnette, investigators Derrick Wester, Donnie Branch, and Ronnie Austin, Professor Matt Aresco, and several of Mike's friends and co-workers.

On December 15, 2006, a day shy of the six-year anniversary of Mike's disappearance, the *Democrat* published a trilogy of stories about Mike under Portman's byline. The banner headline across the top of the front page was: "Six years ago, this hunter disappeared." The same photo of Mike that Cheryl had used in her ad appeared just below the headline. The main section of the newspaper included a biographical sketch of Mike entitled "Nice guy, hard worker, avid hunter, devoted dad" as well as a story focusing on the now-debunked alligator theory.

Portman's front-page, feature article was subtitled, "Did Mike Williams walk away, drown or get killed? Frustrated investigators can't say for sure." She quoted Austin as saying, "My gut feeling is Mike did not die in Lake Seminole, which is the shared feeling of all law enforcement working this case." Wester told her of their frustrations in investigating a case that wasn't initially handled as a criminal investigation. "Now we're trying to make up for that," he told her. Austin said they felt like they were pounding their heads against a brick wall, lamenting, "It's really frustrating."

"The vexing case for investigators is a cruel sentence of uncertainty for Williams' friends and family," the talented journalist wrote. "Many remain haunted by unanswered questions."

Brian and Denise had refused to comment for any of the articles. In his email—which Portman quoted in the feature story—Brian wrote, "'We love Mike and miss him terribly and would ask that our privacy be respected through what continues to be a very difficult time.'"

Damon Jasper provided an interesting, perhaps prescient

comment, telling Portman he couldn't believe Mike would have been wearing his waders while in the boat. "The experienced outdoorsman was obsessed with safety," he told her, "and always waited to put them on until he reached his hunting spot—to avoid the very accident that officials first presumed killed him." Jasper told her Mike—who he had looked up to as a mentor—had preached that to him relentlessly.

Portman credited Cheryl's persistence: "If it weren't for Cheryl Ann Williams, her son's disappearance would not have gotten a second look. In the absence of an investigation and lacking money for a private detective, she became her own sleuth, tracking down leads, cross-checking stories and uncovering inconsistencies."

The senior writer reported that some people had called Cheryl crazy for continuing to pursue what to them seemed to be an obvious, accidental drowning. Even cold-case investigators, the article stated, weren't returning her calls the way they had in the past. "She'll put up new missing-person signs but doesn't plan anything special Saturday to mark the sixth anniversary of her son's vanishing," Portman wrote. "She will wake up and wonder, as she has for more than 2,000 mornings now, what really happened."

Wester told Portman investigators had Cheryl's best interests at heart, despite the obstacles and difficulties they were trying to surmount. And that they had persons of interest in their sights, though he wouldn't provide her with any names. "Wester is confident the mother will get the closure she seeks," she wrote. "But he can't say when. 'I'll give it until 2023,'" he said, which Portman noted happened to be the year Wester would be eligible for retirement. And when Mike Williams would have turned 54.

Portman's six months of research had convinced her Mike wasn't in Lake Seminole. And wouldn't be found there. Using the only tool at her disposal—investigative journalism—she joined Cheryl in her crusade for answers. And justice. Even though she didn't know Cheryl's son—or anyone who had been carrying the weight of his loss for years—the story of what had happened to Mike quickly became personal for her.

She even tacked a missing-person poster bearing Mike's photo to the bulletin board above her desk at the *Democrat*. Before long, her zeal to solve the mystery became almost as passionate as his own mother's.

If cold-case investigators weren't going to work the case hard enough to find out what actually happened to Mike, with the power of the press, Portman vowed to keep the pressure on. With as many newspaper articles as it took. If there was nothing to report in a given year, Portman would be sure to pen a new column each December 16, to remind the public—and everyone who knew and loved Mike—that he hadn't been forgotten. And that there was still more to discover and learn. And each December 16, a beautiful arrangement of holiday-themed flowers would land on her desk at the *Democrat*, from Cheryl and Nick, thanking her for keeping Mike's story alive.

····

Investigators continued to work with Kathy Thomas throughout 2007. She reported to them periodically about her interactions with Brian—which occurred frequently as the divorced parents shuffled Stafford back and forth between their households.

Kathy told them about an encounter she had with Brian at North Florida Christian the afternoon of April 20, 2007. Brian asked her why she thought *Denise* had killed Mike. Kathy told her ex that she was aware he and Denise had been having an affair—and that Mike had discovered it. Though she didn't actually know for certain either was true, she was hoping her answer would scare Brian and cause him to blurt out something incriminating.

Kathy also told her ex-husband he and Denise were doing a horrible disservice to Anslee by not allowing her to visit with Cheryl—and that withholding Anslee from her grandmother made them look guilty. Brian responded that even Mike had a "horrible relationship" with his mother, found her "rude and disrespectful," and dreaded having to take Anslee to see her—implying Mike would be perfectly content with his and

Denise's decision to end Anslee's visitation with her grand-mother.

Brian expressed his concern that afternoon that he could be arrested any day and his fear that Kathy would testify against him. He told her that word of *her* affairs would then come out and cause immeasurable harm to Stafford. Brian threatened to destroy her credibility as a potential witness by posting on the internet video and photos of her engaged in sexual activities with another female.

He implored her to explain to investigators that she "didn't remember" what happened the morning Mike disap-peared, leaving little doubt he wanted her to lie to protect him. Which backfired almost immediately, as Kathy shared his threats with Austin and Wester—in meticulous detail.

On December 14, 2007, Brian asked to meet with his ex-wife again. He told her it was urgent. This time, the FDLE out-fitted Kathy with a secret recording device, hoping to catch Brian making incriminating statements. The pair met at a Mc-Donald's restaurant at 2:30 p.m.

Brian asked her to get into a taxi and talk with him while they rode together. But she refused, fearful of what he might do to her. He then asked her to get into his vehicle instead, but she refused again. Finally, he asked her to follow him to the courthouse in her own vehicle, where they could both walk through metal detectors, just in case she was wearing a wire. Again, she said "no." That made him very suspicious. Brian told her he knew she had been talking to the police and be-lieved he was being framed for something he didn't do.

Kathy was the only person who could help him, he said, and pleaded with her to do so. He tried to convince her they had ridden together to her family's Christmas gathering in Cairo, Georgia the day Mike disappeared. Yet his ex-wife told him that wasn't so, and he knew it. "Stafford's going to go down because of your principles," he replied angrily, his exas-peration boiling over.

The timing of Brian's request to meet that afternoon was no accident. He had received an email from Jennifer Portman requesting a comment about an article the *Democrat* planned to run on December 16—the seven-year anniversary of Mike' disappearance—under the headline "Man still missing after 2,556 days." Her story, Portman told him, would include a sentence indicating there had been "online whispers" that a grand jury might be called in soon to issue criminal indictments in Mike's case.

Portman began the article stating, "Investigators say they're closer than ever to a break in the case of the Tallahassee hunter once thought accidentally drowned and eaten by alligators." She quoted Cheryl as saying she was "more optimistic something is going to happen." And Derrick Wester as well, who told her, "The ultimate goal is always to put someone in jail."

For the first time, Brian issued a comment for himself and Denise, which he agreed Portman could print. "For seven years we have prayed and hoped to find out with certainty what happened to Mike," he wrote. "Nobody wants Mike found more than we do. We continue to love Mike and miss him every day. We ask again that our privacy be respected and that our family be allowed to live our lives in peace." The content and tone of his email couldn't have contrasted more sharply with his recent interactions with his ex-wife.

••••

With Jennifer Portman and the *Tallahassee Democrat* now in her corner, Cheryl felt invigorated. Between her advocacy and Portman's journalism, she believed she could mount a pressure campaign that would ultimately cause Denise or Brian to crack. Whether the FDLE, Jackson County Sheriff's Office, or State Attorney's Office uncovered another lead or not.

During the Greyhound lockout that began in March 1990, Cheryl had learned everything there was to know about the art and science—and legality—of picketing. Every weekday evening from 6:00 to 10:00, following a full day of work with her kids, Cheryl took to the streets in front of the bus terminal—where scabs had all too gladly filled the positions of drivers like her husband. She marched with other wives, hoisting signs they'd attached to yardsticks telling potential customers: "Don't Ride Greyhound. Go Trailways." As a union representative, J.J. fully supported her efforts. She walked the picket line every weekday evening *for more than four years.*

By late 2006, Cheryl was picketing again—this time a solo effort. She stapled a giant sign to a yardstick, with an enlarged photo of Mike in the middle, the words "MISSING since December 16, 2000" above the photo, and his full name below it. Every Sunday, she picketed in front of Four Oaks Community Church where Denise and Brian were now attending, in front of the churches Brian's and Denise's parents attended, or just outside the gate of Midyette Plantation, a stone's throw from Brian and Denise's home at 5017 Centennial Oaks Circle. Some weekends, she also marched up and down Miccosukee Road, occasionally spotting Brian or Denise as they entered or exited their subdivision. She even carried her sign near Doak Campbell Stadium before and after Florida State football games.

Cheryl timed her picketing for maximum impact—marching in front of the churches when parishioners were leaving the early service and arriving for the late service. On several occasions, the ministers exchanged sharp words with her, threatening to call the police, telling her she wasn't welcome on church property. An expert on the rules from her days picketing Greyhound, Cheryl corrected them, telling the preachers she was picketing on public property, and that there was nothing they could do to stop her.

Parishioners—supposedly Christians—would scream and cuss at her as they walked by. Others told the pigtailed grandmother she was crazy or insane. "Why don't you just admit your son is dead and get on with it?" they would shout in an ugly, menacing tone.

She received similar treatment from Brian and Denise's neighbors as they entered and exited their subdivision. Yet the more commotion she stirred up, the more she knew she was having the desired effect. She was intent on getting under the skin of those who Brian and Denise counted on for comfort, support, and refuge. No one had provided those things to her son Mike in his greatest moment of need. It was now Brian and

Denise's turn to feel the heat.

Picketing was just one component of Cheryl's pressure campaign. She had missing-person posters of Mike printed. By the thousands. With the help of Nick and some loyal grown-up kids from her daycare, she had the posters stapled and tacked to trees and telephone poles up and down Miccosukee Road every week—mile after mile—and at grocery stores, restaurants, and other places she knew Brian and Denise frequented. To ratchet up the pressure, she would force the two to look at Mike's face as they drove to and from work, dropped off and retrieved Anslee and Stafford from NFC, or were out and about trying to enjoy themselves in town.

Cheryl's theory was that the last thing someone who had killed another human being would ever want to confront was a photo of his victim staring back at him. She wanted Mike's photos to torment the people she believed had killed him—Brian and Denise Winchester. The posters would quickly disappear, likely due to Brian and Denise enlisting friends and neighbors to tear them down. But they would serve their purpose nonetheless.

Weekend after weekend, month after month, year after year, the tenacious grandmother escalated the pressure in every way she knew how. Slowly, over time she believed, her efforts would bear fruit.

Eventually, she raised enough money to pay for billboards on Thomasville Road near a flyover—again, creating maximum exposure. Like her posters and picket signs, the billboards included Mike's picture and noted he had been missing since December 16, 2000. Phone numbers of investigators with the FDLE, JCSO, or State Attorney's Office appeared on each and every one—reminding Brian and Denise of the ongoing investigation.

The billboards would run for two to three weeks, usually timed around Anslee's birthday, Mike's birthday, or the anniversary of his disappearance. Even with the help she received from contributions, the billboards would drain Cheryl's bank account every time a new one went up. Yet with the mounting exposure—and pressure—resulting from the billboards,

Cheryl Ann Williams was prepared to spend every penny she earned.

••••

By 2011, the investigation into Mike's disappearance had all but ground to a halt. Stone cold. Derrick Wester had retired and the other detectives and agents who had been working the case had been replaced. The new investigators had been stymied by Brian and Denise's refusal to talk. And by the marital privilege, which insulated their conversations from law enforcement scrutiny. For her part, Kathy Thomas had retreated from her willingness to provide assistance—scared off by Brian's incessant threats, increasingly concerned about the effect a criminal prosecution would have on her 12-year-old son.

Though Cheryl's crusade for justice—picket signs, posters, and billboards—continued unabated, she was deeply frustrated. Especially by the FDLE, who had stopped returning her calls.

But there was one person she believed might be able to help: newly elected Florida Governor Rick Scott. On January 1, 2012, she launched a letter-writing campaign in which she scrawled out a new letter to him each and every day, her first letter pleading with him to "Please ask F.D.L.E. to investigate properly my son's case."

On December 15, 2015, after sending the Governor nearly 1,500 letters—not one of which had been answered—the 71-year-old grandmother scraped together another huge pile of cash for an ad in the *Democrat*, this one entitled "An open letter to Governor Rick Scott."

Her letter stated that FWC officers had told her two weeks after Mike disappeared "that my son fell out of his boat, drowned, and was eaten by alligators," even though that was later determined to be impossible. She noted that "Mike was declared dead six months after he disappeared when (planted) evidence surfaced in the lake. His wife collected millions of dollars in life insurance and then married his best friend."

"I still do not know what happened to my son," she lamented. "His case is now considered an active cold case, nothing being done to find Mike or his murderers." The FDLE was no longer helping her, she said, because she wasn't doing things "the right way" and talked too much.

She told the Governor, "You do not see my letters because they are sent over to FDLE, the very agency I am complaining about." She implored him to appoint a "Special Prosecutor from another part of the state to investigate my son Mike's disappearance[.] As a parent yourself, can you imagine the undying agony of not knowing where your daughters are for the past fifteen years, while simultaneously being lied to, ignored, and being called crazy by law enforcement officials when the facts clearly prove otherwise?"

The same day Cheryl's ad was published on page 6 of the *Democrat*, its newly promoted News Director, Jennifer Portman, penned a poignant column commemorating the 15th anniversary of the day her son vanished. Portman noted she had been writing about Mike's mysterious disappearance for a full nine years. "There's not much to write about anymore," she wrote. "It's now a stone cold, missing person case and Mike, a suspected victim of foul play."

Portman noted Anslee—19 months old when her father vanished—had celebrated her Sweet 16 earlier that May. "Cheryl was not invited. She hasn't seen her granddaughter in years after Mike's former wife, upset by Cheryl's tenacity, cut her off."

For her part, though, Cheryl was still holding "out hope her son is still alive. Even though no one else does. On this point she has never wavered." Cheryl told Portman on the phone "God has not told me that child is dead." Though she realized that he might have perished, his mom told the journalist, she didn't "feel it."

"Today she'll mark the day doing what she does every day," Portman concluded. "Work from 6 a.m. to 6 p.m. taking care of other people's children at her in-home daycare. She'll tend to her herd of 21 cats. And she'll write another letter."

Both women felt an overwhelming sense of hopelessness and despair. Despite their relentless efforts spanning an entire decade, they were no closer to learning what had happened to Mike. Or to bringing those responsible to justice.

But that was all about to change.

Photo courtesy of Marya Denmark.

Cheryl with her soulmate J.J. in 1970.

Photo courtesy of Marya Denmark.

Cheryl with Mike in 1973. She could hardly ever keep him still.

Photo courtesy of Marya Denmark.

Mike loved the outdoors from a very early age.

Photo courtesy of Marya Denmark.

Christmas 1975, Mike with Cheryl and J.J., first holiday at their Jeffrey Road home.

Photo courtesy of Marya Denmark.

Cheryl and Mike in 1980.

Photo courtesy of Marya Denmark.

**The blonde-haired brothers,
Christmas 1976.**

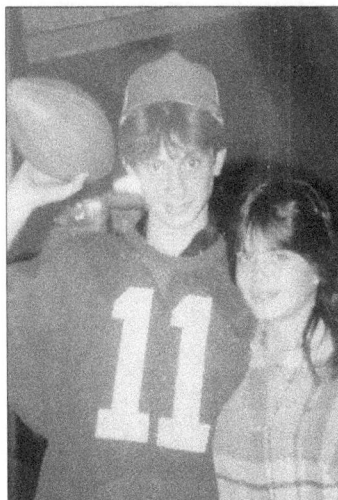

Photo courtesy of Marya Denmark.

**Mike with his first girlfriend,
Denise Pate.**

Photo courtesy of Marya Denmark.

**Mike and his new Denise before
an NFC ninth-grade dance.**

Photo courtesy of Jennifer Stinson.

Brian Winchester as a youngster.

Photo courtesy of Jennifer Stinson.

Brian with his trusty shotgun and hunting dog.

Photo courtesy of Jennifer Stinson.

Mike's second girlfriend and Brian's eventual wife, Kathy Aldredge.

Photo courtesy of Jennifer Stinson.

Denise Merrell's Student Council yearbook picture.

Photo courtesy of Marya Denmark.

Denise, cheerleader for the NFC
Eagles.

Photo courtesy of Marya Denmark.

Mike and Denise at the NFC
Sweetheart Dance, junior year.

Photo courtesy of Marya Denmark.

Mike's high school graduation
picture.

Photo courtesy of Marya Denmark.

The happy couple ready for the
senior prom.

Photo courtesy of Marya Denmark.

Mike, cornerback for the NFC Eagles.

Photo courtesy of Jennifer Stinson.

Mike voted "best personality" by his classmates.

Photo courtesy of Jennifer Stinson.

When it rains, it pours.

Photo courtesy of Jennifer Stinson.

Denise's NFC yearbook photo.

Photo courtesy of Marya Denmark.

Mike's NFC yearbook photo.

Photo courtesy of Jennifer Stinson.

Kathy's NFC yearbook photo.

Photo courtesy of Jennifer Stinson.

Brian's NFC yearbook photo.

Photo courtesy of Marya Denmark.

Mike and Denise opening Christmas presents with J.J. and Cheryl,1996.

Wedding party: Nick seated, Brian to Mike's left with Kathy in front, Rachel Drew and Shannon Norris (Bream) first and second from left.

"Till death do us part."

Warren and Johnnie Merrell couldn't have been prouder of their beautiful daughter.

Photo courtesy of Jennifer Stinson.

10th NFC reunion May 1998: Denise seated next to Shannon Norris, Mike standing between them with Kathy and Brian to his right.

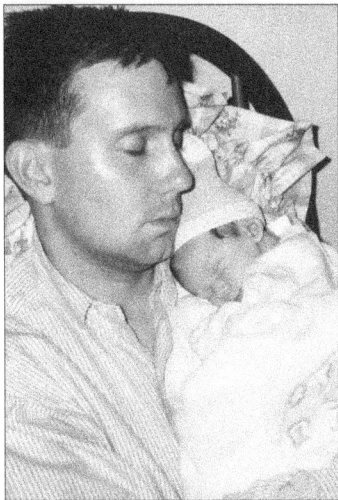

Photo courtesy of Marya Denmark.

Nothing changed Mike's life as profoundly as Anslee's birth.

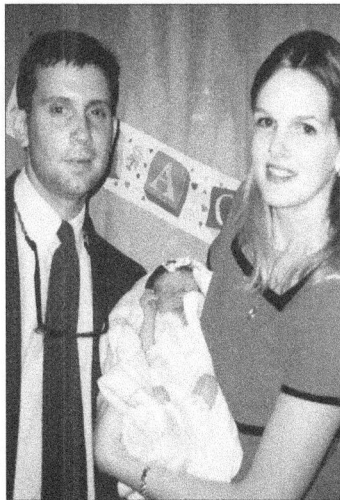

Photo courtesy of Marya Denmark.

The proud parents ready to leave the hospital.

Photo courtesy of Marya Denmark.

Denise all smiles as she holds An-slee's tiny hand.

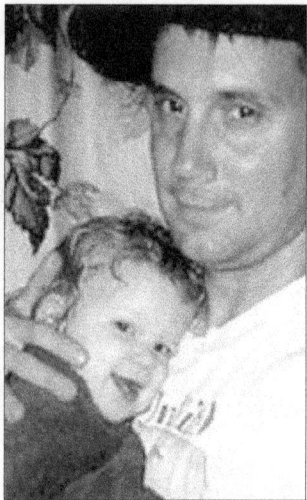

Photo courtesy of Marya Denmark.

Nothing made Mike happier than time with his baby girl.

Photo courtesy of Marya Denmark.

Anslee's first birthday party at Centennial Oaks.

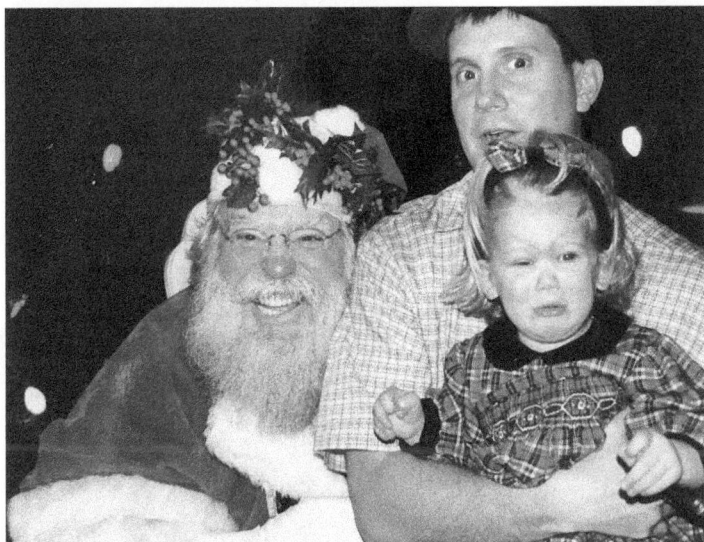

Photo courtesy of Marya Denmark.

Mike holding Anslee in a vice grip, the 19 month old clearly no fan of Santa.

Photo courtesy of Steven B. Epstein.

The fruit of Mike's labor: 5017 Centennial Oaks Circle.

Photo courtesy of Scott Dungey.

Mike showing off his catch after deep-sea fishing with Scott Dungey.

Photo courtesy of Marya Denmark.

The last picture ever taken of Mike: Family Christmas portrait, December 14, 2000.

Photo courtesy of the Florida Second Circuit State Attorney's Office.

Mike's Ford Bronco and boat trailer were found at Lake Seminole, but no Mike.

Photo courtesy of the Florida Second Circuit State Attorney's Office.

Brian "found" Mike's Gheenoe motorboat on the western shoreline.

Photo courtesy of Marya Denmark.

Already a public couple in September 2004—prior to rehearsal dinner for Nick's wedding.

Photo courtesy of Marya Denmark.

Nick and Anslee during one of the 90-minute visits Denise allowed at Centennial Oaks.

Photo courtesy of Patti Ketcham.

To Clay and Patti Ketcham, Mike was more than an employee.

Photo courtesy of Marya Denmark.

Already Stafford's dad, Brian became Anslee's stepdad in December 2005.

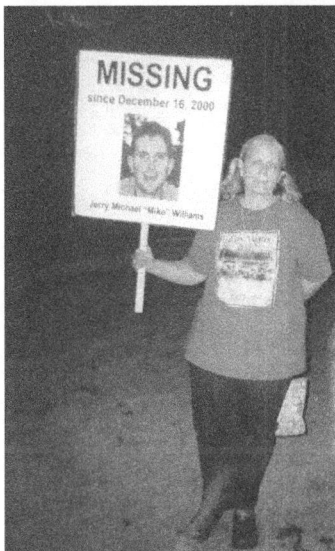

Photo courtesy of Marya Denmark.

Cheryl refused to believe Mike had drowned and been eaten by alligators.

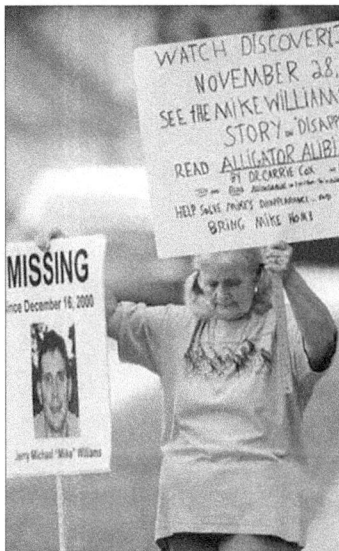

Photo courtesy of Marya Denmark.

Cheryl picketing in front of Four Oaks Community Church in November 2011.

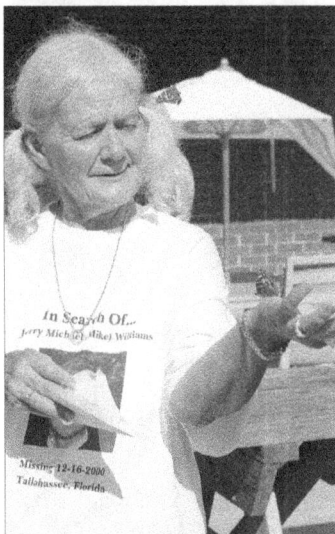

Photo courtesy of Marya Denmark.

Cheryl at a public rally for Mike.

Photo courtesy of Jennifer Portman.

The *Democrat's* crackerjack News Director, Jennifer Portman, kept Mike's story alive for more than a decade.

Part 2
Cold Case No More

7

Rock Bottom

Brian Winchester sat alone at a remote table at the far corner of TGI Fridays' dining room, barely touching his dinner, drowning his sorrows with hard liquor. He arrived at the restaurant resolved that this would be his last night on Earth. The suicide notes he had scrawled on a legal pad were intended to force his own hand, to ensure he didn't chicken out.

It was Thursday, August 4, 2016. The last four years had been a slow but steady descent into Brian's personal Hell.

When he and Denise purchased a luxurious, 5,000-square foot waterfront home on Lake Jackson in August 2012—the $656,000 price-tag depressed significantly by the lingering recession—he felt reassured their often tumultuous relationship had turned an important corner.

To Brian, the picturesque, three-acre Miller Landing estate symbolized more than just their financial good fortune. It was the type of home he had dreamed he would be living in at the peak of his career, one in which everything was possible—including a happy life with his wife, son, and stepdaughter. In his mind's eye, Brian could envision himself tending to the grill at family cookouts on the back deck overlooking the water, and at the wheel of his ski boat—pulling Anslee, Stafford, or their friends as they slalomed across the lake.

But that dream would come crashing down less than three months later, when Denise told him she was done with the marriage and angrily demanded that he move out of their Centennial Oaks home. They hadn't even spent a day in their new home on Lake Jackson—not a single piece of furniture had been moved into the empty house.

To make matters worse, Denise had issued a long list of demands if Brian harbored any hope of repairing the damage his infidelity and drinking had inflicted on their marriage: First, he and Stafford would have to move in with his mom and dad at his childhood home, rather than at the Miller Landing estate; she and Anslee, she said, would continue to live at Centennial Oaks.

Second, he would need to go to counseling with the pastor at their church, as well as with a licensed therapist.

Third, she wanted him to attend 12-step meetings and multi-day workshops to address his addictions to alcohol, pornography, and sex. She even asked him to take a polygraph exam.

Though over the next few years Brian did much of what his wife had asked, it wasn't enough to save the marriage. Denise filed for divorce on August 7, 2015, her handwritten petition contending the marriage was "irretrievably broken." She asked that her former name—Denise Merrell Williams—be restored.

By then, Brian and Stafford had moved into the Miller Landing home on Lake Jackson. But it no longer had the glitz or glamor—or held the promise—it did when they purchased it. All that empty space served as a constant reminder of all the things wrong with Brian's life—making him that much more depressed, especially during the evenings Stafford was with his mom. Which led to even more drinking. And to prostitutes parading in and out of the house to feed his sex addiction. His counseling clearly hadn't worked. He was quickly spiraling into a pattern of destructive behavior, hopelessness, and despair.

That November, however, a ray of hope emerged—seemingly out of nowhere. Denise invited him to join her on a trip to New Orleans. Just the two of them. They actually enjoyed each other's company—almost like old times. The following month, they started attending church together and even celebrated Christmas as a family, with Anslee and Stafford now high school juniors—Anslee at NFC and Stafford at the prestigious Maclay School. But as the calendar turned to 2016, the fleeting hope their marriage could be repaired quickly evaporated.

In April, Denise hired a lawyer, who started pushing forward with the divorce. Her attorney demanded a financial settlement Brian viewed as draconian—especially considering that Denise had entered their union already dripping with wealth from nearly $2 million in life insurance proceeds resulting from Mike's death. Brian wouldn't be entitled to any of that in the equitable distribution of their marital property, as it was all Denise's "separate property."

But she wanted a lot more than that, including the property management business they had created together in 2010 named Barrington Road Business Center, LLC. Denise was moving forward with the divorce aggressively, damn the torpedoes, full speed ahead. Precisely what Brian had been hoping to avoid.

And then, just when it seemed things couldn't get any worse, they did. Much worse. In mid-May, Brian received an urgent call from his dad, Marcus Winchester, who told him to get over to his home right away. Marcus sat him down in the living room when he arrived.

"Stafford got into your cell phone," he said, a father's look of disappointment etched into his face. "He saw a bunch of pictures of you and women. Lots of women."

"Oh no!" Brian thought, his stomach instantly beginning to churn. The pictures were of him in assorted poses—with scantily clad prostitutes. On nights Stafford was with his mom. They were awful. He had completely forgotten they were on his phone.

But that wasn't the worst of it. "He told Kathy all about it," Marcus added. "And Denise and Anslee as well. Your boy is moving in with his mom. For good."

In the blink of an eye, all that was left for Brian to live for was violently ripped out from under him. He was mortified and humiliated. Horrified. Not only at the thought of his

17-year-old son swiping through photos of his father engaged in debauchery with total strangers, but at what he saw as he peered into his own future—without Denise, his stepdaughter, or his only child. His immediate thought was to drive home and kill himself.

His desperate texts to Stafford begging him to talk, so he could explain how horrible life had been in the wake of his impending divorce with Denise, went unanswered. Anslee—whom he had just taken to dinner for her 17th birthday days before—also wouldn't respond. Any hope he could somehow convince Denise to suspend her push for a divorce was clearly now gone for good. He was being shunned by them all as if he were the devil incarnate. Though it seemed like a horrible nightmare, it was all too real. A dumpster fire of epic proportions.

In July, yet another shoe dropped. Marcus told Brian his mom had been diagnosed with a rare and aggressive form of stomach cancer. She didn't have long to live. The abyss into which he was being sucked grew deeper and wider still.

By the summer of 2016, Brian was in full-blown depression, unable to will himself out of bed at times. At work, he would lock himself in his office and lay on the floor, unable to think, much less work. He would dread the thought of going home to his palatial—but empty—house, knowing full well he would self-medicate with booze and hookers to make it to the next day. And that he would wake up the following morning having to endure yet another day just the same.

Because his depression made it nearly impossible to work, Brian's income was beginning to dry up, at the very time Denise's divorce lawyer was going for the jugular. She was pushing for an appraisal of the Miller Landing estate, which Brian believed would eventually put him out on the street. He felt certain he would be ruined financially—in addition to losing every human being, apart from his dad, whom he had ever loved.

With each passing day, suicide became an increasingly attractive option. At least Stafford would inherit everything he had and would be able to start his life fresh, Brian mused, as he sat in front of his computer searching for the least painful way to end to his sorry life.

Google provided a consistent answer: gunshot to the temple. He purchased a handgun at a local sporting goods store, loaded it, and stored it in a backpack together with a pair of sheets still in their plastic wrapper. He intended to use the sheets to cover the sight of his body with his brains blown away. Somehow that would minimize the horror for whoever discovered the carnage, he thought, rationality long since replaced by desperation.

By July 2016, Brian's contact with Denise had been reduced to cryptic texts and communications between their lawyers. One day while he was at work, she left a huge box at his front doorstep at Miller Landing. When he discovered it later that evening, he was knocked down further still. It was filled with their wedding pictures and lingerie he had purchased for Denise in happier times. She also left him a vitriolic letter—spewing her grievances—telling him how much she hated him for everything he had done to her and Anslee.

That "gift" prompted Brian to drop by unannounced one mid-July morning at the parking lot outside of Denise's office at Florida State's iconic Doak Campbell Stadium—which also housed the university's administrative offices—where she had been working as an accountant and tax specialist in the Controller's Office since 2013. He saw her pull up into her usual parking spot and began walking toward her.

Denise saw him approaching and screamed, running toward the elevator before he had a chance to speak. Brian then called her, letting her know he had stumbled across $40,000 in savings bonds—in her name—while rummaging through some boxes he hadn't yet unpacked and was there to deliver them to her. She agreed to return to the parking lot and approached Brian, now seated in the driver's seat of his truck. He rolled down the window and began talking, asking Denise to get into the truck so they could discuss "some things" in private.

"Where are they?" Denise demanded, ignoring his invitation, instead asking to see the savings bonds.

When Brian held the blue-colored documents outside the window, she snatched them from his hand, confirming they were in fact savings bonds in her name.

Brian had been hopeful this gesture might diminish her anger and restore some level of civil communication between them. But it did just the opposite. Denise demanded that he leave at once, threatening to call the campus police. Frustrated, Brian put his truck in gear and drove off. From that day forward, Denise blocked his phone calls and texts and ignored his emails. He was completely cut off.

Not long after that, Brian prepared a will and carefully crafted ten lengthy suicide notes, including to Denise, Anslee, and Stafford. What he wrote to Denise was bitter, telling her to "enjoy your riches and your daughter—I hope they make you happy." Yet he also told his estranged wife she was all he ever wanted: "You were my best friend—I wanted to grow old with you. I realized too late I wanted kids with you. I have so much regret and pain and remorse. I can't take it."

To Anslee he wrote: "I loved my life with you and your mom and Stafford. As it unraveled over the past few years, I lost hope in this life." He told her, "I always raised you and considered you my daughter. Your dad Mike was my best friend and I tried to raise you like I thought he would have." He was proud of her, he said, "and the woman you have become."

His note to Stafford was the hardest. Brian told his son he was "so sorry for what I have done" but explained he had been struggling for years. "I just could not take the pain and the loneliness anymore. I am just ready to leave this painful world and go to heaven." He told Stafford he was a "horrible sinner," but was now in heaven because, "God is merciful and through Jesus, I am saved, thanks be to Him." Brian expressed hope his 17 year old would forgive him "and remember the good times," telling him, "I hope you know I loved you and I meant well ... I am so proud of you, Stafford."

••••

It was after 1:00 a.m. when Brian paid his check at TGI Fridays, now thoroughly inebriated. He staggered out of the restaurant and found his GMC Sierra crew cab truck in the parking lot, eying his backpack in the backseat as he got in, recalling the presence of his loaded handgun. He knew what he wanted to do and how he wanted to do it. He just didn't know where. Brian decided that before doing the deed, he would try to talk to Denise one last time. So he headed toward the Centennial Oaks property where once upon a time they had a good life together.

Despite his intoxication, he was able to find his way to the subdivision's entrance. The gate, however, was locked. In his drunken state, Brian couldn't remember the passcode to open it. He backed out and parked just down the road by the greenway across Miccosukee Road. He stumbled his way back to the entrance gate, backpack slung over his shoulder, a spray bottle filled with a clear liquid in hand.

••••

It was just after 9:00 on Friday morning when Denise opened the driver's side door to her gold Chevy Suburban, dressed in a loose-fitting black tank top and fuchsia pants, a long gold necklace dangling from her neck. Her bleach-blonde hair was pulled back into a tight bun. She dropped her purse in the passenger seat and began driving the SUV out of the circular driveway in front of her home.

At the stop sign just past the entrance gate, she turned left onto Miccosukee Road to begin her familiar 25-minute drive to her office at Florida State. She picked up her cell phone and dialed her younger sister Deborah, as she did most every morning on the way to work.

Just then, Denise was startled by a sudden movement behind her she detected in her peripheral vision—a large man had jumped out from the back of the truck, pouncing onto the bucket seat directly behind her. Her heart began pounding furiously.

"Help!" she screamed into the phone, slamming on the

brakes, hoping her sister would call 911.

"Give me the fucking phone!" her soon-to-be ex-husband demanded, as he leaned forward, forcefully yanking her left hand away from her ear—his hand grazing against her face. He hung up the phone and tossed it onto the floorboard at his feet. "Drive the fucking car!" he yelled.

"What are you doing?" Denise screamed.

"Just drive!" Brian repeated.

"And what are you going to do if I don't?" Denise shot back.

Brian turned around and reached for his backpack, pulling out his weapon. Leaning forward again, he stuck the barrel of the gun into Denise's ribs, repeating, in a menacing tone, "Drive, or you're gonna get hurt." His face was now inches from hers, allowing her to take in a whiff of the putrid smell of alcohol on his breath.

Though she continued driving, Denise ignored Brian's demand to exit at the roundabout, instead driving down Miccosukee Road until she reached a nearby shopping center that included a CVS. She remembered the drugstore had security cameras facing the parking lot and pulled into a spot near the front door, hoping someone watching the video feed would come to her rescue.

"What are you doing?" Brian screamed at her.

"This is the *only place* I will talk to you," she screamed back.

"I just want to talk to you," Brian said, beginning to calm down. "You've blocked my texts. You've blocked my calls. You won't answer my emails. I just want to talk to you Denise!" he whimpered, his anger gradually morphing into despair.

"I'll talk to you *right here*," Denise responded, trembling with fear and beginning to sob. "I'll talk to you Brian."

"Stop crying!" Brian demanded, fearful someone walking by would notice them. His right hand grasped firmly onto the seatbelt buckle by her right hip, just to be sure she didn't try to make a run for it.

"What do you want to talk about?" Denise asked.

"I want you to call off the divorce Denise. Please, I'll do

anything. I'm so miserable. My life is in shambles. I don't have anything left to live for. Please don't do it, Denise."

She glanced behind her toward Brian, noticing his gun for the first time. "What is that?" she asked, her fear escalating once again. "Is that a gun?"

Brian showed her the pistol. "Oh my God!" she cried out. "Is that what you were poking me with?"

"Yes," he replied. "I'm sorry. I don't want to hurt you, Denise. I bought it to kill *myself*." He put the firearm between his legs on the back seat to convince her he was no longer a threat.

"Where did you get it from? Why do you have it?" Denise pressed him.

"I got it to kill myself."

"Did you plan on killing both of us?" she asked, beginning to sob once again.

"No, just myself," he said, now weeping himself. "I swear, Denise. I've lost everything—I've lost my son, I've lost you, and soon you're going to take the house. My mom is dying of cancer. Your lawyer keeps taking me to court. I have nothing left to live for. Why shouldn't I kill myself?"

"Are you sure you really want to die today?" she asked.

"Like 98 percent sure," he answered.

"Well, if you're not 100% sure, then don't do it. I'll talk to you, Brian," Denise said, sensing that the more she talked, the more he was calming down. She swiveled around in her seat to face him, placing her hand on his knee.

"I know you want to talk," Denise continued, "but this isn't the way to do it."

"I know, I know," Brian said, sobbing. "What have I done? What have I done?"

"It's going to be okay," Denise said, now calming down herself. "Brian, you let go of my seatbelt a while ago and I haven't gone anywhere. I'm still here. I'm listening to you."

"Thank you," Brian said tearfully. "I just don't know what to do."

"Let's talk to your dad," Denise suggested. "I'm not going to call the police. I promise. I don't want to see you arrested—I just want to get past this. I won't tell anyone what happened.

This could be your rock bottom. Do you think this is your rock bottom?"

"I don't know. I'm so sorry, Denise," he said, still sobbing. "I'm so sorry."

"Well, let's talk to your dad. We're going to get through this. We will." Denise said she really needed to get to work, as her coworkers would be concerned she wasn't there yet. But if Brian's dad would meet with them after work, she told him, she was willing to do that.

"Go ahead and call your dad," she said.

Reluctantly, Brian dialed his father at his office and put him on the speaker phone. He told him that he and Denise had an altercation, but were now talking and thought it would be a good idea if they included him in their discussion. Denise chimed in that she agreed. They decided to meet at Marcus's office after work.

After they hung up, Brian and Denise continued talking. He confided in her how his life had been spiraling out of control with excessive drinking and hookers to feed his sex addiction. She suggested he get help in a residential rehabilitation facility. He agreed that was a good idea. As they talked, he started feeling better just knowing Denise was taking an interest in his life again. Maybe, just maybe, he thought, all wasn't lost.

They pulled out of the parking lot, Brian directing her back to the greenway by Miccosukee Road, where he had parked early that morning after leaving TGI Fridays. In view of everything that had just transpired, that now seemed like years ago.

Denise pulled up alongside Brian's truck. He climbed into the rear cargo area of her vehicle and retrieved two sheets and what sounded to Denise like a large piece of plastic material. He also grabbed a large spray bottle she believed was filled with bleach, and some type of tool. He placed the items in his backpack.

"Where's the gun?" she asked.

"Right here," Brian said, pointing to it lying on the floorboard behind her. He picked it up and placed it into the backpack.

"I didn't mean to scare you Denise. I'm so sorry. Really, I am. I just wanted to talk to you and couldn't figure out any other way," Brian said with genuine remorse, large teardrops rolling down his cheeks. "I'm so sorry," he reiterated.

"I know you are," she said. "It's not too late. All isn't lost. I have to get to work, but I'll meet you and your dad later."

Brian opened the rear passenger door of her SUV and closed it behind him, unzipping the front compartment of the backpack to retrieve his car keys. He gave Denise an awkward wave as he opened the driver's-side door of his truck. It had been nearly an hour since he sprang up from the back of her Suburban and poked a steel barrel in her ribs. An hour that would be seared in their memories forever.

Denise pulled away, driving down Miccosukee Road in the left lane, toward Florida State. The traffic light up ahead was red, causing her to pull to a stop. A moment later, Brian pulled up beside her in the right lane. He rolled down his window, trying to get Denise's attention. When she saw him, she rolled down her passenger window and turned in his direction.

"I'm so sorry. I'm so sorry," Brian said a final time, sobbing.

"I know," she responded. "It's going to be okay. I'll see you after work."

When the light changed to green, Brian turned right and drove off. Denise continued straight ahead, in the direction of her office at Florida State, fully intending to comply with the plan she and Brian had just made.

But she would never make it into work that morning. Rather, her sister Deborah somehow tracked her down—scared that something awful had happened when their phone call abruptly disconnected. They met in a parking lot outside a medical office building.

Denise sat in her sister's car, recounting in meticulous detail her horrifying hour-long encounter with Brian. She was visibly shaken, sobbing uncontrollably. Denise told her sister she needed to get to work because Brian would be calling there soon to make sure she was following through with the plan they discussed—and not going to the police.

Yet Deborah insisted that she contact the police immediately—suggesting she call her husband Dave McCranie, a 20-year veteran with the Tallahassee Police Department (TPD), who was at home on his day off.

Following her sister's advice, Denise did just that, barely able to get her words out as she told her brother-in-law about the morning's events. He implored her to get back in her truck and drive directly to the Sheriff's Office.

So instead of continuing to her office at the football stadium as she had planned, Denise drove to the Leon County Sheriff's Office—where a cascade of events was about to begin that would forever alter many lives, and would once and for all reveal what actually happened to Jerry Michael Williams.

8

Big Break

$\mathbf{B}$rian reached out for help the moment he parted ways with Denise. He called his treating psychologist and sex addiction counselor, Dr. Ron Rickner, to try to schedule an emergency session. When Dr. Rickner didn't answer, he drove directly to his office. On the way, Denise's estranged husband passed by the Apalachee Mental Health Center and tried calling there as well. No answer yet again. And when he arrived at Dr. Rickner's office, the psychologist wasn't there. He also placed a call to Tallahassee Memorial Hospital's mental health center but, once again, received a recorded message. He contemplated calling 911.

Finally, however, Brian made actual contact with a live human being—Steve Mnookin, a friend who was also a practicing anesthesiologist. Dr. Mnookin served as Brian's addiction group sponsor, having battled his own demons over the years. Dr. Rickner was also his therapist. He and Brian frequently had lunch together during the work week.

As they spoke on the phone, Brian confided in his friend that he had hit rock bottom—a "new low"—and desperately needed someone to talk to. He wanted his advice, Brian said, on the best place to seek treatment. Dr. Mnookin agreed to drop everything and meet his friend at the Village Pizza & Pasta off of Thomasville Road.

The two entered the restaurant about noon and ordered

lunch. Brian recounted the sordid details of his morning adventure with Denise, admitting he had kidnapped her at gunpoint. He had been intending to commit suicide, Brian said, and needed to speak with Denise one last time before he did. He then broached an additional subject. "And this part is confidential," Brian said. "Like privileged because you're my doctor."

"Sure," the physician replied, humoring his friend, fully aware there was nothing at all privileged about their conversation because it had nothing to do with medical treatment. He thought Brian was about to reveal a new sexual escapade—a topic they frequently discussed.

Yet Brian brought up a different subject altogether—Mike Williams. He told Mnookin the police had been hounding him, coming to his house repeatedly. They were telling him that once he and Denise were officially divorced—and the marital privilege protecting the confidentiality of their communications gone—they were going to put pressure on her to tell them what she knew about Mike's December 2000 disappearance. They wanted him to believe, Brian told his friend, that once he and Denise had officially split, she would squeal on him about what had actually happened to Mike.

"They're trying to get me to say something," he told Mnookin, clearly worried. "Or get her to." He was desperate to discuss the matter with his estranged wife, to convince her not to allow the divorce to go through—if only to protect them both from the police. But he had no way to talk with her since she had blocked him on her phone, he said. That is why he had hidden in her truck that morning—to make sure he could finally speak with her.

This wasn't the first time he had pulled such a stunt either, Brian shared with his friend. He told the physician how he had ambushed Denise and her boyfriend Chuck Bunker at an Atlanta hotel many years earlier—before he and Denise got married.

"You can't keep doing this stuff," Mnookin remarked when Brian finally took a breath—not sure of what to make of what his friend was saying about his interactions with the police.

"I know. You're right," Brian acknowledged, beginning to tear up. "I really messed up."

As they sat at the table, the pair called mental health providers, trying to find somewhere Brian could either get a quick appointment or check in for inpatient rehab. Finally, they were able to make an appointment for him to see Dr. Rickner—their mutual therapist—at 5:00 that afternoon.

"Are you sure I can't take you to the hospital right now?" Mnookin asked, the two standing beside Brian's truck in the parking lot. He was afraid Brian might try to kill himself before day's end.

"No, no, I'm going to be okay," Brian responded. "I'm going to go speak with my dad."

"Okay my friend," Mnookin said, as he gave Brian a warm embrace. "Please take care of yourself and get help."

"I will," Brian assured him. "Thanks so much for everything."

About an hour later, Brian called his friend again, thanking him once more for meeting on such short notice. "Listen," he said. "What we talked about at lunch, you know Steve, I would really appreciate it if, you know, we never had that conversation. Okay?"

"Sure, Brian. Whatever you want," the doctor agreed.

••••

Denise sat patiently in an interview room at the Sheriff's Office. She texted with friends, likely unaware of the tiny camera in the corner of the room capturing her every move and projecting a live video stream into a nearby room chock full of law enforcement officers.

It had been nearly 16 years since her husband Mike went missing—and over a decade since the FDLE launched its suspicious missing-person investigation into his disappearance. Investigators' efforts to fill in the puzzle pieces had been halting and frustrating, turning up precious few leads—largely because neither Denise nor Brian would talk.

But now, after all that time, and by sheer serendipity—thanks to Brian's actions that morning—Denise was sitting in a room in the Sheriff's Office seemingly eager to talk. Her estranged husband was likely only hours behind, sure to be arrested and brought into custody later that afternoon. Investigators who for years had been stymied by the Mike Williams case had just received their biggest break imaginable.

Would this be the day they would crack the case wide open? Was being held at gunpoint for nearly an hour enough to cause Denise to break her silence—or any pact she had with Brian? The law enforcement officers gathered that afternoon just a few steps away from where Denise was sitting certainly hoped so.

••••

The door finally opened. Detective Paul Salvo with the Sheriff's Office sat down across the desk from Denise, his back to the camera. She shared with him how Brian had abducted her at gunpoint, holding her hostage for nearly an hour. Though she was quite animated—speaking rapidly and gesticulating forcefully—Denise was eerily detached as she described the kidnapping incident, almost as if she were sharing details of what had happened to a stranger, rather than herself.

"He pulled out a gun—like not a hunting gun, but like a gun you would kill someone with—and he put it right here in my ribs," she explained, demonstrating with her right hand where the gun had been pressed against her body.

"So I'm driving and he's right here," she continued, using her left hand to show how Brian had gotten right up against the right side of her face. "He was like, 'I had to do this because you won't answer my texts or calls. Please just call the divorce off. I've lost everything.' You know, blah blah blah."

She recounted for the detective their interaction in front of the CVS. "He's screaming and I'm just like shaking," she said, reliving the experience. "And he's telling me to stop crying—that people are going to notice. I was like, 'Are you planning on, you know, ending both of our lives today?' 'Well, mine. I'm planning on mine.' And then he would say … he must have said a million times, 'I want to kill myself.'" She described Brian as being "crazed."

"And then, as we were just talking, I was just kind of agreeing with whatever he was saying and I was like, 'I know that you love me.' He recently lost his son. His son had decided to move in with—he had joint custody and now he doesn't. And so he said, 'I lost my son, I lost you, I have nothing to live for.' And I was like, 'You can get us all back if you'll just turn your life around.' Because he was a Christian at one point, and I was like, 'If you'll just turn back to the Lord.'"

Denise explained how she had finally calmed Brian down, turning to face him and putting her hand on his knee, and how he "kind of woke up, saying, 'What have I done? What have I done?'" She placed her hand on her forehead to demonstrate Brian's recognition of how badly he had messed up.

After discussing the kidnapping incident with Detective Salvo for about 90 minutes, Denise's brother-in-law Dave McCranie—who had been watching the video stream down the hall—took over the questioning. McCranie had driven to the Sheriff's Office shortly after hanging up with Denise, initially intending to provide her support and comfort. But once there, his role quickly morphed into that of an interrogator—as if Denise were a total stranger.

The TPD officer deftly changed the subject from his sister-in-law's kidnapping that morning to Mike's disappearance 16 years before, suggesting that Brian wasn't just a kidnapper, but a murderer as well. "I know Denise, he did it and you know exactly what I'm talking about … and he held that over your head forever," he insisted. "He wasn't gonna kill himself Denise. He was gonna kill you so that you didn't talk about him later. That is the truth."

Denise finally began losing her composure, shaking her head side to side, tears cascading down her cheeks.

"Fifteen years ago," McCranie continued, "he walked in and told that you he had done something. Didn't he?"

Now sobbing, Denise reached for a tissue, wiping her eyes, still shaking her head side to side.

"No," she finally replied.

"Denise?"

"No," she whimpered.

"I'm telling you. He killed Mike, and he was going to kill you to make you go away. The person you saw today, he killed Mike, didn't he?"

Denise didn't respond.

"And he did. And that's who he was then," McCranie said. "He has conned you to no end." He tried to get her to agree that Brian was very capable of committing such a heinous act.

"I mean, that person today could have done anything, and uh, anything," she reluctantly agreed, but quickly added, "That's not the person I married. It's not the person I knew." She told her brother-in-law she had married Brian because "he was living for the Lord and he was a Christian."

Refusing to accept her answer, the TPD officer shot back, "We can't put it back in the bottle. He killed Mike and I'm pretty sure the reason he was going to kill you today was he was afraid you were going to say something." But his sister-in-law wouldn't budge.

"This is not going away. Okay? He's going to kill you," McCranie insisted, rising up from his seat, leaving Denise to stew.

Officer McCranie walked down the hallway and tagged FDLE Special Agent Mike DeVaney—a bearded, gray-haired man wearing a blue hooded jacket—who rose from his seat, determined to get Denise to cough up whatever she knew about Mike's disappearance.

The veteran agent, who had been involved in the investigation into Mike's disappearance since 2007, had raced over to the Sheriff's Office after being tipped off Denise was sitting in an interview room spilling her guts about Brian. He had been listening intently to her responses to her brother-in-law's questions, chomping at the bit to interrogate her himself—before a lawyer showed up by her side. As he walked down the corridor, DeVaney believed her presence that afternoon represented a golden opportunity to finally crack the stone-cold case wide open.

Reaching out to greet Denise, he explained that he had been looking into Mike's disappearance for a long time and had "dissected" everything he could about her, her family, Brian, and his family. He told her there were "a lot of people" involved in the investigation.

Denise listened, nodding her head occasionally, but not saying a word. Her emotional affect had changed 180 degrees in just a few minutes—no more tears, just a distant expression.

For nearly twenty minutes, the two engaged in a verbal tug-of-war that yo-yoed uncomfortably between Denise trying to focus on that day's events and DeVaney seeking to probe her about the 16-year mystery of Mike's disappearance.

With hopes of cracking the veneer that to then had been unbreakable, the special agent began by informing Denise she had been under near constant surveillance. He actually knew the gate code to the Midyette Plantation subdivision "by heart," he boasted, and had been around her house so frequently he even knew when she had some carpeting removed.

Denise finally broke her silence, but only to clarify whether he was talking about carpeting she removed to expose the hardwood floors on the second floor of the house. He confirmed he was.

DeVaney tried to shake some sense into Denise, imploring her to let it "sink in that today was going to be your last day. *Please* let that sink in," he said. He inquired about the items Brian had with him, implying her second husband was going to use them to dispose of her body. He asked whether Brian had been trying to get her to turn around as she was driving toward the CVS. Denise responded that he kept telling her he wanted her to go to the roundabout—her finger making a circle to illustrate her point.

Then, seemingly out of nowhere, the veteran agent began an entirely new line of questioning. "Where do you think Mike's buried at?" he asked, intending to catch Denise off guard.

Revealing no discernible reaction to the abrupt change of subjects, she responded, almost casually, "Oh, I have no idea."

"Any speculation on that?" DeVaney pressed.

"On where he's buried?"

"You don't really believe he died at—on the lake?"

"*I* do," she replied, nodding her head slightly.

"*Why*?" DeVaney asked, incredulous at her response.

"I just, I just always have," she said, nervously crossing her arms, dropping them onto her lap. "That's what I believe." She then attempted to pivot back to the roundabout Brian was directing her to take, again, drawing an imaginary circle with her right hand. But her efforts to steer the conversation back to that topic were met with stiff resistance.

"No, no, no, that's not what I'm talking about," Agent DeVaney said. "Why do you think Mike perished in the lake? I mean, he didn't die at Lake Seminole, okay."

Arms crossed more tightly now, leaning forward uncomfortably, Denise responded, "That's what I believe. That's what I've always believed."

"Again, why?"

"I've never been proven anything different," she answered, now becoming visibly frustrated with where their conversation was heading.

Agent DeVaney told Denise it was literally "an impossibility" Mike had died in the lake, as there had never been anyone who had fallen overboard or drowned there whose body wasn't later recovered.

"That's just what I believe," Denise insisted.

"Really?" the agent pressed her, again incredulous.

"Really."

The waders appearing out of nowhere, despite a "big monstrous search," he told her, was a red flag that "kind of led investigators to go in different directions than what they initially thought."

Denise, showing increasing signs of discomfort, began nervously rubbing her crossed arms with her hands.

The agent then disclosed some additional tidbits: that the FDLE had recovered Mike's Ford Bronco from a junkyard in Alabama, and his boat from Monticello, so investigators could "get a good look at it." They had torn Mike's truck apart looking for clues, he told her.

"I mean, there's a whole lot of stuff and you don't have *a clue* of what we've looked at," he said, his tone now more menacing. Denise remained mute, her left hand nervously scratching her left leg, seemingly more annoyed with each additional question.

DeVaney told her the FDLE had reached the conclusion "that Mike did not perish or die on Lake Seminole. Please understand that." Denise merely nodded to signal she was listening.

"You seem to say you don't have a clue what happened to Mike?" he asked.

Denise just stared straight ahead, a blank expression concealing her thoughts.

The FDLE agent then abruptly transitioned to her relationship with Kathy and Brian: "Apparently you were *really* close, okay? Do you know what I'm talking about?" he asked with a slight smirk.

Denise acknowledged she and Kathy were very close—and remained so—apparently not getting the gist of his lurid question. "We're still very close," she said, noting she had been texting with Kathy just before he had walked in.

"If I say that we're totally aware of all the videos, you'd probably know what I'm talking about?" he asked, pushing his subject to acknowledge the existence of some risqué footage involving herself, Brian, and Kathy. Denise shook her head side to side, telling him she had no idea what he was talking about.

"You're clueless when I say videos?"

"I don't, yeah," she repeated, a perplexed expression washing over her face.

"Of you, Kathy, and Brian?"

"I would have to see 'em," she said, her frustration with the interrogation now reaching a boiling point.

"You have no idea what I'm talking about?" Agent DeVaney asked yet again, well aware—and seemingly pleased—he was getting under her skin.

"No. I'm just starting to feel very uncomfortable," she finally confessed, her right hand nervously rubbing her left arm.

"Well I've been uncomfortable for a long time," the agent shot back, "because we've needed some things on this case." He told her they'd been hoping either she or Brian would help them put the puzzle pieces surrounding Mike's disappearance in place.

Denise pointed to the paperwork on the desk between them, trying to shift the conversation back to her mission. Not only did she want the agent to focus on what had transpired that morning, she also was trying to petition the court for a domestic violence protective order before it closed at 5:00 p.m. "I want me and my daughter to be safe," she said.

There was no need for her to worry, Agent DeVaney replied, telling her he had no doubt "Brian will be located and put in jail for the crimes he has committed."

And that led him right back to the subject of her first husband's disappearance, a topic he told Denise was likely to be discussed while Brian was being held in jail: "What if he starts talking about the past?" he mused. "*Way* in the past."

"I don't know," Denise responded. "I have no idea what he's going to say."

"No idea?" the agent asked, incredulous yet again.

"No," she insisted, shaking her head.

"What if he starts talking about the disappearance of Mike?"

"I hope he admits this morning. I hope he admits what he did," Denise replied, "because that's what he did. If they ask him about Mike, I have no idea. I mean we'll see."

The seasoned law enforcement officer then raised a related, but different topic, asking Denise if she knew anything about *Brian's* disappearance the day Mike went missing. He inquired whether Kathy had ever discussed that particular subject with her. Denise said she didn't recall anything about that, but offered to text Kathy right then and there.

"I'd rather hear it from you, okay?" Agent DeVaney told her. "You knew, I mean, Brian just disappeared."

"I don't know about that," Denise said, reiterating her rush to get the domestic violence petition filed, noting to the agent it was already 3:30 p.m. "I just want to make sure that I have time to do that. That's my priority right now."

Not backing down, DeVaney pushed her again: "I wish I could just fill in some of the pieces of the puzzle. I'd much rather get it from you than from Brian but, once he's arrested, I'm going to talk to him too. And we're going to see what he says, okay? He may say something you don't want to hear."

Denise refused to take the bait, replying she had no idea what Brian would say. "But I guess what I'm saying about Mike's situation that you want to talk about," she added, "I don't want to talk about this right now." Rather, she wanted to get the domestic violence petition taken care of first. "So, I understand that you want to talk about this, but this is what I want to do," she said, pointing again to the paperwork. "This is what has to be done—today," she insisted.

But the veteran agent wouldn't let her off the hook. "You know why it's so important to talk to you about Mike?" he asked. "I mean this was *your husband*. He simply vanished. I hope you still have an interest in that."

"I'm just, I'm not comfortable talking about this right now," she repeated, now losing what little patience she had left. "I've had an *unbelievable* day and—it's just all too much right now," she said, gesticulating forcefully with her hands. "I just really want to focus on this," she said, again pointing to the domestic violence petition.

Denise told Agent DeVaney she was worried what might happen to her and Anslee if Brian were released from jail—especially because she had promised him that morning she wouldn't tell anyone what happened or report him to law enforcement. Persisting with his questioning, DeVaney used her fear to try, once again, to steer their conversation back toward Mike. "We've seen a side ... of Brian that we knew was there, and it surfaced again. Okay? Because, again, we've kind of tracked his history. And we also know, you know, Mike vanishes."

"Well, I myself, have never seen anything like I saw this morning," Denise retorted, her left hand touching her chest for emphasis. "*Never*." But she also acknowledged, "I would never have thought he would have done this. I mean, obviously, he's capable of what he did today," she said with a nervous laugh.

"Do you think he's responsible for Mike's disappearance," DeVaney interjected, finally demanding a "yes or no" answer to his central question.

"I do not, and I never have," Denise answered, shaking her head side to side. "I would have never married him if I thought that. I would have never wanted so bad to have children with him. I would have, I mean, in my mind, in my heart, *no*."

Denise said she was open to looking back "on that situation" with the benefit of hindsight, especially knowing what Brian had done to her that morning. "But do I believe right here in this moment that he had anything to do with that? Absolutely not," she said emphatically. "Does that mean I'm not gonna try to process this and look back? Of course I am."

Their conversation ended with Agent DeVaney telling Denise, "We knew that one day there'd be a blowup. We predicted that … I don't think it's finished yet as far as people talking about different things," he said, an ominous—perhaps prescient—prediction that Brian, once in custody, might have a lot to say about Mike's mysterious disappearance.

As he left the Sheriff's Office that afternoon, the FDLE agent was likely disappointed he hadn't succeeded in getting Denise to spill the beans. Based on her nervous reaction to some of his questions—and fairly incredible responses to others—he was supremely confident Denise knew a whole lot more about Mike's disappearance than she had let on. He also had the luxury of knowing that, any minute, Brian Winchester—the other person he had been dying to speak with for years—would be waiting for him in another interview room just down the hallway.

••••

While Denise was wrapping up her interview with Agent DeVaney, a slew of armed sheriff's deputies were staking out the parking lot at Winchester Financial Group—waiting for

Brian to exit. Eventually the suspect walked out of the building toward the parking lot and entered the passenger side of a truck owned by his cousin, Kevin Winchester.

The officers immediately surrounded the truck with their vehicles—preventing it from moving—and took Brian into custody without incident or resistance. They transported him to the Sheriff's Office, leaving him in another interview room not far from where Agent DeVaney had just grilled his estranged wife. Before long, Sergeant Salvo walked in, fully aware of Brian's criminal conduct that morning.

Yet Brian feigned ignorance, acting as if he had no idea what the detective was talking about. Realizing he wasn't about to hear anything resembling the truth, Salvo placed him under arrest, reading him the required Miranda warnings. He informed Brian he was being charged with kidnapping, domestic assault with a deadly weapon, and armed burglary. Brian invoked his right not to speak further until accompanied by his attorney, Tim Jansen.

He was then transported to the county jail—officially the Leon County Detention Center—where Brian was promptly fingerprinted, photographed, and provided a standard-issue navy blue jumpsuit.

Rather than a posh 5,000-square-foot waterfront house, for the next 16 months, a dark, foul-smelling jail cell would be the place Brian Winchester would call home.

9

Deal with the Devil

The *Tallahassee Democrat's* News Director Jennifer Portman began her Monday morning the same as any other—by scrolling through the list of arrests in Leon County since her last check on Friday. As she got to the bottom of the list, one of the names nearly jumped off the page: Brian Winchester. As Portman read more closely, she was even more astonished to learn Brian had been arrested for kidnapping his estranged wife, Denise.

"Oh my God!" she thought to herself, fully aware the ensuing legal proceedings held the potential to finally solve the mystery of Mike Williams' disappearance. Brian's arrest was by far the biggest break, she believed, to come cold-case investigators' way since they begrudgingly acceded to Cheryl's incessant demands to open an investigation some 12 years before.

In an article released later that day in the *Democrat*, Portman wrote that a "man with ties to one of the area's most vexing unsolved crimes is in jail, accused of kidnapping his wife at gunpoint." She informed newspaper readers that investigators—who initially believed Mike had been eaten by alligators—now believed "the 31-year-old father was the victim of foul play but have named no suspects or persons of interest in the cold case."

News of the arrest spread through the Sunshine State's

capital city like wildfire. Two days later, spectators, reporters, and media crews behind a bank of video cameras packed a downtown courtroom, waiting in rapt attention for Brian's initial appearance.

As was customary in Leon County, newly charged defendants remained in the county jail for the quick proceeding, communicating with court officials through a closed-circuit TV. A video stream projected his image onto a large TV monitor near the judge at the front of the courtroom. From his side of the video feed, Brian could see the entire courtroom and hear every word spoken about him.

His lawyer, Tim Jansen, asked Judge Stephen Everett to release him on bond. Jansen argued that his client's arrest was based solely on his estranged wife's statement and that Brian was innocent of the charges. It was appropriate for him to remain out on bond pending trial, he insisted.

With a victim's advocate by her side, Denise stood before Judge Everett, begging him to keep her estranged husband locked up until trial. Seemingly tormented by anguish over the kidnapping incident, she appeared terrified about the prospect Brian might be released.

Her hands trembled as she read to the judge from a prepared statement. "He was waiting for me in the back of my car with a gun. He grabbed the steering wheel," she said through her tears. "He shoved the gun in my rib cage, screaming profanities uncontrollably at me. I will never be the same," she added, her voice quavering with emotion.

As he watched his estranged wife's statement through the TV monitor, Brian's facial expressions and furrowed brow conveyed a different narrative—suggesting Denise was embellishing what had actually transpired.

"I would never wish this on anyone," she continued. "I can't sleep, I can't eat, because I only see him rising up out of the back of the car and because all I can feel is the gun shoved in my ribs. I can't have peace because I only hear his voice screaming and cussing at me. Please don't let him out," Denise pleaded in a high-pitched whimper. "He could have killed me."

She then read a typed statement from her 17-year-old daughter Anslee, which said: "Judge, I am scared. My mom is scared. He had a gun. He could have killed her. She is all I have. Please don't let him out. He will come for her and then I will have no one. Please."

As Denise walked away from the center of the courtroom, wiping tears from her eyes, Judge Everett stated he was finding probable cause as to the charges of kidnapping, aggravated assault with a deadly weapon, and armed burglary. He denied bond, noting the defendant could reapply at a later time.

Two days later, Brian formally entered a plea of not guilty.

••••

In early January, Jansen made a second run at securing Brian's release. This time, the defendant was in the courtroom, sitting at counsel table beside Jansen and his associate Adam Komisar. Brian was clad in a drab blue jumpsuit with the words Leon County Jail written across the back—feet shackled together beneath the counsel table. A different circuit judge, James Hankinson, peered down from his perch on the bench. Denise, seated beside her victim's advocate and members of her family, watched from the gallery.

The defense team called Sergeant Paul Salvo to the witness stand. Through his sharp questioning, Komisar—a former Assistant State Attorney himself—forced the detective to acknowledge that Denise bore no signs of any injury the day she reported the incident, that she was unable to identify what type of firearm had been used, and that she later changed her story about what Brian had been wearing.

Salvo also conceded that the liquid in Brian's spray bottle—which had been widely reported by the news media to contain bleach—had never been tested to determine its contents. The detective also testified that the video footage from the CVS security cameras didn't show much of anything—not even Brian's presence in Denise's vehicle.

As Salvo stepped down from the witness stand, Denise came forward, her victim's advocate again by her side. Facing

Judge Hankinson for the first time, she implored him to keep Brian locked up, telling him how certain she was that he would find some way to harm her and Anslee were he to be released. After she finished, a young Assistant State Attorney named Andy Rogers asked the judge to keep Brian locked up behind bars.

Next to address the court was Jansen. Arguing that his client didn't pose a danger to the community, and should be released on bond until trial, the defense attorney suggested the safety of Denise, Anslee, and the larger community could be assured by having Brian placed under house arrest with strict GPS monitoring. He wouldn't be an unreasonable danger to the community, Jansen contended.

Judge Hankinson disagreed, stating from his perch on the bench, "These facts show that he is very much a danger to the community. I think it would be foolish on my part to grant him bond." He denied Jansen's request.

Having uttered not a single word during the entire proceeding, Brian was whisked away by uniformed sheriff's deputies and deposited into a patrol car for the 15-minute ride back to the county jail, now certain to be his home until trial.

••••

On May 4, 2017, the marriage between Brian and Denise Winchester officially came to an end with the entry of a divorce decree. Four days later, Denise Williams—as she would now be known once again—celebrated the 18th birthday of her daughter, Anslee, who was just a few weeks away from graduating from NFC, the very high school where Denise and her father had met more than 30 years before.

Brian's trial date on the kidnapping, assault, and burglary charges was fast approaching—scheduled for October 23. The former financial planner was finding everyday living in the rigid confines of his jail cell intolerable, and knew things would only get worse in prison.

With the trial looming ominously, desperate to find a way out of his predicament, Brian initiated discussions with several people he believed might provide "assistance." He approached a fellow inmate, Wade Wilson, who offered to lend a hand—for a certain price, of course. Their discussions continued for some time, Wilson plotting various scenarios with him. But when the inmate—a self-described hitman—said he could make Denise and other witnesses "go away," Brian got cold feet and ended his discussions with him. Another person he approached through an intermediary was a woman named Kimberly Adams, who seemed agreeable to fabricating evidence and tampering with witnesses on his behalf. He also solicited assistance from his own sister, Jennifer.

Meanwhile, Tim Jansen's attempts to engage the State Attorney's Office in plea negotiations were going absolutely nowhere. He had pled out many a client facing aggravated kidnapping charges to five years in prison, followed by another five of probation. Yet prosecutors in the State Attorney's Office didn't seem interested in negotiating any deal at all, insisting they would be seeking a life sentence for Brian. They did hint, however, that if Brian decided to tell them what he knew about Mike Williams' December 2000 disappearance, there just might be something to discuss.

By early fall of 2017, FDLE agents had caught wind of Brian's various conversations and schemes. Word filtered back to Jansen that prosecutors were contemplating leveling additional charges against his client for obstructing justice and tampering with witnesses. With Brian's situation looking more bleak with each passing day, Jansen played the only card he held. He let his counterparts in the State Attorney's Office know his client might be interested in making a deal.

Jansen hadn't just fallen off the turnip truck. He had been practicing for 30 years following his graduation from law school at the University of Florida. His career path included stints on both sides of the courtroom, beginning with five years as an Assistant United States Attorney in both Tampa and Tallahassee, prosecuting drug dealers and white collar criminals. In 1994, he opened his own firm and, for the next 25 years, concentrated on criminal defense work. During that time, the hard-nosed lawyer had represented numerous high-profile clients, including Heisman Trophy winner and future NFL quarterback Jameis Winston. He was also a frequent TV analyst and commentator during significant Florida trials, working with the likes of Greta Van Susteren and Nancy Grace.

In view of Brian's shenanigans with thugs like Wade Wilson, it was now clear to Jansen his client was going to spend hard time in prison. The only way to limit the length of his sentence, he believed, was to make a deal that would let prosecutors and law enforcement agents question Brian about Mike's disappearance. Over the course of several weeks in September—shrouded under a tight veil of secrecy—Jansen and Assistant State Attorney Andy Rogers negotiated the contours of a deal, which they labeled a "proffer agreement."

The agreement, eventually typed up and signed by Rogers, consisted of two single-spaced pages, 12 bullet points in all. The key provisions were as follows:

First, Brian would be required to "fully and truthfully answer questions … regarding the circumstances and his knowledge of the disappearance of Mike Williams."

Second, the State would be prohibited from using any information Brian provided to prosecute him for any crime, including any crime associated with Mike's disappearance. He would essentially have immunity no matter what his own involvement had been in bringing about Mike's death—even if he had killed his best friend in cold blood.

Third, the State would agree not to seek a life sentence on the pending aggravated kidnapping charges or any other charges related to his August 5, 2016, altercation with Denise.

Fourth, the State would agree not to present any evidence related to Brian's nefarious interactions with Wade Wilson in any further proceedings in the kidnapping case.

Fifth, the State would agree to continue the trial of Brian's case until December or January to provide law enforcement agents ample time to question him about the details of Mike's disappearance.

Finally, the State would be prohibited from using any statements Brian made against him so long as they were truthful; any untruthful statement, however, could be used against him in any future criminal proceeding.

Plain and simple, in the eyes of State Attorney Jack Campbell, this was nothing short of a deal with the Devil. The recently elected lead prosecutor of the Second Judicial Circuit—a six-county area that included Tallahassee's Leon County—was fully aware the news media and public would question his decision to make this deal. After all, under the agreement, if it turned out that Brian was Mike's killer, he would avoid even the slightest punishment for his despicable crime. Campbell recognized that his next political opponent would likely vilify him for making a deal that gave someone a pass for a vicious murder.

But without this agreement, the State Attorney was convinced Brian would take to the grave everything he knew about the events of December 16, 2000. Even if his office couldn't convict anyone for killing Mike, Campbell believed, the proffer agreement allowed the mystery surrounding his disappearance to finally be solved. Most importantly, Cheryl and Nick Williams could finally have closure. And, with any luck, perhaps justice as well.

••••

On October 4, Brian Winchester and Tim Jansen placed their signatures on the proffer agreement. Law enforcement agents met with them both in a secure room at the jail on October 9 and again on October 12—the second meeting conducted by Special Agent Mike DeVaney. Assistant State Attorneys Andy Rogers and Jon Fuchs—Rogers' supervisor—watched via Skype.

The meetings hardly qualified as interrogations. When Brian was asked what had happened on December 16, 2000, his answer lasted for more than an hour, with barely an additional question being asked.

Brian literally spilled his guts, every word recorded by sophisticated audio equipment. He was emotional, breaking down in tears as he revealed detail after detail. It was as if he had been itching to finally break his silence and release himself from the sordid story he'd locked deep inside his soul for more than 15 years. His time with the investigators was almost like cathartic therapy.

To the investigators seated across from him—and prosecutors watching remotely—Brian seemed forthcoming and truthful. Moreover, by mid-October, they were able to corroborate the most critical details he had shared, confirming he had lived up to his end of the bargain.

The deal between Brian and the State Attorney's Office—as well as the information shared in his proffer statements—would remain secrets more closely guarded than the formula for Coca-Cola. For nearly eight months. Neither Jennifer Portman nor the news media writ large had the slightest inkling of what had been going on behind the scenes—or of the massive excavation project Leon County Public Works had undertaken in broad daylight at Carr Lake. Not even Cheryl Williams would learn those details for over two months.

Thus, when Brian appeared before Judge Hankinson on October 19 to plead "no contest" to the charges of aggravated kidnapping and burglary with a firearm, neither the prosecutors nor defense attorneys uttered a word about the proffer agreement, Brian's statements at the jail, or the excavation project that had wrapped up just the prior day. Indeed, the proceeding lasted only a few minutes. To the media and larger Tallahassee community, why Brian had suddenly agreed to accept criminal responsibility for kidnapping Denise was as much a mystery as the disappearance of Mike itself.

••••

As she did every year on December 16, Jennifer Portman penned a poignant column in the *Democrat* to commemorate the 17th anniversary of Mike's disappearance: "He's the one who supposedly went duck hunting alone before dawn on Lake Seminole, fell from his boat, was sucked by his waders to the bottom and eaten by alligators, never to be seen again," she wrote. "Not a trace of him. I keep retelling his story because I'm missing one critical fact: what actually happened to Mike

Williams."

Her piece intimated Brian Winchester held the key to unlocking the 17-year-old mystery: "If Brian knows anything about what happened to Mike, a man he was friends with since 9th grade, now might be a good time to talk."

She pushed State Attorney Jack Campbell to explain why more wasn't being done to get Brian to share what he knew. "There has not been a day I didn't want to solve [Mike's] case," Campbell told her. "Yes, I'm certainly interested in [Brian] and I would love to be able to use his case to solve this case."

The Second Circuit's lead prosecutor suggested to Portman the prospect of a long prison stay might prove a "tipping point. We aren't stopping," he told her, "we aren't quitting." What he didn't tell her, however, is that prosecutors in his office had known for nearly two months exactly what happened to Mike. And that Brian was the one who told them.

••••

Three days later, a downtown courtroom was once again packed, this time for Brian's sentencing hearing. TV cameras, reporters, and friends and former NFC and Florida State classmates of Mike, Denise, and Brian filled the gallery. Denise and her family members attended as did Brian's father and sister. His mother Patricia had died of stomach cancer just weeks before—Brian missing her funeral due to his unfortunate circumstances. Mike's former boss Clay Ketcham sat with his wife Patti, hopeful the day's proceedings might yield some clue as to what had happened to Mike.

A few days before the hearing, Jansen submitted to Judge Hankinson a 13-page handwritten letter his client had written from jail. In the letter, Brian expressed his profound apologies to Denise, his dad and now deceased mom, and everyone he had let down by his actions. "I was a good Dad, and for the most part I was a good husband," he wrote, "but I had moral failings that led us into a lifestyle that I knew was wrong. My selfish choices to allow and encourage the lifestyle we were leading led and contributed to the destruction of our marriage.

I will always regret them."

Brain shared in his letter how he often read the obituary section of the newspaper, appreciating the "words of admiration from the families of the deceased." He acknowledged his own obituary, if written right then, "wouldn't be good. I am 47 years old and when I look in the mirror I am ashamed of myself. This is not the reputation and legacy I want to leave behind. I want to give my son reason to be proud of me." His goal, he told Judge Hankinson, was to "change my obituary in the time that I have left in my life."

He closed his letter noting a litany of events he had already missed out on, and would continue to miss in the future: holiday traditions, Stafford's high school graduation—which had occurred earlier that year—his son's college years, career choices, wedding, and in all likelihood, "the birth of my first grandchild. All these things lost because of my selfish stupid choices." He asked for "whatever mercy" the judge might be willing to grant him.

Notably absent from his letter, however, was any reference to his best friend Mike Williams and whatever he might have known about his disappearance.

Brian's wasn't the only letter Judge Hankinson received. More than 40 friends, hunting and fishing buddies, business acquaintances, coworkers, former neighbors, and extended family members wrote the judge asking for leniency on Brian's behalf.

Among the themes expressed in those letters were how kind, generous, and gentle Brian had always been; what an amazing father he was to Stafford; how he had devoted significant time and energy teaching his sons' friends and other neighborhood youth how to hunt and fish; his devotion to living a true Christian life, serving as a "model citizen" prior to the events of August 5, 2016; and how his actions on that date were completely out of character, caused by the stress of losing his wife, son, and his mom's terminal cancer diagnosis.

The letter writers expressed confidence that Brian's kidnapping of Denise was a momentary lapse in judgment, rather than a sign of a deeper character flaw. Many ended their letters assuring Judge Hankinson that Brian posed not the slightest threat to society.

During the hour-long hearing, Brian's father, uncle, and sister all spoke on his behalf. Even Stafford wrote a letter in support of leniency—describing his father as a "troubled man who had lost his way." It had been his discovery of the photos of his dad with prostitutes, after all, that helped set off the cascade of events culminating with his father being sentenced for kidnapping.

Through a steady stream of tears—and gut-wrenching anguish—Brian stood before the judge, reciting a prepared statement which appeared both remorseful and heartfelt. Though he freely admitted his wrongdoing in kidnapping Denise, his state of mind on August 5, 2016, he said, was greatly affected by his mom dying of cancer, the failure of his marriage, and his sense that he was "financially ruined."

Gasping for air, sobbing, Brian told the judge how losing his son "was the nail in my coffin. I lost all hope when I lost him." Barely able to maintain his composure, with his voice catching, he confessed, "I wanted to end my life that day."

"Never, ever, did I have any intentions of harming Denise," he insisted. "Nor would I."

With her victim's advocate by her side—rubbing her back for comfort—Denise, dressed entirely in black, told the judge she had relived the kidnapping incident "every single day and it is always with me … He is the reason," she continued, "he has been sitting in jail the past 16 months … He is the reason that he lost me and the children," she said, wiping tears from her eyes.

Denise told Judge Hankinson that since the incident she had been diagnosed with PTSD and extreme anxiety. She began each day, she said, with the memory of Brian jumping out of the back of her car and ended each day "feeling the gun shoved in my ribs when I turn on my right side trying to sleep."

"We all have a right to feel secure and safe and he took my sense of security and safety from me," she added. "He stole it from me. I live each day with the fear of retaliation for my decision to tell. He will finish what he has started no matter what age he is when he is released."

Denise implored the judge to sentence Brian to life in prison. "It comes down to my life or his," she closed, sobbing hysterically, "and I am asking you please to choose mine."

Assistant State Attorney Jon Fuchs argued that Brian had intended to harm Denise that August morning, the very reason he had the gun in her car and was lying in wait, suggesting that only Denise's quick thinking had thwarted a planned murder-suicide. He asked the judge to sentence Brian to 45 years in prison.

Not only was that request far longer than the 15 years recommended by the probation report, it also appeared to renege on the deal State Attorney Jack Campbell had made in the secret proffer agreement not to seek a life sentence. As Brian was already 47, a sentence of 45 years constituted a life sentence in all but name.

Jansen, miffed that Fuchs's request ignored at least the spirit of their agreement—about which Judge Hankinson was completely unaware—argued that the transcript of Denise's interviews following the incident made clear she didn't believe her estranged husband was going to harm her. He asked the judge to sentence Brian to the statutory minimum of ten years.

Having listened carefully to both sides, and to the emotional statements from both Brian and Denise, Judge Hankinson settled on a sentence of 20 years. With credit for time served, Brian would be eligible for release by the age of 65. With that, the bailiff adjourned court and the courtroom crowd began to disperse.

Deputies surrounded Brian, ready to begin the process that would ultimately land him in the Wakulla Correctional Institution, about 20 miles southeast of Tallahassee. Shackled at the waist and ankles as he was being escorted from the courtroom, Brian, upon making eye contact with his dad Marcus, mouthed, "I love you."

As they got up from their seats to leave the courtroom, a frustrated Clay Ketcham lamented to his wife Patti, "Well that's it. The door has just been slammed on whatever happened to Mike. There will never be an answer. We will never know."

For her part, as she jotted down her final notes—ready to head back to the office to file her story for the *Democrat*—Jennifer Portman felt equally deflated. She had been so hopeful 16 months earlier when Brian was arrested and placed in jail. Surely, she believed then, he would offer up what he knew in order to obtain a more lenient sentence.

But now, three days after the 17th anniversary of Mike's disappearance, it appeared he hadn't. And that what had happened to Mike would likely remain a mystery forever. Portman could only imagine the heartbreak Cheryl Williams was about to feel upon learning that the 16 months between Brian's arrest and his sentencing had shed no light on what had happened to her son. Not even the faintest glimmer.

But what neither Portman nor the Ketchams could possibly know as they left the courtroom that morning was that investigators, FDLE agents, and prosecutors had known for over two months precisely what had happened to Mike at Lake Seminole. And what they knew with absolute certainty was that the long lost duck hunter hadn't been eaten by alligators.

••••

Though the name Mike Williams hadn't been uttered a single time during Brian's sentencing hearing, it would be referred to repeatedly the next afternoon at an impromptu news conference at the Tallahassee Regional Operations Center of the FDLE. Jennifer Portman was notified first thing that morning the FDLE would be providing an "update" on its investigation into Mike's disappearance. A throng of local, state, and even national media quickly assembled, satellite trucks stationed in the parking lot outside to broadcast whatever news might be revealed.

The podium at the front of the briefing room had an FDLE logo etched into the wood veneer. An easel was just off to the side with Mike's smiling face at the center of a large poster board. The word "update," written in large, upper-case yellow letters, was just above his image.

The photo of Mike in a blue-and-white plaid shirt was the same one his mother Cheryl had been using for over a decade to bring attention to the unsolved mystery in newspaper ads, on billboards and posters—and on the signs she had so courageously carried outside of Brian and Denise's church and the Centennial Oaks home in which she hadn't been welcome since October 2004.

As the clock struck noon, a man named Mark Perez took his place behind the podium to address the assembled crowd. Assistant State Attorney Jon Fuchs stood off to the side, just to his left. The bombshell they were about to share was actually only a small fraction of what Brian had revealed to investigators in October.

"Good afternoon," Perez said, introducing himself as the Special Agent in Charge of the FDLE's Tallahassee regional office. "Seventeen years ago, Mike Williams disappeared hunting on Lake Seminole near the Georgia state line," he said, reading from prepared remarks, cameras flashing as he spoke. It was a "special day," he noted, Mike and Denise's sixth wedding anniversary. He was to be home at noon that day, Perez added. "Unfortunately, he never returned. His boat was recovered the following day, and it was initially believed that Mike had drowned."

The law enforcement investigation commenced some three years later, he said, in an effort "to find out what happened to Mike Williams. After years of interviews, forensic and investigative analysis, we finally got the break that we needed. Standing here now, I can tell you that we know what happened to Mike Williams. *He was murdered*."

Perez alluded to "new information" investigators had recently received—without disclosing that its source was none other than Brian Winchester. Those details, he reported, led investigators to conduct a days-long search "at an undisclosed location." He revealed that "human remains" had been recovered which, through DNA analysis, were confirmed to be those of Mike Williams.

"It was also determined that 17 years did not hide how Mike Williams died. Further forensic analysis concluded that

Mike Williams was in fact murdered," Perez added, stating that his department's focus had now "shifted to bringing those responsible for his death to justice, and we will not stop until that is done."

The special agent acknowledged the information he had just disclosed would raise many questions, including how Mike had been murdered, the source of the new information, and whether there were any suspects. "Right now, I cannot, and will not, answer any of those questions," he said, much to the disappointment of inquiring minds like Portman's.

"I know you've waited years to learn what happened, and while this case is 17 years old, it just recently turned into a homicide investigation." Investigators were already conducting interviews and following leads, he explained. "This case is moving forward," he assured those gathered, with significant time and resources being devoted to bringing it to a successful conclusion.

"When Mike was killed, he was only 31 years old. He was a husband, a father, a son, and a brother," Perez said, reminding the press of the victim's biography. "As a property appraiser, Mike had a promising and bright future ahead of him. I ask the public to remain patient as we work diligently to bring the person or persons responsible for Mike's death to justice." Perez then moved aside, inviting Fuchs to the podium to share his remarks.

The Assistant State Attorney began by thanking a long list of people who had made the afternoon news update possible, inadvertently providing a cryptic hint as to where Mike's remains had been discovered when he thanked employees of Leon County Public Works—an agency whose jurisdiction extended only as far as the county's borders, nowhere near Lake Seminole. Another hint was Brian's defense attorney, Tim Jansen, who was in the audience trying to his best to blend in with the assembled media.

"I often tell the victims and the victim's family," Fuchs continued, "that the wheels of justice sometimes turn slowly. But they do turn. I cannot think of a more perfect example than this case involving Mike Williams." He provided his assurance that "we will do everything within our power to bring justice for Mike Williams and his family."

Though Fuchs told those gathered his office stood ready to prosecute anyone deemed responsible for Mike's death, his statement wasn't fully accurate. The secret proffer agreement with Brian left the State Attorney without any recourse to prosecute *him* for whatever role *he* might have played in Mike's murder. But it would be many months before that information would be revealed to the press and the public—and before he and State Attorney Jack Campbell would have to explain why they felt compelled to make that deal.

Five minutes into the press conference, members of the media began directing questions toward the podium. Not surprisingly, the questioning was dominated by the reporter who had kept the story of Mike's disappearance alive for more than a decade, Jennifer Portman.

She began her litany of questions, asking whether Mike's remains had been found at Lake Seminole or in the Tallahassee area.

"We don't believe it adds value to our investigation to release that information," Perez answered, assuring her it would be released "at the appropriate time." The special agent apparently hadn't heard or appreciated Fuchs's slip of the tongue when he thanked Leon County Public Works for its assistance in helping solve the mystery. That tidbit intimated Mike's remains hadn't been found at Lake Seminole after all.

"You won't say how long you guys have known that you had Mike's remains?" she asked.

"No we will not," Perez answered. He did, however, respond to Portman's question about whether Cheryl Williams had been notified, disclosing that Mike's family had been informed that morning and provided with a victim's advocate.

Portman pleaded with the special agent for more information: "I have been writing about this for a really long time … You all have said you don't think that Mike Williams was ever in that lake or ever went to that lake. Can you say now if he ever went to that lake and if his body was found at that lake?" Telling Portman he appreciated her and other reporters' dedication to this story, Perez said he just couldn't reveal that information and had to withhold it "for the best interest of the case." He promised to release it "at the appropriate time."

She asked if he had any idea how much longer it would be until suspects were named and arrests made. Perez responded that they couldn't establish a definite time frame, but hoped it would be "very soon."

The *Democrat's* News Director asked whether there was any correlation between the timing of the press conference and Brian Winchester's sentencing the prior day. Perez would only say that it was appropriate for the kidnapping case "to run its course" before providing their update about the discovery of Mike's remains.

"This is a good day," he insisted, despite his inability to answer virtually every question asked. "It brings closure to some of the families that the remains were found and new information was received that allows us to move forward."

The news conference came to an abrupt close—lasting a mere nine minutes. Yet in those few minutes, more information—at least more accurate information—had been disseminated about Mike's December 2000 disappearance than in the entire 17 years that preceded them.

Though not himself a member of the press, Clay Ketcham sat through the news conference—having been tipped off that morning by Portman—perhaps even more interested in what was being disclosed than any of the assembled media. As discouraged as he had been when he left the courthouse just the prior day, he was greatly relieved the marathon for justice for his protégée hadn't come to a screeching halt with Brian's sentencing. And that it now seemed inevitable that the truth would finally be revealed.

As he told Portman for her article that appeared in the *Democrat* the next day, "This news, on one hand, is so encouraging … Now we have hope that we are on the way to opening the final chapter in Mike's story and that he will not be forgotten by any of us that loved him," he said, tears dribbling down his face. "And on the other hand, I really want the people that are responsible to be held accountable to the fullest extent that the law allows."

A few days later, having had time to absorb and reflect on the news, Portman penned a powerful column in the *Democrat* under the headline, "Break in the Williams Case Blows Open New Door."

"Mike Williams isn't missing anymore," it began. "I've got to say it again. Mike Williams is not missing. He didn't vanish without a trace, wasn't eaten by alligators, didn't hightail it to Bainbridge and jump on a Greyhound Bus to oblivion."

She wrote that, from the very beginning, she "knew it in my heart to be true" that Mike had been murdered. But the press conference making it official, she acknowledged, was taking time to sink in. She had dreamed for years of how she'd learn the news, "but never could quite conjure how I would find out." There was no way "I could have imagined how discovery day would play out. What's curious is during all that time reporting and writing, waiting and hoping, I never gave much thought to what would happen after."

"Last week's revelation," she wrote, "was no resolution. Not even close. The nearly dozen years I've been working on the missing Mike story were a prelude. The discovery of murdered Mike doesn't bring closure. It blows open a new door."

Turning to Mike's mom Cheryl, Portman wrote that some people were of the view that she "must be happy to finally know." But upon receiving news that "your son is dead, murdered no less," she observed, "happiness is not what you feel."

After all, it was Cheryl's fervent belief Mike was still alive that fueled her drive all those years, enabling her "to withstand ridicule, downright hatred and the most undeserved punishment of all, the loss of Mike's daughter, told all these years her grandmother was crazy."

"Believing Mike wasn't dead kept Cheryl alive," Portman added. "I'm not sure she could fathom what would happen after she was proved wrong."

She ended her column with these penetrating thoughts: "That bereaved, brave mother is going to walk, roll or crawl through that blown-open door, and I'll be right behind her. There is light ahead, and it just might be justice."

••••

As Special Agent in Charge Mark Perez had acknowledged during the press conference, there were many things he and Jon Fuchs couldn't disclose as they met with the media. Chief among them was that Brian Winchester had entered into a proffer agreement in early October—an agreement which wouldn't allow them to prosecute Brian for any role he had played in Mike's disappearance.

They also were unable to disclose that Brian had spilled his guts about Mike's disappearance on December 16, 2000—even the smallest details of that day's events still seared in his memory all these years later. And that Perez and his colleagues were now fully aware of the horrifying events that snuffed out the life of Jerry Michael Williams long before his time.

10

Murder

The high-pitched blaring of an alarm clock woke Mike Williams from a deep sleep. It was Saturday morning, December 16, 2000, hours before daylight. He had slept in the guest bedroom after getting home late following an evening that included ringing the Christmas bell beside the Salvation Army's red kettle, greeting shoppers in a Santa hat while seeking donations as they entered and exited the Walmart. The last thing he wanted was to awaken his wife in the wee hours the very day they were heading out to the coast for their special, anniversary weekend. Sunday would mark six years since they tied the knot.

Mike had been looking forward to this trip for some time. He had been working ridiculously long hours, often past midnight, with only a few hours of sleep separating one stressful day from the next. It hadn't been easy keeping up with all the work. Though he made sure to get home for dinner each night to squeeze in precious time with his beautiful baby girl—before heading back for the night shift—it was hardly enough. The hours at work were taking their toll. Not only on his time with Anslee, but on his relationship with Denise as well.

Since Denise had become pregnant, their marriage—once exciting and vibrant—had gradually evolved into a mundane, platonic partnership. Sex had been a regular part of their relationship before Anslee's birth, but had vanished altogether since. Though she claimed it was nothing more than post-partum depression, Mike sensed the problem ran deeper than that. As time marched on, his wife had become more distant, even cold.

But Mike was hopeful nonetheless. They were parents of an amazing daughter, who at 19 months was starting to speak in full sentences. And to his pleasant surprise, Denise had agreed to his suggestion of a weekend getaway to the Gibson Inn at Apalachicola Bay—an iconic Victorian-style hotel with wrap-around porches situated right on the Gulf of Mexico.

The thought of spending a romantic evening with his bride at the charming, seaside resort brought a smile to his face and warmth throughout his body. Mike felt hopeful his long dry spell would end that night, and that he and Denise would at least begin to rekindle the magic that fueled their relationship throughout their high school and college days, and earlier in their marriage.

Mike was also looking forward to his hunting excursion that morning with his best friend of the last 16 years, Brian Winchester, who had mentioned a "secret, special spot" they would try out at Lake Seminole. Lots of ducks there, he assured Mike.

Brian suggested that they meet up at a gas station on Thomasville Road and drive caravan style to Sneads, some 50 miles away, right at the Georgia border. That way, Brian said, they could each head to their afternoon plans as quickly as possible after hunting. He also told his friend to make sure to bring his waders, which Mike grabbed before heading out the door along with his hunting jacket and his winter gloves. He inventoried the contents of his boat as he hitched the trailer to his Ford Bronco: dozens of decoys, life jackets, paddle, and anchor. Everything they would need.

It was nearly 4:00 a.m. when Mike pulled into the rear parking lot of Ketcham Appraisal on Thomasville Road. Since Anslee's birth, he had stored his collection of hunting guns in a closet in his office—not taking any chances with a mobile, curious child in the house. He opened the back door to the converted home, disarmed the Sonitrol security system, and walked upstairs to his office. He grabbed the shotgun he thought would be perfect for the morning duck hunt, carefully zipped it up in its case, scooted back downstairs, and re-armed the security system just before walking out the back door. It was 4:03 a.m.

As he headed down Thomasville Road, Mike spotted Brian's white Chevy Suburban waiting at the gas station by the McDonald's near the I-10 interchange, exactly where he said he'd be. He pulled up alongside Brian's SUV and greeted him. Brian told him the battery on his cell phone had died, which would prevent them from chatting along the way as they often did. He checked to make sure Mike had brought his waders. Mike confirmed he had. They started their hour-long drive to Sneads, Mike leading the way.

When they arrived, while Brian parked his truck along River Road, Mike backed his Bronco down a secluded dirt ramp and unhitched his canoe-shaped motorboat from the trailer. After parking his truck beside Brian's, he walked back down the hill, waders, hunting jacket, and shotgun in hand. He left the gun in its case and placed it in the boat.

There was an eerie calm as they stood together at the shoreline. It was dead quiet, the water still as glass, early-morning fog blanketing the lake. Not another human being was anywhere in sight. They had the lake entirely to themselves.

Brian said they were running late and needed to put their waders on before getting into the boat. Mike did what his friend asked and both men—waders on—jumped in the boat and pushed off the shoreline into a cove locals had nicknamed Stump Field. Brian sat in the back, steering the boat with the tiny motor, a lamp on his forehead guiding them through the darkness. Mike sat up front.

As they got into deeper waters, maybe a couple hundred yards from the ramp, Brian told Mike something seemed to be wrong with the motor. He stopped the boat, motor still running, and asked his friend to come to the back to take a look. Mike rose from his seat to see what the trouble was.

Suddenly, without warning, Brian shot up from his seat

and—with tremendous force—shoved Mike overboard. He revved the engine and steered the boat away from his friend, who began thrashing wildly in the frigid water, desperately trying to free himself from his waders.

As Mike continued to wrestle with his waders—which were quickly filling with water and beginning to tug him under—Brian circled the boat around him, like a wild animal stalking its prey.

After struggling frantically for some time, Mike somehow managed to free himself from both his waders and hunting jacket, but was still flailing in the water, panicking. As he was about to go under for good, miraculously, he grabbed ahold of a tree stump and clung to it desperately, his head barely protruding above the water.

Seeing Mike find safety, Brian circled the boat closer. But rather than reaching out to help, he grabbed his 12-gauge shotgun and pumped it full of ammunition. With Mike's wide-open eyes staring at the best friend he had ever had—frozen in terror and screaming for mercy—Brian calmly pointed the gun at his face. And then, drawing the boat to a distance of about three feet, he squeezed the trigger.

A bright flash lit the blackened sky as the sound of gunfire echoed across the lake. Mike's screaming ceased the instant the weapon discharged. Though Brian couldn't bear to look when he fired the shot, it was apparent he had hit his target. Mike was no longer clinging to the stump. Rather, his lifeless body was sinking into the lake.

Brian quickly reached into the water before Mike, with the life blown out of him, plummeted to the depths of the lake. He tightly grabbed one of Mike's legs. With his free hand, Brian guided the boat toward another dirt landing, his friend's lifeless body floating beside the boat—feet first—the entire way. The rapid flow of the water caused Mike's shirt to wrap tightly around his head by the time Brian powered down the boat.

When he got to the shore, Brian pulled the boat up onto the landing, but left Mike's corpse submerged in the shallow water close by. He ran up the hill and down River Road to his truck—still sitting next to Mike's. He then drove back to where he had left the boat.

At the edge of the water, he dropped down the tailgate to his Suburban. With adrenalin coursing furiously through his veins, Brian summoned all the strength he could muster, hoisting Mike's 170-pound body into the back of the truck — shoving the upper half of his anatomy into a large, plastic dog crate.

He then pushed the boat back into the water and sped away, just as daylight began peeking over the horizon. As he rushed down River Road, he broke down the shotgun and threw the pieces — one by one — out the window, into the woods.

••••

Brian had agreed to meet his father-in-law, Jimmy Aldredge, for a hunting trip that morning to establish an alibi. But as he sped through Tallahassee and drove by the TJ Maxx parking lot where they were supposed to meet up, Kathy's father was nowhere in sight. "Damn," he thought. "Too late."

Just then, as Brian pulled up to a red light, things went from bad to worse. He spotted a State trooper at the stoplight just across the intersection. Less than 50 yards away. The body of his best friend — who he had just shot and killed at point-blank range — was stowed in the back of his truck. His heart was racing so fast, he thought it might leap out of his chest.

The light remained red for what seemed like an eternity. Finally, it turned green. When it did, the trooper drove off in the opposite direction. Brian breathed a huge sigh of relief and headed home. "Close call," he thought, relieved to have survived his first brush with the law.

He pulled into his driveway and quietly entered the house, hoping Kathy hadn't yet awakened. His good luck continued — she was still asleep. He took off his clothes and crawled into bed next to her, hoping she would believe he had been there all along.

He had to get up with his father-in-law to explain why he hadn't been there to meet him. He called him from the house phone and spoke in a whisper to avoid rousing Kathy.

Brian apologized for oversleeping and missing their hunting trip. He nudged Kathy, telling her he had overslept and didn't make the trip and that he was heading out to train some dogs. She rolled over and went back to sleep, seemingly none the wiser.

When he walked out the side door, Brian's heart leapt yet again, this time from what he saw under the back of his truck, which was sitting at an angle on his sloped driveway, the front a good bit higher than the back. Something was dripping from the tailgate onto the surface of the driveway.

As he got closer to the rear of the truck, he realized it was blood. Mike's blood. He quickly grabbed a garden hose, spraying down the concrete to remove any traces of the red liquid, all the while gripped by fear a neighbor might be watching. Or worse yet, that someone might approach him. Mercifully, no one did.

Mike's assassin knew he needed to dispose of the body. Quickly. But he had no tools or shovel. So Brian headed to the Walmart, parked his truck, and scurried into the store. Mike had been there some 12 hours earlier, cheerfully greeting customers as he rang the Salvation Army's Christmas bell. He was back again—just a few yards from that very spot—this time as a bloody corpse stuffed into a dog crate in the back of a Suburban.

Brian feverishly rummaged through the aisles, tossing items he thought he might need into his cart: a shovel, a tarp, and a pair of dumbbells.

Before he could make it to the checkout area, though, panic set in again. Mike Phillips, a friend of his and Mike's from their high school days, was also shopping that morning and struck up a conversation with his old pal. Though he wasn't in uniform at the time, Phillips worked as an agent with the FDLE. Brian tried his best to conceal his deep anxiety as he made small talk, desperate to get out of there to go bury their classmate.

Somehow, he survived his interaction with Phillips—eluding the suspicion of a law enforcement officer for the second time. He successfully checked out of the store, jumped back into his truck, and headed toward the southeastern side of Carr Lake, about four miles from his home. He drove down Gardner Road until it turned into a dirt road, found a landing, and backed his truck down to the edge of the water—some 50 miles from where he had murdered his best friend earlier that morning.

The water level at Carr Lake was very low. Portions were nearly completely dry, with only puddles of water and mud. Brian intended to drag Mike's body out to one of the big mud puddles at the center of the lake and bury him there, believing the water would eventually rise high enough to submerge the corpse in the lakebed forever.

He quickly spread out the blue tarp behind the tailgate, pulled the now-stiff corpse out of the truck, and dropped it in the middle of the tarp. He used the tarp to wrap Mike's body like the filling inside a burrito.

But when he began pulling the tarp—and its filling—he had an instant epiphany. Two in fact. First, that there was no way on earth he'd be able to drag 170 pounds of dead weight all the way out to the middle of the lake. And second, that there wasn't nearly enough time to do that without being detected.

While pondering his dilemma, Brian caught sight of a more accessible spot by a willow tree at the lake's edge—and decided to dig the grave there. He was still hopeful that when the water level rose, Mike's body would be buried underwater in that spot forever. Brian began digging, his whereabouts hidden by the steep hill between him and the road above. He was hopeful he could finish the job without being seen.

But even digging the hole proved much more onerous than he anticipated. He was exhausted from the day's events. The adrenalin that earlier had given him the strength to hoist Mike's body into his truck had vanished and been replaced by lactic acid—which made his muscles extremely lethargic.

Worse still, as he dug deeper into the mud, Mike's killer sensed something crawling on his legs, soon swarming all over them. Ants. Vicious fire ants. They began stinging him with abandon, sinking their venom beneath the layers of his skin. Somehow he persevered, but fretted over how he would explain the ant bites to Kathy, who was sure to notice them later that day.

Those worries were quickly replaced by more urgent trouble. Brian heard a vehicle approaching on the road above—in the direction of his truck. His heart thumped louder and louder as the engine cut off and a mysterious silence hung in the air. He dropped the shovel and quickly ran back up the hill, now completely drenched in sweat.

An older man got out of the vehicle, grabbed a rifle, and began walking toward Brian, whose heart was pounding furiously. Though the man wasn't in uniform, Brian suspected he was an off-duty wildlife officer. The man told Brian he had come to the lake to go deer hunting. They made small talk, Brian trying his best not to appear like a man who had just brutally murdered his best friend and literally was in the midst of burying him.

Amazingly, he didn't arouse the deer hunter's suspicion, who he went on his way relatively quickly. Brian waited by his truck a few minutes longer, tracking the man's footsteps to make sure he was heading in the opposite direction of his unfinished business down below. Once again, his incredibly good luck prevailed. The outdoorsman was heading away from, not toward, the nearly completed grave—and Mike's tarp-wrapped corpse.

Brian hurried back down to the lake's edge and finally scooped out enough dirt—just wide enough and deep enough—to dump Mike's dead body into and cover him up with tightly packed dirt.

It wasn't pretty. It wasn't as foolproof as he had hoped it would be. But the job was done. Jerry Michael Williams was buried and wouldn't soon be found. Though he hadn't drowned at Lake Seminole as Brian had planned when he shoved him overboard, he would have a watery grave nonetheless as soon as Carr Lake filled in. Hopefully, Brian thought, both Mike and his sinister plot would be submerged in that very spot for eternity.

It was already after noon—time to get going. Everyone in Kathy's family would soon be gathering for a Christmas celebration in Cairo, Georgia. To avoid suspicion, Brian needed to be there. He also knew that, before too long, Denise would alert family and friends, and possibly even law enforcement, that her husband of six years was missing.

11

Found

A caravan of unmarked, government-owned SUVs crept slowly down Gardner Road, approaching its dead end just to the east of Carr Lake's southeastern corner. Seated in the lead vehicle were Tully Sparkman and Jason Newlin—both investigators from the State Attorney's Office—as well as Tim Jansen and his client Brian Winchester, whose feet were shackled and hands cuffed behind his back. Special Agent Mike DeVaney and other investigators followed closely behind.

It was October 12, 2017, Brian's first excursion beyond the confines of the county jail or courthouse in the 433 days since his arrest.

The group had just completed several hours of difficult questioning about Mike's murder. Their mid-afternoon field trip was intended to corroborate Brian's statement that—after shooting and killing Mike at Lake Seminole—he buried his corpse on the shoreline of Carr Lake.

Sparkman had been working on the Mike Williams investigation off and on for ten years—taking over for Ronnie Austin around 2007. Newlin, on the other hand, hadn't had any involvement until Assistant State Attorney Jon Fuchs tapped him to conduct Brian's questioning. The veteran prosecutor wanted the interview led by someone who held no preconceived notions about how Mike had been killed to ensure that not one hint of "confirmation bias" tainted the inquiry.

The vehicles bumped along the unpaved extension of Gardner Road, moving as close to the lake as they could get. The law enforcement officers got out of their SUVs and walked toward the shoreline with Brian leading the way. They were less than five miles from the doublewide trailer where Mike had grown up.

For nearly 17 years, Jerry Michael Williams had alternately been described as a missing person or suspicious missing person. Missing nonetheless. As the investigators stood at the edge of Carr Lake, peering across its calm water, they were hopeful the world would soon know that the husband, father, son, and brother had finally been found. And that Cheryl Williams, in her courageous, tireless crusade to find him, had been right all along.

"I buried him right about there," Brian said, interrupting the chit chat, pointing to a spot several yards into the lake. He knew that was the right place because it was near the willow tree—the one he stood beside as he dug Mike's makeshift grave some 17 years before.

He told the investigators he had been back to this very spot many times over the years, fearful the area would be developed and that Mike's body might be uncovered in the process. He had actually considered moving it, he said, but decided doing so wasn't worth the risk.

"Are you sure it's there, in that general area?" Brian was asked.

"Positive," he replied. Investigators marked the trees closest to where they were standing; they would come back the next day to begin their excavation. Meanwhile, Brian was ushered back to one of the SUVs and returned to jail, where he would await news that whatever was left of Mike's body had been found.

••••

That same day, Agent DeVaney called William Schwoob, Jr., who by then had been with the FDLE for 32 years, mostly assisting with or supervising crime-scene investigations from his office in the crime lab. DeVaney asked Schwoob to drop everything and meet him at the lake.

This wasn't the first time DeVaney had called the crime-lab supervisor for assistance on the Mike Williams case. When the FDLE agent was boasting to Denise on August 5, 2016, that he had Mike's Ford Bronco torn apart after retrieving it from an Alabama junkyard, he was actually referring to Schwoob's handiwork. But even aided by sophisticated chemicals designed to reveal the presence of blood or body fluids years after the crime, Schwoob's efforts failed to turn up anything of value from the remaining pieces of Mike's Bronco.

What the crime-lab supervisor was now being asked to oversee made his work on Mike's truck look like a sixth-grade science experiment. When DeVaney explained to Schwoob they would need to search and find human remains embedded in the lakebed—buried for nearly two decades beneath several feet of water—the experienced investigator instantly recognized the enormity of what would be required.

To his knowledge, the FDLE had never before undertaken such a monumental task. The work was sure to last days and require the efforts of dozens of people from multiple agencies. Cadaver dogs brought to the site had picked up on the scent of human remains wafting through the water, roughly at the spot Brian had identified. Locating them, though, would require removal of an entire portion of the lake—holding the rest of the water at bay while a team searched the exposed area. But before they could even begin their work in the lake, they would first need to remove a huge stand of trees and dense overgrowth that blocked access to the shoreline.

The FDLE enlisted a tree-removal company to clear an area wide enough to stage all of the equipment and people the operation would require. That was the easy part.

The hard part was making a portion of the lake disappear to expose the mud and muck lying at its bottom—where Brian assured the law enforcement officers they would find Mike's remains. That task fell to the Leon County Public Works Department, the very agency Assistant State Attorney Jon Fuchs would later thank inadvertently as he stood before the press alongside Mark Perez.

Gaining access to the lakebed in the area the cadaver dogs had alerted required the construction of a large "cofferdam"—essentially a massive plastic bag to capture the water near the shoreline and pull it back to the center of the lake. Once that was in place, the water the dam left behind was sucked out with sump pumps and redistributed elsewhere. Gradually, the lakebed began to resemble the area Brian encountered when he arrived there as a savage killer some 17 years before.

Holding back the lake with the cofferdam proved a constant challenge, as water continuously seeped over and around the plastic. Those involved in the operation called the exposed area of the lake a "nasty, wicked place." Water moccasins and eels would occasionally spring out of the mud puddles, tormenting the men, women, and canines working tirelessly to find the buried "treasure."

Once the lakebed was exposed, the Public Works Department began its second task. A large excavator was delivered to the site to begin scooping up the wet, gooey muck—just two to four inches at a time. When the bucket at the front of the machine filled with mud, the hydraulic arm would swivel around to dump the bucketload onto any of ten huge sheets of plywood laid out beside it.

Law enforcement officers and members of the FDLE's crime-scene section would then meticulously sift through the mud with rakes, shovels, and their hands—as if they were searching for emeralds and rubies. Though the operation loosely resembled an archeological dig, rather than searching for artifacts from an ancient civilization, what workers at Carr Lake were hoping to find were remnants of Mike's decayed anatomy, or the clothing he was wearing when his body was submerged into its underwater resting place.

The arduous work continued for six solid days, 16 hours a day, with about 30 people and cadaver dogs involved. The joint efforts between the FDLE and Leon County Public Works evolved into the most extensive search for human remains in the 48-year history of the FDLE.

Despite the length and massive scope of the operation—

and number of people involved—neither Jennifer Portman nor the news media ever caught wind of its existence. Neighbors who approached the workers readily accepted the cooked-up story they were told—that the operation was a sophisticated training exercise. The efforts of the FDLE and State Attorney's Office to conceal its actual purpose amazingly didn't result in one single leak.

••••

By the sixth day of the tedious, painstaking operation, Agent Mike DeVaney was beginning to wonder if Brian had led them astray. Had he sent them on yet another wild goose chase reminiscent of the massive search at Lake Seminole 17 years before? With exactly the same result?

Only one area in the exposed lakebed remained unexplored. If Mike's remains weren't found there, DeVaney was seriously considering pulling the plug on the immense operation.

To his and the workers' good fortune, however, after the excavator was moved to that final location, the bucket finally made contact with something besides mud, vegetation, or slimy creatures—its teeth gently scraping across a gnarly, blue fabric. As more and more dirt was scooped away, it became clear that this wasn't the hopeless exercise DeVaney was beginning to fear.

The excavator had uncovered a tarp. Not just any tarp, but the very one Brian told investigators he bought at Walmart, the one in which he had wrapped Mike's body. The buried treasure had finally been found. Yet the ghastly nature of the discovery tamped down the desire of anyone standing nearby to jump for joy.

The find was a remarkable achievement indeed. On October 13, when the giant, complex operation first began, Mike's remains had been covered by three feet of water and an additional layer of mud some three feet thick. Five days later, cameras were now snapping picture after picture of their stomach-turning discovery.

Schwoob had the excavator operator carefully dig a square around the tarp to ensure nothing contained within it would be damaged. They were then able to carefully support it from underneath as the tarp was hoisted onto the plywood and carefully unwrapped to expose the contents inside—the big reveal everyone had been waiting for.

The group stared transfixed at Mike's skeletal remains—an image of grisly carnage more gruesome than anyone could have fathomed. The stench of death had apparently faded away in the more than 6,000 days the corpse had been underwater.

Approximately 98 percent of the bones in Mike's body were ultimately identified. They were incredibly well preserved considering how long they had been submerged. His leg bones and spine were almost perfectly intact—one of his feet still in a thick blue sock. His pelvic bone was covered by red plaid Hanes boxers, frayed and covered in twigs and brush. His arm bones were still intact as well, encased in a long-sleeve, blue Polarmax shirt. The autopsy X-rays of his arms looked no different than an orthopedist might take of a living, breathing human being.

Mike's hand bones were found inside a pair of Charles Duboung Wind Stopper gloves, which kept them together in remarkable condition. A closeup X-ray of his left hand revealed a perfect circle surrounding his ring finger. When Lisa Flannagan, the Medical Examiner, removed the glove covering that hand, she discovered a gold wedding band loosely encircling that bone.

The most significant discovery involved Mike's skull, found tightly wrapped inside his blue shirt—almost like a soccer ball wedged deeply into a small bag. Because it had been sealed so tightly by the fabric, Mike's skull was remarkably intact, despite being fractured in numerous locations.

At the morgue, Flannagan took X-rays of the skull while still held together by the shirt. Aside from detecting fractures throughout Mike's facial bones and cranium, she noticed something which definitely hadn't been part of his anatomy before he was killed. Her X-rays revealed a skull riddled with dozens of tiny, dense circular objects.

When it was dislodged from the shirt, Mike's skull crumbled into more than 30 pieces. As it did, the mystery surrounding the circular objects was solved. More than 70 tiny metallic balls came loose—shotgun pellets. The plastic "cup" section of the shotgun shell that held the pellets together was also pulled out of the remnants of Mike's skull.

Flannagan carefully spread out all of the pieces and fragments from Mike's face and skull on the lab table, a grotesque display staring back at her as she completed her work.

Mike's lower jawbone, or mandible, was in two large pieces. His upper jawbone, or maxilla, was in a handful of smaller pieces. Many of Mike's teeth were still in their sockets, while others were found loose among the collection of bone fragments. His facial bones disintegrated into more than 25 small pieces. His cranium was in several pieces as well, none more than a couple of inches wide. The color of the skull fragments varied from light to dark brown.

Based on the location of the skull fractures, the large number of fragments in the facial area, and the presence of the shotgun pellets and cup, Flannagan concluded the cause of death to be shotgun wounds to the face. The presence of the shotgun cup left little doubt that Mike's face had sustained the blast from close range. Those findings neatly corroborated Brian's account of how he had shot and killed Mike at Lake Seminole.

When the Medical Examiner completed the autopsy, she delivered a segment of one of the bones to the FDLE's crime lab, which was able to extract enough DNA to perform a comparison with swabs Cheryl and Nick provided years before.

In late November, the crime lab was able to establish a match. After nearly 17 years, Jerry Michael Williams was missing no longer.

••••

As it typically was on a Wednesday morning, Cheryl Williams' home on Jeffrey Road was full of infants and toddlers the morning of December 20, 2017. But this wasn't any ordinary Wednesday morning. It was the day both Cheryl and the children had been looking forward to for weeks: their big Christmas party. For an entirely different reason, though, this day would evolve into one Cheryl Williams would remember for the rest of her days.

Just after 8:30 a.m., her phone rang. Nick, from his office at the Florida Department of Revenue, said he had just received a call from the FDLE.

"Mama, I don't know what's going on," he said, "but I've been told to be at your house at 9:00 a.m." He told his mom not to worry about the children as the FDLE had already arranged a babysitter to look after them—Cathy Drew, the wife of Howard Drew, who worked for Special Agent in Charge Mark Perez.

On his way to her home, Nick picked up his wife Jeanne, whom he felt sure he would need for moral support. They arrived just before two government-owned vehicles pulled into Cheryl's front yard. State Attorney Jack Campbell, a victim's advocate from his office, Tully Sparkman, Mike DeVaney, and Cathy Drew got out and approached Cheryl's front door. Greeting them warmly, Cheryl showed them inside.

As Cathy Drew went to the playroom to take care of the children, the rest of the adults moved outside to the backyard patio and settled onto the outdoor furniture. Campbell, seated next to Cheryl on a bench, placed his arm around her and smiled.

"Well, we have some news," he said, somewhat gleefully. "We have Mike's body."

Startled by the unexpected pronouncement and clearly perplexed, Cheryl asked, "What do you mean you have his body?"

Campbell shared details with her that Mark Perez would withhold from the media at the FDLE news conference soon to begin—information that would remain top secret until the following June.

He explained that his office had made a "deal with the Devil." They had entered into an agreement with Brian Winchester in early October, he said. That deal, he told Cheryl, was their only hope of finding Mike's body and learning what had happened to him.

As part of their agreement, the State Attorney explained, Brian had the freedom to tell them exactly what happened to Mike on December 16, 2000, without fear his words could be used against him in court. In fact, the main part of the deal, he revealed, was that Brian couldn't be prosecuted for Mike's murder *at all*. But he would be in prison for a long time anyway, Campbell assured her, having just been sentenced the prior day to 20 years for Denise's kidnapping. Brian, he said, would likely die in prison just the same as if he had been sentenced to life for Mike's murder.

Most importantly, Campbell added, striking such a deal led to Brian spilling his guts about the events of December 16, 2000. "Brian confessed to killing Mike at Lake Seminole," he finally revealed.

For a woman who had spent the last 17 years on a one-person crusade to find out what had happened to her son, the information Campbell was sharing was overwhelming—nearly impossible to digest in real time. Cheryl nonetheless tried her best to understand the significance and gravity of what she was being told.

Campbell told her Brian had led investigators to the spot where he had buried Mike—in Tallahassee, not at Lake Seminole. In mid-October, he said, after the most extensive recovery operation in FDLE history, they found Mike's remains in the very spot Brian had identified. He also told her the Medical Examiner, as she sifted through the remains, confirmed Mike had been murdered. He apologized for having to keep their discovery a secret for over two months, telling Cheryl that any premature release of that information could have jeopardized their continuing investigation.

"Michael is dead?" Cheryl finally blurted out, her shock and disbelief evident to the entire group. "He can't be."

"Mike is dead," the State Attorney confirmed.

"Well you can't just tell me Michael is dead," she retorted. "You have to prove it."

"We have, Ms. Williams," he responded. "We've done the

DNA testing. It's a perfect match to you and Nick."

"There's no mistakes?" Cheryl asked, beginning to tear up.

"There's no mistakes. But this is not the end Ms. Williams," Campbell assured her. "This is just the beginning."

They were very hopeful there would be at least one person prosecuted for her son's murder, perhaps more, he said, adding that their investigation was just beginning. He then offered to take Cheryl, Nick, and Jeanne to the location where Mike's remains were found.

With Cathy Drew remaining behind to care for Cheryl's daycare kids, the group piled into the government vehicles and headed toward Gardner Road.

As she rode with Mike DeVaney, Cheryl tried her best to process what she had just learned. For 17 years, she had clung desperately—and hopefully—to the belief her son was still alive. That belief helped her wake up each morning and get through each day. Campbell's news hit her like a ton of bricks—an excruciatingly difficult blow to absorb.

While standing on the shoreline of Carr Lake that morning, observing remnants of the massive operation undertaken two months earlier to find her son, it began sinking in that she would need to find another reason to wake up each morning.

As Cheryl told a reporter from WCTV the following day, "People say I should be happy, but I'm not. I honestly wasn't looking for a body. I was looking for Mike to come home." She said she had always known Mike wasn't at Lake Seminole and hadn't been eaten by alligators, adding, "This is vindication for me." But it was particularly upsetting to learn "he's been five miles away from me this whole time."

During her interview, the iron-willed grandmother made clear she had already pivoted to the new crusade she would launch now that Mike's body had been found. "Mike was a good person. He didn't deserve this," she said. "Now I have to put everyone involved in Mike's murder in prison. That's my next job."

12

Arrest

Denise carefully pulled her Suburban into her usual parking spot outside Doak Campbell Stadium, ready to begin another workday in the Controller's Office. It was October 30, 2017. The crisp, autumn air made her shiver as she began her familiar stroll to the elevator.

Suddenly, a burly man wearing a hat and green hooded jacket appeared from nowhere and confronted her. He had some kind of paper in his hand.

"Denise?" he said, stopping the accountant in her tracks. Instinctively, she screamed.

"My name is Chuck. I just got out of jail. I served time with Brian. Can I talk to you?"

"Get away from me!" she yelled, running ahead to the elevator like an Olympic sprinter. Scared himself, the man scurried away.

Once ensconced in the safety and comfort of her fifth-floor office—her heartrate having finally returned to normal—Denise called the campus police. A patrol officer was dispatched to meet with her. While at her office, he took down her information and got a good description of the man who had confronted her. Denise also told the officer the man had been trying to hand her a piece of paper.

The following day, she received a call from Sergeant Richard Wooten, a 15-year veteran with the Florida State Police

Department. Sergeant Wooten told her he would be handling the investigation and was using her description to try to find Chuck and apprehend him.

On November 2, as Denise approached her Suburban in the parking lot after work, she noticed something flapping in the breeze under the windshield wiper. She pulled the folded-up piece of paper out from under the wiper and opened it up.

Chuck, the stranger who had tried to talk with her in the parking lot, had written her a note. It read: "Denise, sorry I scared you the other day. I just wanted to talk. I was in jail with Brian and he told me everything. I need money to get out of florida [sic] and back to Missouri." He provided a telephone number for her to call him and warned "DO NOT GO TO THE POLICE OR I WILL CALL THE NEWSPAPER." The note closed with this cryptic reference: "Innocent people don't leave their cell phones in the car in the park."

Despite Chuck's warning for Denise not to go to the police, she took the note straight to Sergeant Wooten, hoping the phone number would lead the campus police officer straight to Chuck. In the weeks that followed, she reached out to Wooten repeatedly, seeking updates on his continuing investigation.

The officer told her they were doing everything within their power to locate the mysterious stranger.

In his last call with Denise, Sergeant Wooten told her that her case had been escalated—and was now being assumed by the FDLE's cyber-crimes unit. An agent named Will Mickler would be calling her, he said.

A short time later, Denise received a voicemail from Mickler, who asked her to call him back. Then another. And another still. Yet Denise didn't return his calls. Finally, on December 18, 2017, Mickler succeeded in making direct contact with her.

"Can we set up a time to meet to discuss what happened in the stadium parking lot?" he asked. Denise told him that, with the holidays approaching, she was very busy and didn't have any time available in the immediate future, but would call him back when she did.

••••

At about 10:00 a.m. on December 20, 2017—the day after Brian's sentencing—while State Attorney Jack Campbell and Mike DeVaney were sitting with Cheryl on her back patio informing her and Nick that Mike's remains had been found, Mickler was knocking on the front door of 5017 Centennial Oaks Circle. He was accompanied by Holly Francis, the same victim's advocate who stood inches from Denise—rubbing her back for comfort—a day earlier as she pleaded with Judge Hankinson to lock Brian up forever.

It was apparent both Denise and Anslee were at home. Denise's Suburban was parked in the garage; her daughter's smaller SUV was parked in the circular driveway a few feet from the front porch.

Mickler knocked on the door several times—to no avail. He also rang the doorbell repeatedly, but no one came to the door. He called Denise's cell phone and left a voicemail. He called her work number and confirmed she hadn't reported to the Controller's Office that morning. Francis also called her cell phone and left a voicemail. They both said they needed to talk with her. The pair waited for ten minutes, but Denise didn't come outside or return their calls.

Finally, they gave up, getting back in Mickler's car and leaving the gated subdivision. But just as they pulled through the gate, Denise finally called.

"Today's just not a good day for me," she said, telling Mickler she had been up for hours throwing up due to her jangled nerves from Brian's sentencing. But the special agent insisted they needed to speak with her in person and that it couldn't wait.

"About what?" Denise asked.

"About your first husband Mike Williams," the FDLE agent responded. "We don't need to come inside. We can talk with you at the front door."

Denise quizzed him about whether any media was with them. Mickler told her it was just him and Francis. She told him she needed just a few minutes to make a call and would then call him back.

A few minutes later, the agent's phone rang. "Where are

you?" Denise asked, telling him she was standing at her front door ready to meet.

"Just outside the gate," he said. "We'll be right there."

When they pulled into the circular driveway, Mickler and Francis saw Denise—in a bathrobe—standing just inside the house at the threshold of the front door. She closed the door behind her and stood with them on the front porch.

"Ms. Williams," Mickler said, "I'm here to tell you that human remains have been recovered." The remains, he told her, were confirmed to be those of her long-missing first husband, Mike Williams.

"Oh my God!" Denise responded, her eyes welling up with moisture. She instinctively reached out to hug Francis. The victim's advocate asked her if she needed to sit down. But Denise backed away, responding that she was "fine."

"When were they found?" she asked, dabbing her eyes with a tissue even though no actual tears had formed.

The special agent informed her there was still an active investigation, and that he therefore couldn't divulge any additional details. "Do you know of anyone who could have possibly wanted to harm your husband?" he asked.

"No," Denise responded. "He was a good man and had no enemies in the world." And then, rather than asking any additional questions about the discovery of her long-lost spouse's remains, she abruptly changed the subject to what she and Mickler had discussed just two days before, asking if he had been able to find "him," apparently referring to Chuck.

"We were," the special agent answered, much to Denise's relief. "Agent DeVaney and I need to meet with you in our office to discuss some of these things further." But Denise said that wouldn't be possible, at least for some time. She suggested that their meeting would have to wait until January because she needed to travel to a funeral for her grandmother.

"Can I speak with Anslee to share the news about her father?" Mickler asked. Denise rejected that idea, telling him that her daughter—now an 18-year-old freshman at Florida State— was fast asleep upstairs, but that she would be sure to inform her once she woke up.

"Very well," Mickler said, sensing Denise had nothing further to ask or say. "Thanks so much for your time Ms. Williams." Their entire interaction lasted just a few minutes, quite the contrast with the death notification Jack Campbell and Mike DeVaney were providing Cheryl and Nick about ten miles across town. Indeed, Mickler didn't offer Mike's widow the slightest hint about where his remains had been found, let alone offer to drive her there to see for herself.

••••

Almost from the moment Denise kicked Brian out of their Centennial Oaks home, she and Kathy (Winchester) Thomas had begun rekindling their friendship, eventually speaking with and texting one another almost daily, even after Kathy, her second husband Rocky, and their daughters moved to the North Carolina mountains. The pair had something very unique in common: they were the exclusive members of the Brian Winchester Ex-Wives Club.

In early February 2018, Kathy called Denise from the road. From the first moments of their conversation, it became clear she hadn't called to chit chat. Kathy said she was very distraught over a subpoena she had just received commanding her to appear at the State Attorney's Office. She was crying, continuing to sob as she and Denise spoke, her painful anguish evident throughout their lengthy discussion. Kathy told her friend she was very concerned about being placed under oath by the State Attorney because of what she knew about Mike's disappearance.

"What do you know?" Denise asked in a surprised tone.

After a long pause and several deep sighs, Kathy told Denise that Brian had called her at the Copy Shop, crying, shortly after he confronted her and Chuck Bunker at their hotel in Atlanta. She said she hadn't been aware of most of the details about what happened in Atlanta until Chuck sent her a letter about it. But when Brian called, she said, he was mad. "Brian had figured out that you were cheating on him with Chuck," she said. "And he just told me about Mike."

"What did he say?" Denise asked curiously. "He called you upset about Chuck, and then he wanted to talk about Mike?"

"He was mad at you … And so, he told me. He told me about what happened to Mike."

"Well, I would love to know what happened to Mike. He never told me. They said they found his remains and that he was beaten or that he was shot," Denise said, though those details departed from what Agent Mickler had told her on her front porch in December.

"Brian told me that y'all planned it," Kathy replied.

"Planned *what*?" Denise asked, ostensibly taken aback by the insinuation. Kathy didn't answer, sighing loudly.

"Oh my God," Denise uttered softly.

Kathy explained that Brian's dad, Marcus Winchester, came by her family's printing business later the same afternoon Brian had told her about Mike, "telling me how I would have to take this to my grave …"

"Wait, wait, wait, so Mike …"

"Apparently, Brian told Marcus that he had talked to me and he went on to …" Kathy paused for a moment to gather herself. "Marcus went on to tell me how my life would be ruined, how I would never be able to start over if Stafford's life was ruined, if …"

"So Marcus knew?" Denise interrupted, expressing surprise. "And when you said Brian … said y'all, you're talking about me and Brian? Or Marcus? Or who?"

"*You and Brian*," Kathy declared, for the second time accusing Denise of having planned her husband's murder.

Denise's initial response to her accusation wasn't shock, disbelief, or umbrage. Or even a tepid denial. None of those. Rather, she merely asked, "And that Marcus is involved? I mean, obviously, if he came and talked to you … What in the world? … But, yeah, that's pretty major, especially with Marcus involved," she said with a nervous chuckle. Yet, for some reason, what she didn't consider "pretty major" was that her friend since the ninth grade had just accused her of murder.

Still processing, Denise said, "And then you got a letter

from Chuck? My parents got a letter too. But you got a letter from Chuck and he's talking about it too, or no?"

"Chuck told me what happened in Atlanta," Kathy replied, without revealing everything he had accused Denise and Brian of, or the urgent warnings he had given her about the two.

"Well, you know, I know that you know something Denise," Kathy continued, "because whenever I was going out to see Marcus, you're like, 'Tell Marcus to tell Brian, *I'm not talking.*'" Kathy's insinuation couldn't have been clearer: Denise and Brian had a pact of silence, she was suggesting, and Denise wanted Marcus to make sure Brian knew she was holding up her end of the bargain—and expected him, from behind bars, to do likewise.

"Yeah," Denise acknowledged softly.

"And I knew what that meant."

Denise finally pushed back, though, telling Kathy that Brian and Marcus had been lying to her, lying to one another, and "playing everybody against each other."

"I don't even care about all that anymore," Kathy said. "Because time has moved on. Mike is in heaven. So, here is my problem. Here is like … My problem is Rocky doesn't know any of this. Rocky doesn't know that I know. In all these years, any time anything came up about Mike, I'd just sit with my mouth shut. He never would have married me if he had known."

"This has nothing to do with you," Denise told her.

"It has *everything* to do with me," Kathy shot back, voiced raised. "I have been lying to him for 15 years!"

Denise disagreed, telling her friend that what she had learned from Brian and Marcus "has nothing to do with you and anything that you did, or anything that you didn't do. You know, I mean, it doesn't," she said, carefully sidestepping the question of her own involvement in Mike's murder.

Now becoming hysterical, Kathy asked Denise, "If I lie, if I lie whenever they ask me, 'Do you know what happened to Mike?' if I lie, then now, now what happens when I go home and Rocky says, 'Why didn't you ever say anything?' Like, how do I explain that? How do I explain that I just decided to forget it? He never would have married me." She trailed off, sobbing uncontrollably. "I've never lied to him about anything, but any time anything comes up about Mike, I just ... That is a *lie*." She told Denise Rocky was "good and honest ... not like us."

Denise deflected once again, asking Kathy if she and Marcus had ever again spoken about the subject of Mike's death. "Has he ever said anything to you?"

"No, it's just been understood if I ever said anything then everything, then all of the stupid shit we did, that everybody would know ..."

"Yeah," Denise agreed, without either of them specifying the "stupid shit" they had done.

"Everybody would know and wouldn't that be awful and, you know, Mike's in a better place and so ..." Kathy sighed heavily, trailing off again.

"I mean, him saying that to you," Denise said, "again, that's using fear and the unknown to try to control you and that's typical, you know?"

Kathy then pivoted to a different topic. "I was going to ask you this, because I've been thinking about it, but, not long before Mike's [disappearance] he called me. Mike called me. And he had found a bunch of money in your wallet." She sighed, filled with deep emotion. "And he said, 'I think Denise has a boyfriend.'"

The startling revelation that Mike believed she was having an affair prior to his December 2000 disappearance provoked only a barely audible "mhmm" from his widow. No denial. No, "that's crazy!" Not even mild surprise.

"And he said you told him something then about Deanna," Kathy continued, "that you had told him that Deanna had paid you back for something" and that Mike had found out from Deanna "that wasn't true."

"Yeah, yeah, yeah, I remember all that," Denise responded, ignoring altogether the topic of whether she had a boyfriend while Mike was still alive.

"But I remember thinking," Kathy continued, "'Mike, he

knows, he knows that Denise and Brian like each other,' and like … She trailed off again, sobbing. "I've always thought to myself, if I had said, 'Mike, I think Brian has a girlfriend,' I've always wondered if he would still be here. Why? *Why couldn't y'all just get a divorce?*" she asked through her tears.

Though she didn't come right out and say it, Kathy was now implying Denise had decided to have Mike murdered rather than divorcing him. Her question hung heavily in the air, no response at all from Denise even remotely suggesting that she believed the implication untrue, let alone outlandish.

"I've always known that you and Brian loved each other," Kathy added, intimating again their relationship dated all the way back to Denise's marriage to Mike. This additional declaration also elicited no audible reaction.

"Brian told me one time that you were his best friend and that was just the way it was always going to be," Kathy added, again, without any hint of a response.

"Did Mike find out?" Kathy asked through her tears, now directly posing the question of whether Mike had ever learned she and Brian were cheating on him behind his back.

Finally, Denise broke her eerie silence, though once again evaded her friend's question. Speaking in a monotone—no emotion in her voice whatsoever—she replied, "No, that was all … I remember him calling Deanna. I think I remember, I'm pretty sure that he told me that he had called you, um but I know for sure he called Deanna because we talked about it. And, um, I remember the conversation … I remember us talking about it. I remember that we were talking about … the pot and stuff like that."

"I remember talking about that with him," Denise said. "And I don't remember how much money it was; I do remember money and I do remember a conversation about pot … And he had talked to Deanna too, so I had to tell her all of that. So I do remember that, yeah. I guess I didn't know that he had talked to you, but …"

She paused a moment before continuing.

Denise then blurred Kathy's question about why she hadn't divorced *Mike* with her divorce many years later from

Brian, stating, "I just can't do anything with the, I couldn't do anything with the divorce without talking to an attorney."

She told Kathy she followed the directions of the lawyer she had hired to divorce Brian—not even acknowledging her friend's insinuation that she and Brian were having an affair while Mike was still alive.

Denise eventually steered their conversation to her interview with Agent Mike DeVaney the day Brian kidnapped her. "Marcus's name didn't come up or anything like that," she said. She speculated that law enforcement officers might have issued a subpoena to Marcus similar to the one they had issued to Kathy.

"I don't know," Kathy said, "but when I get back, I'm going to get just like … a throwaway phone because God, who knows? I mean, I don't know. I'm just scared. I just feel like, why do they keep calling me? Like calling me this weekend and left a message that they knew I was in town. I think that they are listening to me."

"Probably," Denise agreed. "I mean, I don't know, but they could be."

As their conversation neared an end, Denise assured Kathy she could tell her husband everything she knew without fear of any repercussions to their marriage. "I just don't think it's going to be what you think it's going to be. I really don't. And I don't know how you can be married to him for the next however many years and not say anything if it's [been] bothering you that bad."

"It wasn't bothering me until I got a subpoena, until I have to do it," Kathy whimpered.

"Yeah. That's the only thing I can think of," Denise said, her emotionally distant tone in sharp contrast to Kathy's blubbering. "But I don't think he would be like *goodbye*," she said, using a high-pitched voice for emphasis.

"It's starting to be really hard," Kathy said. "I'm going to have to go."

Before hanging up, Denise assured her friend everything would be okay with Rocky, whatever happened. "I think you're right about him being a kind and good person, but I mean, these are things that people told you years after Mike died. I just don't think he's going to be like, 'We're getting divorced; I'm never talking to you again.' I really don't. But you know him better."

Their 23-minute telephone conversation was most illuminating, Denise evading or ignoring Kathy's questions about whether she had been having an affair with Brian before Mike's death or had planned his murder instead of divorcing him.

Tellingly, she didn't deny a single one of Kathy's insinuations—or express affront or outrage upon hearing her friend of over three decades assert them. Her stunningly unemotional responses and ramblings—particularly in view of how deeply troubled her good friend was on the other end of the line—made it seem most unlikely that Denise Merrell Williams was merely an innocent bystander to the events of December 16, 2000.

••••

What Denise had no way of knowing as each of these events unfolded was that she had been the primary target of the FDLE's investigation into Mike's murder—following Brian's proffer statements and the recovery of Mike's remains. Between late October and February, Denise had been the subject of a well-coordinated, multi-faceted sting operation.

The man who approached her in the parking lot at Doak Campbell Stadium on October 30—and who had left a note on her windshield three days later—wasn't actually named Chuck. Nor had he been one of Brian's fellow inmates. Rather, the mysterious stranger was an undercover FDLE agent named Lon Green—whose encounter with Denise that late October morning had been a carefully orchestrated "bump."

Even the campus police officer, Sergeant Wooten, was in cahoots with the FDLE. The Florida State Police hadn't actually investigated the parking lot incident. Instead, the only ongoing investigation centered on Denise herself, the bump designed to elicit information from her about Mike's murder.

For his part, Special Agent Mickler had nothing to do with the FDLE cyber-crimes unit, despite what Sergeant Wooten told Denise. Rather, along with Mike DeVaney, Mickler was a lead case agent assigned to the Mike Williams murder investigation.

When Agent Mickler appeared on her front doorstep on December 20 with Denise's victim's advocate, the tandem wasn't there to console her as she learned the news of Mike's remains being recovered. Rather, the FDLE's primary goal that morning was to witness what Mickler and his law enforcement colleagues expected to be an unnatural, contrived reaction—one that might prove helpful to prosecutors in a murder trial. He was even wearing a miniature, hidden video camera to capture that moment for posterity.

For her part, though on the surface Kathy Thomas may have been Denise's friend, by February 2018, she was also working as a confidential source for the FDLE, receiving detailed instructions from both Mickler and DeVaney. The FDLE had outfitted her with sophisticated audio equipment to record her calls with Denise.

Kathy hadn't actually received a subpoena to appear in the State Attorney's Office. That fact—and many others that permeated her recorded conversation with Denise—were all part of a well-crafted script Mickler had her follow, a script designed to elicit reactions and statements from Denise to help prove her active involvement in Mike's murder. Upon reviewing the audio recording of the conversation Kathy later provided him, Mickler couldn't have been more delighted with the results.

"Quite the performance," he marveled.

••••

It was nearly quitting time at the Controller's Office on the fifth floor of Doak Campbell Stadium. Denise eyed the clock, counting the minutes until the workday ended. The last three months had been a long, difficult slog following her mother Johnnie's death in early February. Both of her parents were now gone, her father Warren having succumbed to brain cancer in 2011.

This particular evening, however, had been marked on Denise's calendar for quite some time. A happy occasion, finally. Not only had Anslee just completed her freshman year at Florida State, this was also her 19th birthday. She and her mom had a special dinner planned to celebrate both milestones.

But the events of Tuesday, May 8, 2018, were about to take a most unexpected twist, one Denise in her wildest dreams—and most frightening nightmares—couldn't have seen coming.

Just after 4:00 p.m., there was some kind of commotion out in the lobby, not far from her office. Will Mickler's boss, FDLE Special Agent Supervisor David Wells, asked to be directed to Denise's personal office. He was accompanied there by a uniformed campus police officer, Kimberly Tyus, and FDLE Special Agent Sean Wheeler. The three found Denise sitting at her desk working, looking down.

"I'm David Wells with the FDLE," Agent Wells interrupted, drawing her attention. "We have a warrant for your arrest. Stand up and place your hands behind your back."

Without saying a word, Denise did as she was told—staring straight ahead with a blank expression—the agent quickly cuffing her while Officer Tyus patted her down. Agent Wells informed Denise she had been charged by the grand jury with first-degree murder, conspiracy to commit first-degree murder, and accessory after the fact in relation to the death of Jerry Michael Williams.

After Denise was read her Miranda rights, Agent Wells, Officer Tyus, and Agent Wheeler led her to the office lobby. Denise asked if she could leave her purse with one of her colleagues. Beyond that, she didn't say a word. Officer Tyus took her by the elbow and escorted her down the hallway to the elevator, her accounting colleagues gawking at the spectacle in shock and amazement.

As the elevator doors opened on the ground floor, another group of Florida State Police officers joined the procession—including one whose face Denise surely recognized: Sergeant Richard Wooten. The group of officers and their catch marched out into the bright, afternoon sun, led by Officer Tyus and the 48-year-old arrestee. Her perp walk from the stadium to the waiting Florida State Police patrol car extended just about the same length as the 100-yard field around which the iconic stadium was constructed.

A throng of reporters and photojournalists who had raced to the campus after learning of the grand jury's indictment lined the red-brick sidewalk as Denise was paraded by them in an unflattering bluish-purple patterned dress, Army green leggings, and flip-flops.

She was also having what could only be described as a bad hair day, her bleach-blonde hair desperately in need of a refresh. Overall, head to toe, not exactly the image she would have preferred to be splashed across the internet and evening news broadcasts. Had they still been alive, Johnnie and Warren Merrell—to whom appearances mattered more than just about anything—would have been mortified.

Denise stared straight ahead or looked down at her feet the entire length of the perp walk—assiduously avoiding even the slightest eye contact with the media and curious onlookers.

The *Democrat's* Jennifer Portman did her level best to elicit a comment from the newly-charged criminal defendant. "Denise, did you kill Mike?" she asked.

Denise ignored the question altogether, her eyes cast down toward the brick pathway.

"Did you and Brian plan to have him killed?" the seasoned reporter pressed. "Do you have anything that you want to say to Cheryl?"

Denise didn't even look up as these questions flew by.

"Anything you want to say at all?" Portman tried again.

Denise didn't acknowledge the question.

Seated in the backseat of a caged vehicle, hands still cuffed behind her, Denise was escorted to the Leon County Detention Center to be booked and processed. The irony of her situation was lost on no one. She was about to be housed in the very place that her second husband—the man doing time for kidnapping her—had called home for more than 16 months. In hindsight, it was that kidnapping incident that had led inexorably to her own trip to the clink. Poetic justice, perhaps.

••••

Jack Campbell and Jon Fuchs arrived at Cheryl Williams' Jeffrey Road home at about 4:30 p.m., hoping to make it there in time to break the news. But the prosecutors were a few minutes too late—news of Denise's arrest having already reverberated all across town. Cheryl gladly accepted their hugs and comforting thoughts nonetheless. A flood of emotions poured out as she and Nick chatted with the seasoned prosecutors.

For Cheryl, the moment was bittersweet. "I'm thankful she is arrested," she told Portman for her article in the *Democrat*. "But I have a granddaughter and that's her mother. My heart goes out to Anslee. I cannot imagine where that baby's head is at." Indeed, as she always did on her granddaughter's birthday, Cheryl had taken out an ad in the *Democrat* that very day wishing Anslee a happy 19th birthday—knowing full well her love and good wishes wouldn't even be acknowledged, much less reciprocated.

Her thoughts also turned to her other baby—Mike. "I want justice for Mike. I want every single person involved in his murder, even if they just knew about it and didn't come forward, to be prosecuted," she told Portman. "They did not have a right to kill my son." Denise "may not have pulled the trigger," she added, "but she killed Mike and I want her to pay for that."

For his part, Clay Ketcham was gob-smacked upon learning the news of Denise's arrest. "Oh my gosh!" he exclaimed when Portman caught up with him. He told her he thought the day would never arrive. "We are getting to the end of the story," he said. "It's horrible. But it's a feeling of coming to resolution with it."

"I'm thrilled," he added. "I'm ecstatic. I just can't believe it."

May 8, 2018, turned out to be quite the remarkable day indeed.

Part 3
Justice

13

Prelude

Murder is a unique crime. Not just in severity or depravity, but also in its treatment under the law. Unlike virtually all other crimes, murder—being the most heinous of all—has no statute of limitations. That is how some of the most vicious, racially motivated killings of the civil rights era could first be prosecuted in the 2000s. And also how Leon County's grand jury was able to indict Denise Williams for her husband's murder more than 17 years after the fact.

Though the indictment wasn't terribly specific about the three homicide charges leveled against her, it did contain a few interesting details. First, the conspiracy charge alleged that Denise and Brian had conspired together to kill Mike for more than *nine months*.

Second, the charge of Denise having been a principal in the murder revealed that Brian had killed Mike by shooting him with a firearm—in Jackson County, where the cove in Lake Seminole known as Stump Field is located.

Third, and perhaps most curiously, the accessory after-the-fact charge focused on Denise aiding and assisting Brian—and helping him avoid detection and arrest—from August 1, 2014 until December 19, 2017, a time period that commenced nearly 14 years after the murder, long after the couple had separated. It also included the 16 months Brian had been housed in the county jail.

One of the first people to lay eyes on the criminal charges was Ethan Way, a 1998 *cum laude* graduate of Florida State's law school and board-certified criminal defense lawyer. Way had opened his own Tallahassee firm in 2005. Over the course of the dozens of cases he had tried, he had garnered the reputation of being a solid courtroom lawyer and aggressive advocate, his bulldog style often evident in his cross-examinations of prosecution witnesses.

Way was a larger-than-life character as well, full of machismo—often sporting cowboy boots in court—quick to brag to fellow attorneys and courtroom staff about his big-game hunts in Africa. He had proudly mounted several large animal heads on the walls of his law office. Fittingly, his prized possession during his younger days was a crotch rocket motorcycle capable of reaching speeds of nearly 200 miles per hour.

The criminal attorney carried that same swagger into the courtroom and during his interactions with the media, often using the press as an additional outlet to advocate for his clients. He could be cavalier and smug at times. Even arrogant. As full-throated a defense lawyer as someone charged with first-degree murder could ask for.

He wasn't cheap either. Fortunately for her, as of May 8, 2018, Denise Williams was a millionaire—and had been since Mike's life insurers had paid her nearly $2 million in 2001. She had invested wisely since then and did quite well in her divorce with Brian. With her life on the line, she wasn't about to spare any expense. Way was on her case within hours of her arrest.

Though the death penalty was still on Florida's books as of May 2018, it had waned in popularity since Florida's most notorious execution, when serial killer Ted Bundy met his fate in the electric chair in January 1989 for a murderous rampage on the Florida State campus. Unlike Bundy, Denise—a freshman at Florida State at the time of his execution—was facing the prospect of a life sentence without the possibility of parole, the State Attorney having decided at the outset not to pursue the ultimate punishment.

In his customary, brash style, Way wasted little time seizing the offensive for his new client. Interviewed in the hallway outside the courtroom following Denise's first appearance the day after her arrest, he was asked, "What's the defense here?"

"What do you mean, 'What's the defense here?' Way responded, seemingly annoyed by the question. "Brian Winchester did it. I mean the true bill speaks for itself. Brian Winchester shot Mike Williams in Jackson County and my client's the one being held without bond right now," with Brian receiving only a 20-year sentence. "So it appears, you get a homicide, you get a 20-year sentence. I mean, it's ridiculous. We're going to fight it, and we're going to get acquitted."

When the reporter suggested Brian had "flipped" on Denise, Way retorted that he hadn't flipped, but instead "made something up. That's the big difference between flipping and fiction."

Later in the day, sitting with the *Democrat*'s Jennifer Portman for a more formal interview, Way continued his rant: "My client had nothing to do with Mike Williams' disappearance and had absolutely nothing to do with the crimes that Brian Winchester committed," he told her. He said Brian was lying about Denise's purported involvement in the crime. "We will fight this until the end." Way even predicted Denise would testify in her own defense, telling the ace reporter, "I'm certain when a jury hears from Denise Williams, and the facts come out, the inescapable conclusion is that Brian Winchester killed Mike Williams"—alone.

He ridiculed Brian's story, upon which the indictment against his client was premised. "Mr. Winchester was sentenced to prison, went to prison, he's in prison, and now six months or so after he got into the Florida Department of Corrections, lo and behold, there is a story that conveniently closes a 17-year-old mystery about something nefarious that happened involving a gun." That story, he noted, "is made by a man who is in prison for committing a violent offense with a gun."

The "one thing we know the grand jury got right," Way told the journalist, was that "Brian Winchester killed Mike Williams." With chest-thumping bombast, he expressed certainty that the jury, "when it gets an opportunity to hear Denise's defense will find her not guilty. I have absolutely no doubt of that."

For his part, Brian's attorney Tim Jansen told Portman he didn't anticipate his client being charged with Mike's murder — despite the indictment making very clear he was the one who pulled the trigger. Of course, Jansen didn't tell her about the October 2017 proffer agreement which gave him complete confidence in his prediction. Rather, he simply told her that, if subpoenaed and given immunity, Brian would testify truthfully. Against his ex-wife.

••••

Judge James Hankinson had served as a circuit court judge in the Second Judicial Circuit since January 2002, following a distinguished 22-year career as a prosecutor. After his graduation from law school at Florida State, he served three years as an Assistant State Attorney in Pensacola before moving to Tallahassee, where he served nine years as a state prosecutor and other ten as a federal prosecutor.

Outside of work, Hankinson was deeply engaged in the community, building wheelchair ramps, working with the Adopt a Highway project, and spending time at the Lighthouse Children's Home. He was active in the local Kiwanis Club. He also refereed football games at Leon High School, where he met a young man who played center for the Lions named Jack Campbell, the very same Jack Campbell who was now the elected State Attorney overseeing the Denise Williams murder case.

As a judge, Hankinson was as no-nonsense as they came, running a tight ship, but also known for his fairness. He had tried some of the most high-profile cases in Leon County history. Judge Hankinson expected the lawyers appearing before him to be thoroughly prepared and to present their evidence quickly and efficiently, without wasting his or jurors' time. Somewhat ironically though, of late he had developed a noticeable speech impediment, resulting in him speaking in labored, halting sentences, his cadence slow and shaky.

A packed courtroom sat in rapt attention at 3:00 p.m. on June 18, 2018, a TV camera ready to record highlights of Denise's bond hearing—her first time in a public setting since her arrest weeks before.

The tables had turned significantly since her last appearance before Judge Hankinson the prior December. On that occasion, Denise wore flattering clothing, makeup, and jewelry, had a victim's advocate by her side, and was flanked by prosecutors, as she pleaded with the judge to send her ex-husband to prison for the remainder of his life. Whereas Brian had departed the courtroom that day escorted by sheriff's deputies in handcuffs and shackles—headed to prison for 20 years—she had left of her own volition, to return to the familiarity and comfort of her 3,000-square-foot home.

On this late spring day, however, Denise was the one seated at the defense table in a jail-issued jumpsuit—sans makeup and jewelry—her hands now cuffed, feet shackled. The very same prosecutors who had worked with her as teammates the prior December, Jon Fuchs and Andy Rogers, now sat on the opposite side of the courtroom—aligned against her. At this hearing, Denise would have no speaking role at all.

For Jon Fuchs, the Denise Williams murder case would represent the biggest, most media-intensive of his 16 years as a lawyer—a career in which he had risen steadily through the ranks of the State Attorney's Office following his law school graduation from Nova Southeastern in Fort Lauderdale. As a college student at Florida State, Fuchs had actually briefly overlapped with Mike, Denise, Brian, and Kathy.

Andy Rogers would play the role of second-chair prosecutor, having gained knowledge about Denise and Brian from his work on the kidnapping case—when Denise had been the one working with him and Fuchs, rather than Brian. Just six years out of law school, Rogers was by far the youngest attorney in the courtroom, having been a Florida prosecutor for less than two years.

For his second chair, Way had retained Phil Padovano, who for more than 25 years had served as both a circuit judge and an appellate judge. In the 1990s, he regularly presided over trials in the very same courtroom. And during his 18-year stint on the First District Court of Appeal in Tallahassee—which ended in 2015—it was standard fare for Padovano and his brethren to review Judge Hankinson's decisions. Those tables were now turned as well.

Had they not chosen law as a career, Way and Fuchs could just as easily have been gladiators on the gridiron. Way, a burly 6', 240 pounds, had a beer belly and thick, bushy beard. At about 6'4" and 260 pounds, Fuchs had more of a barrel-chested physique, his face typically stubbly and unshaven, his voice deep and gravelly. The prosecutor carried himself very differently from Way, often shying away from the media spotlight, hardly any swagger at all.

By that Monday afternoon, the cat had finally been let out of the proverbial bag. The provocative news about the proffer agreement between Brian and the State Attorney's Office had been released to the media a few weeks earlier. In her June 1 article in the *Democrat*, Portman credited that agreement for solving the mystery of Mike Williams' disappearance. "State Attorney Jack Campbell," she wrote, "gave Winchester a pass in exchange for the truth about what happened to Williams when he disappeared while purportedly duck hunting alone the morning of Dec. 16, 2000."

Interviewed for the article, Campbell told her, "I'm quite confident we would have never found him if I had not taken this step," calling his decision a hard one, but "the right one." Way, not surprisingly, viewed it very differently, telling Portman the deal was a "Christmas present" to Brian Winchester.

After the bailiff called the courtroom to order, Judge Hankinson asked Fuchs if he had any evidence to present. To the surprise of nearly everyone assembled, the prosecutor told the judge he intended to play the entirety of Brian's October 9, 2017 proffer statement. In open court.

After the judge overruled Way's meek objection, Fuchs hit "play" on the audio recording, allowing the judge, Denise, and family members—including Denise's sisters, Brian's father and sister, and Mike's brother—to hear for the very first time the gruesome details surrounding the murder. Details that included Denise's personal involvement both before and after Mike's best friend killed him in cold blood.

The media and spectators cramming the gallery sat in complete silence for nearly two hours—transfixed—as they listened to Brian's riveting confession. For her part, Denise stared straight ahead as the recording was played, showing no visible reaction whatsoever—as if Brian's blood-curdling description of the murder was about a complete stranger, rather than her husband and the father of their now 19-year-old daughter.

When the audio recording ended, Fuchs put investigator Jason Newlin on the witness stand, having him describe how Brian, just a few days after making that statement, had led investigators to the location at Carr Lake where Mike's remains had been uncovered. Newlin also testified he had met with Cheryl and Nick Williams and obtained sworn affidavits from each, in which they described how Denise had threatened them about not being permitted to see Anslee if Cheryl persisted in seeking publicity and an investigation into Mike's disappearance.

Toward the end of his testimony, Judge Hankinson asked Newlin if the Medical Examiner had been able to draw any conclusions from Mike's remains. The investigator responded that it had been confirmed through DNA testing that the remains were those of Mike Williams. And also that he had been shot in the face with a shotgun. Newlin explained the Medical Examiner had found "projectiles" from birdshot lodged in Mike's skull, the most graphic public revelation to date surrounding his murder.

Ethan Way put Brian's attorney, Tim Jansen, on the witness stand—turning the tables on the lawyer who was the one typically asking the questions. Through Jansen, Way introduced the proffer agreement between the State Attorney and Brian. Beyond that, however, Jansen wouldn't answer any questions, telling the judge the information Way was requesting—about potential witness tampering charges against Brian involving his fellow inmate Wade Wilson—was protected by the attorney-client privilege.

With Jansen on the stand, Fuchs couldn't resist the temptation to ask a few questions of his own—the first time in his career he was provided the opportunity to question one of his adversaries under oath. Under Fuchs's questioning, Jansen agreed the primary goal of the proffer agreement was to learn how Mike had died and to locate his body. And further, that there was "absolutely no discussion about what Denise Williams' role was … until Brian Winchester stated it in the course of the proffer."

Way also called FDLE Agent Will Mickler and Detective Paul Salvo as witnesses, each confirming a separate investigation had been opened into Brian's dealings with Wade Wilson. Salvo testified he had confirmed Wilson was paid in excess of $20,000 through an intermediary in order to obtain coerced or falsified statements regarding Denise. Though interesting, that point seemed to have little to do with whether the newly charged defendant should be released on bond.

With the evidence closed, Fuchs stood up to argue against Denise's release. As much for the assembled media as the judge, he made clear the decision to enter into the deal with Brian was one he made with a heavy heart. "In the end, I may be proven wrong," he said, "because, in fact, he was the murderer. However, in this situation, we had, first and foremost, closure for family members [and] the location of Mike Williams."

"Cheryl Williams was right for 17 years," he added, "that it was not a disappearance, that Mike Williams was not eaten by an alligator, that he was in fact murdered. Denise Williams tried, by holding her granddaughter hostage, to keep that from happening." That forced separation, he argued, demonstrated better than anything else her consciousness of guilt. He asked the judge to deny her request to be released on bond.

Taking center stage with his typical bravado and flair, Way portrayed his client in a very different light, calling her a "victim, not only of kidnapping and armed burglary, but she was also the victim of the murder of her husband at the hands of Brian Winchester. The State Attorney's argument is passionate, Your Honor, because the person who shot Mike Williams at close range with a 12-gauge shotgun, apparently, will not be charged with that crime nor forced to enter a plea."

The defense lawyer argued forcefully in favor of Denise being released on bond. "The disappearance of Mike Williams has been a matter for great local and national media speculation and interest for 17 years," he said. "If Denise Williams was intending to flee the jurisdiction, Your Honor, to show a consciousness of guilt, that would have happened a long time ago." Based on her strong ties to the community and her reputation, he argued, Denise presented neither a flight risk nor a danger to the community. He asked the judge to set bond in the amount of $100,000.

Taking only a few seconds to consider his decision, Judge Hankinson announced: "I'm going to deny the motion to set bond. I believe the evidence presented is sufficient to show the proof of guilt as evident. Her presumption is great. I've considered my discretion to set bond anyway, and I decline that opportunity. She'll be held without bond."

In the blink of an eye, the lengthy hearing was over. As sheriff's deputies quickly ushered her out of the courtroom, Denise barely had time to glance at her sisters and friends who had turned up to show their support. It would be nearly six months before they would see her again. When the stakes would be considerably higher.

Despite the setback, Way's enthusiasm for his client and his case was seemingly undiminished as he spoke with the media. "We are looking forward to our trial," he said. "Denise will be exonerated after the jury sees the evidence or the lack of evidence against her. We feel supremely confident." Only time would tell if that confidence were warranted.

••••

Mourners began arriving at Immanuel Baptist Church long before the 11:00 a.m. funeral on Saturday, September 8, 2018 was set to begin. Unlike Mike's February 2001 memorial service at Thomasville Road Baptist Church—at a time Cheryl Williams fervently believed her son was still alive—this service would have her seal of approval and full participation.

Not only did the Merrell family not participate in planning this particular service—Warren and Johnnie having already passed on themselves—not a single one of Denise's sisters or brothers-in-law attended. Though Marcus Winchester wasn't there either, his daughter—Brian's sister Jennifer—did come to pay her respects. About 150 people attended in all.

Mike's dark brown, oak casket sat at the front of the sanctuary, near the pulpit, adorned by greenery and flowers, wooden mallard ducks just off to the side. Inside the coffin were the skeletal remains and bone fragments recovered from Carr Lake the prior October. It was actually somewhat miraculous Cheryl and Nick were able to obtain them at all as, under Florida law, with Denise in jail, Mike's adult child Anslee had full control over their disposal.

At Cheryl's request, Jon Fuchs had written to an attorney representing Anslee asking her to permit law enforcement to release her father's remains for the funeral and a proper burial. Surprisingly, the 19-year-old agreed, her attorney noting her two conditions: first, no media would be permitted inside the church or at the burial; second, she asked to be invited to the service. After checking with Cheryl, Fuchs agreed to both conditions.

It was a bittersweet day for Cheryl and Nick Williams, representing closure in some respects of their harrowing 18-year odyssey. Denise's December trial would hopefully bring more closure still, and perhaps justice as well.

More than anything, as they steeled themselves for the excruciating day ahead, Cheryl and Nick were hopeful this would be the day they had been waiting for since their January 2005 altercation with Denise and Brian in Cheryl's kitchen—the day Anslee would finally accept their love once again. But as the funeral progressed, those hopes were dashed. Cheryl's estranged granddaughter was nowhere to be found.

Photo displays of Mike's childhood greeted mourners in the narthex. The program each guest was handed was filled with pictures of Mike at various points in his life—his baby pictures, young Mike hunting for Easter eggs, his elementary and high school graduations, and Mike looking athletic as a high school football player.

The back of the trifold was the most heart-wrenching of all: a photo of Mike and Anslee both asleep in a chair just after her birth, another of his daughter snuggled up against his chest, and a third taken just a few days before his murder—of a terrified toddler in Mike's vice grip while her picture was snapped with Santa. Conspicuously absent from the program were any photos from his wedding or life with Denise.

Having difficulty walking any distance, Mike's 74-year-old mother was wheeled into the church, her gray hair uncharacteristically resting freely behind her head. Nearly two dozen of her "kids" from over the years made it to the service, as did her son's former colleagues from Ketcham Appraisal, including Clay and Patti.

The pews were also filled with investigators, detectives, and prosecutors who had worked so diligently for more than a decade to learn the truth and bring closure for Cheryl and her family: Jack Campbell, Andy Rogers, and Tully Sparkman from the State Attorney's Office, Mark Perez, Mike DeVaney, and Will Mickler from the FDLE, and Derrick Wester from the Jackson County Sheriff's Office.

During the service, Howard Drew provided pearls of wisdom and funny anecdotes about Mike's early days hunting. A family friend sang a beautiful rendition of the 1929 hymn, *I'll Fly Away* beginning with the words, "Some glad morning, when this life is o'er, I'll fly away, to a home on God's celestial shore, I'll fly away." Considering Mike had spent his last morning on earth at Lake Seminole—his favorite place to hunt ducks soaring over the water—the song was most apropos. The pastor offered a moving message of hope, assuring mourners Mike was at peace.

After the service ended, Mike's casket was carried into the awaiting hearse by Nick, Cheryl's brothers Jimmy and Mike, and friends of Mike's from NFC, Florida State, and adulthood. His best friend from those days, however, was unavailable to serve as a pallbearer. Or to attend the service. Brian Winchester, now better known as Prisoner N32301, spent the day instead in his cell at the Wakulla Correctional Institution, none the wiser to the goings on at the Baptist church. Yet more than anyone else in the world, he was the primary reason why 150 people had crammed into the church sanctuary that morning and shed so many tears over such a beautiful life ended far too soon.

Cheryl's closest family members and friends accompanied her to the Roselawn Cemetery, where Mike's coffin was lowered into its final resting place close to a stunning oak tree, on top of a lush, green hill. Though those assembled on the hillside likely didn't dwell on it at the time, this was actually Mike's second burial—the first one, nearly 18 years earlier, the final act of a despicable crime.

The gray headstone placed at Mike's grave months later did more than just mark the site. It contained a short, but fitting, illustrated biography of his life. Ducks with outstretched wings were etched into the upper corners of the marker. "Loving father," "loving son," and "loving brother" furthered the narrative under his name.

Most atypically, however, the stone didn't include the date of Mike's death. Rather, it finished the story of his life the horrific way it actually ended: "Murdered December 16, 2000."

With Mike now laid to rest—for the final time—Cheryl Ann Williams was more than ready to move forward with the concluding chapter of his story. One that would play out just a few days before the 18th anniversary of his brutal slaying. In Courtroom 3G of the Leon County Courthouse. Where justice, she hoped with all her might, would finally be delivered.

14

Showtime

Despite the immense pretrial publicity swirling around the Denise Williams murder case, jury selection took only a single day—blazing speed considering the magnitude of the stakes for both sides. Just before 6:00 p.m. on Monday, December 10, 2018, a jury composed of six men and six women—evenly split between white and African-American jurors—was empaneled to hear the evidence and determine whether Denise was guilty of murder. As a whole, the jury was very young, five jurors under the age of 30—none of whom were even teenagers in December 2000. Only four were over 40.

The next morning, the courtroom was filled even beyond capacity, a throng of local, state, and national media packed into the gallery along with friends and family members of Denise, Brian, Mike, and Cheryl. Denise's sisters sat directly behind the defense counsel table. Brian's father, Marcus, was also there as was Mike's first love, Denise (Pate) Brogdon, who sat among some of Cheryl's "kids" and their parents behind the prosecution table along with Nick's wife Jeanne. Because anyone appearing on either side's witness list was sequestered, Cheryl and Nick—and Clay and Patti Ketcham—weren't permitted to attend or even watch the proceedings remotely.

Denise sat at her table flanked by Ethan Way and Phil Padovano. Permitted to wear civilian clothes for the first time since her arrest—freed of her jail-issued jumpsuit, handcuffs, and shackles to prevent any unfair taint that might arise from that image—she wore a light pink cardigan over a white blouse. The hair on her scalp was now completely brown—pancake flat—the bleached portion beginning near her temples, limply extending just past her shoulders.

The 48-year-old, wearing glasses but no noticeable make-up, looked beaten down—bearing no resemblance to the attractive woman capable of turning heads just a few years before. Her vacant expression made it appear as if her soul had been sucked completely out of her body.

The tension in the courtroom hung heavily as Judge Hankinson delivered his preliminary instructions to the jury. Cocking his head toward the prosecutors, he invited Jon Fuchs to make his opening statement. The veteran prosecutor slowly approached the wooden podium and greeted jurors—just a bit nervous as he gathered himself for the most significant opening statement of his career.

Behind his left shoulder, a PowerPoint presentation was queued up on a projection screen, the title "State of Florida vs. Denise Williams" in large yellow lettering against a blue background. He spoke in a calm, matter-of fact, unemotional tone—almost as if he were having a dinner conversation with the 12 people seated in the jury box. As he proceeded through his 35-minute presentation, his massive frame was a blur of motion as he paced between the podium and projection screen.

Fuchs opened with a truncated version of Mike's duck hunting trip to Lake Seminole some 18 years earlier and the massive search to find him. Investigators, he said, quickly surmised his boat had hit a stump and that he had fallen overboard—clicking the PowerPoint to a slide of Mike's empty boat against the tall reeds on the lake's western shoreline to illustrate his point.

The prosecutor explained that the search eventually focused on a small "hole" in the lake about 12 feet deep—where Scott Dungey felt something give way when he was using his PVC pole. The spot was marked for further exploration, he said, first with a bamboo shoot, and later a pole. He told the jury about the discovery of the camouflage hat and—six months later—Mike's waders. "And what you are going to hear is not only were there waders found, but there was a jacket found, a flashlight, and a hunting license. That hunting license belonged to Mike Williams."

Surprisingly, Fuchs didn't suggest these items were planted—as investigators had all but concluded many years before. Throughout the trial, he would instead use these discoveries as evidence corroborating Brian's account of the murder—as if it made perfect sense that all of these items had been missed in the extensive, months-long search following Mike's disappearance.

The case went cold, Fuchs told the jury. There was no evidence "of any foul play in any way, shape, or form. It's simply a duck hunting, boat accident. A body was never found. There were even theories of alligators possibly had eaten him."

The Assistant State Attorney fast forwarded to 2003—after Brian and Kathy divorced—telling jurors Brian and Denise had started dating. "There are suspicions and law enforcement takes another look." But the investigation was hampered, he said, because those were the days of flip phones, home answering machines, and long-distance telephone calls. He reminded jurors that, back then, texting required mashing numbers on cell phones until the correct letters appeared on the screen. By the time investigators finally reclassified the missing-person case as one involving suspicious circumstances, he said, it was too late. The phone records had been purged.

What investigators were able to learn, however, was that Denise had collected $1.75 million in life insurance from three different policies. "She was the sole beneficiary," he revealed. "No one else."

In 2005, Fuchs told jurors, "Brian and Denise get married. At this point, there are definitely suspicions going on, but there's no evidence other than what you've heard and the case goes cold again." The couple separated in 2012, he recounted, never living together in the $650,000 house they purchased on Lake Jackson. "Then in 2016, everything changes."

Fuchs described how Brian kidnapped Denise at gunpoint, projecting Brian's mugshot onto the screen. "The agreement is she is not going to go to law enforcement, but she does."

The veteran prosecutor told jurors that the morning of the kidnapping incident, Denise's brother-in-law, TPD Officer Dave McCranie, urged Denise to report Brian to law enforcement and was "on the phone with her the whole way" to the Sheriff's Office. It was because of her brother-in-law's insistence that she report the crime, he said, that Brian was ultimately arrested.

With jurors now on the edges of their seats, Fuchs revealed that, while in jail, Brian confessed to murdering Mike. His confession went much further, he told them. Brian told investigators he and Denise had been having an affair for *three years* as of December 2000, admitting he had personally written the $1 million insurance policy on Mike's life on which Denise had collected.

"What he is also going to tell you," Fuchs added, "is that during that time period of writing that policy, there's discussion between him and Denise about how they can be together. Keep in mind, at this point, they've been dating two years behind the backs of Mike and Kathy, their respective spouses. So they talk about it for a long time, different scenarios." Denise didn't like the stigma associated with being a divorcée, Brian told investigators, and wouldn't consider divorcing Mike. That, Fuchs said, left them with just one option for them to be together. Mike had to die.

One of the scenarios they discussed, the Assistant State Attorney told the jury, was killing both Mike and Kathy. "There was a discussion about going out fishing on the boat offshore and that somehow Mike and Kathy would fall overboard and miraculously Denise and Brian would be the ones that were rescued and therefore be together." But Brian rejected that scenario, not wanting to harm the mother of his child. "Apparently killing his best friend is okay, but killing the mother of his child was not."

"So they settled on killing just Mike. Denise likes the sound of being a widow much more than a divorcée," Fuchs said, his voice laden with divorcée disgust. "The widow gets sympathy from the community, the center of the attention, and they talk about how to do it." The plan they hatched, he said, was that Brian would go hunting with Mike in the early morning hours and push him overboard, resulting in Mike's waders filling with water and him drowning.

Brian established an alibi—to go hunting with his father-in-law, he said. His plan was to meet up with Kathy's father right after pushing Mike into the lake, leaving him to drown in his waders.

Pivoting to his description of the murder itself, the veteran prosecutor recounted how Brian and Mike met up at a gas station and drove to Lake Seminole in separate vehicles. Before launching Mike's boat, Brian got his best friend to put on his waders. Once they got out to the deepest water, "Brian pushed him over. But it didn't go as planned," he said. "Mike is able to get out of the waders and now he's not drowning like he is supposed to. As a result, Brian picks up a shotgun and shoots him in the head."

Brian realized he couldn't leave Mike to sink into the lake full of bullets, Fuchs explained, so he pulled him ashore and put his body in the back of his Suburban. "At this point, he's taken much longer than he has anticipated and his alibi with his father-in-law was blown. So, instead, he goes all the way home with Mike in the back of his truck and crawls in bed with his wife Kathy, trying to establish an alibi or reestablish an alibi at that point. Later on that day, you are going to hear that he took Mike to Carr Lake and actually buried him."

Following his confession, Fuchs revealed, Brian led law enforcement officers to the very spot where he had buried Mike all those years ago. "And there they found Mike exactly where Brian said he would be," he said, pausing for emphasis as a photo showing Mike's grisly remains appeared on the screen.

"His boots are still on. Amazingly, the boxers are still bright red. An autopsy is conducted, X-rays are taken," the Assistant State Attorney continued, an X-ray image of Mike's bullet-ridden skull now displayed on the screen. "And all of these little dots are all of the birdshot, shot in the head just like Brian said. Mike still had his wedding ring on," Fuchs said softly with a hint of emotion, as an X-ray image of Mike's hands and forearms appeared on the screen.

At that point, he told the jury, the investigation went into high gear. Kathy Thomas agreed to work together with the FDLE. She also confided in law enforcement that she, Denise, and Brian had sex together in Panama City *prior to* Mike's death—confirming, Fuchs said, that Brian's relationship with Denise began before the murder. How and why Kathy was part of their secret affair, however, he left confused jurors to figure out for themselves.

Kathy also shared with the FDLE, the prosecutor added, that Denise had approached her just after Brian was arrested for her kidnapping, asking her to "'tell Marcus to tell Brian that I didn't say anything to the FDLE.' Say anything about what? Why would that have to be a message that you would have to send?" he asked rhetorically, intimating that Denise's message was the continuation of a 17-year pact between her and Brian.

Fuchs then previewed the controlled telephone call between Kathy and Denise—the one in which Kathy accused her friend of having planned her husband's murder. "And you are never going to hear flat-out admissions. She never says, 'Yeah, I was involved in the murder.'" But jurors would hear enough to make clear, he said, that Denise and Brian had plotted the murder together.

The Assistant State Attorney then advanced his Power-Point to the final slide, which revealed Denise's enlarged, unflattering mugshot, with large red lettering scrawled across her face spelling out "21 Years of Sex, Lies and Deceit. $1.75 Million."

"In the end," he told jurors, "the State is going to ask you to end the 21 years—three years plus the 18 years—of the sex, lies, and deceit, and find her guilty of these particular crimes. Thank you."

His opening statement complete, Fuchs took his seat next to Andy Rogers, content he had begun moving jurors down the path he hoped would lead to Denise's conviction.

••••

Apart from arguing legal motions to Judge Hankinson, Phil Padovano was assigned very few tasks during the trial. But he was the one to deliver Denise's opening statement. Considerably older than the other three lawyers in the court-room—having graduated law school before they were even born—the 72-year-old retired judge presented his remarks old school, sans technology or any other show-and-tell theatrics. Unlike Fuchs, Padovano remained planted behind the podium for his entire presentation, though his voice was filled with a touch more emotion than the prosecutor's.

"Let me begin by saying that there is no dispute about the fact that Mike Williams was murdered," the grandfatherly law-yer told the jurors, looking at them through his hornrimmed glasses. "The evidence is going to show beyond any doubt that he was shot in the face and killed by Brian Winchester, a man he thought was his friend." He reminded jurors Brian wasn't the one on trial—having "never been charged with the mur-der."

Padovano wasted little time getting to the crux of the mat-ter: Brian's testimony couldn't be believed. It would be given under a grant of immunity, he revealed. "The kind of immu-nity that was given to him is that he will be able to say—he will be able to testify *as he pleases* about this without any fear that the State will be able to use that testimony against him."

He told jurors, "Brian Winchester's testimony is totally uncorroborated. In plain English, there isn't anything to back it up. You are not going to hear evidence from a witness who said that he or she saw Denise Williams participating in the planning or the execution of this murder." There would be no DNA or fingerprint evidence or other physical evidence, he said, "to connect Denise Williams to this crime. No confession. No admission. *Nothing*. All you are going to have to go on is the word of a man who actually committed the murder."

The silver-haired lawyer transitioned to Mike and De-nise's marriage, telling jurors it was a happy one. "The evi-dence is not going to suggest any reason why Mrs. Williams would have been unhappy with her husband. Mike Williams was a good husband, he was a good father, and he was most certainly a good provider." No evidence would be presented, he added, "to suggest that Denise Williams was having any sort of marital problem with Mike Williams."

He suggested the prosecution's focus on insurance was misplaced, telling jurors Mike had been guided by a financial advisor named Dick Gainey. "Mr. Gainey advised Mr. Williams that he should have at least a million dollars in life insurance."

Padovano told jurors it was Marcus Winchester, not his son Brian, who sold that policy to Mike. Though that increased his total coverage to $1.75 million, he added, "You are going to hear evidence that this was not too much insurance for a person in Mike Williams' financial situation," a real estate appraiser with an annual income of $185,000.

"There's no evidence that Denise Williams participated in any of these discussions about the insurance," the retried jurist said, "and there's no evidence that she did anything to influence her husband Mike to buy this insurance. The only evidence you are going to hear on this point was that the matter was initiated by Mike Williams himself, with the advice of his advisor, Mr. Gainey, his friends, and with the assistance of two insurance agents, Brian Winchester and his father, Marcus Winchester."

Padovano then pivoted to the murder itself, suggesting Brian's statement that Denise was "opposed to divorce for religious and personal reasons"—but perfectly willing to commit murder—made no sense at all. And even according to Brian, he told jurors, Denise didn't have any actual role in the crime other than giving Mike permission to go hunting that morning.

The defense lawyer then described how Brian killed Mike at Lake Seminole—almost precisely as Fuchs had—including the additional details of Brian purchasing a shovel and tarp at Walmart and later cleaning the back of his Suburban with bleach.

"I preface this account by saying this was Mr. Winchester's version of how this murder occurred," he continued. "I think when you hear the evidence, you are going to have some questions about whether it happened where he said it happened, whether it happened the way he said it happened. But what I think is not in question is that he did, in fact, shoot and kill Mike Williams. And there's no evidence—absolutely no proof—that Denise Williams had anything to do with that or that she even knew about it."

Shifting gears again, the most senior lawyer in the courtroom told jurors they would hear no evidence corroborating Brian's testimony that he and Denise had been having an affair prior to December 2000, telling them investigators uncovered no such evidence. "You are not going to see any phone records to verify that Denise Williams was calling Brian Winchester or vice versa. You are not going to see any security camera footage of them going in and out of buildings. You are not going to hear from any witnesses that they saw them in a private setting. You are not going to see credit card receipts for dinners or hotel bills."

Jurors would also hear evidence, Padovano said, that would "flatly contradict what Mr. Winchester says, that his claim—his claim that he was having an affair with Denise Williams and that they cooked up this plan to kill Denise's husband so that they could be together." He pointed out that, following the murder, Brian had actually worked hard to save his marriage with Kathy. At the final divorce hearing with Kathy, he said, "Brian Winchester, the man who was supposed to have done this to be with Denise, was sitting in the back of the room sobbing, begging her, begging her not to go through with the divorce."

For her part, Padovano revealed, Denise was in her own relationship, with a coworker named Charles Bunker. "You will hear from him too. That started a couple of years after her husband disappeared." As time went on, he told jurors, the relationship "got more serious, and, you know, they had some things in common. Mr. Bunker was a single parent. He was caring for a child and so was Denise."

Curiously, he shared with jurors how, during Denise's

trip with Bunker to Atlanta, Brian showed up unexpectedly at their hotel and threatened them—an action that seemingly contradicted the notion Brian and Denise hadn't already been involved in a relationship of their own.

"Now, Mrs. Williams did eventually marry Brian Winchester," Padovano acknowledged, "but that was five years later, five years after her husband disappeared." He downplayed the significance of their marriage, telling jurors they had gone to high school and college together, had been friends for many years, and had children the same age.

More importantly, he said, "before the marriage, Denise Williams laid down some very strict rules. Brian Winchester had to be baptized. In fact, he was. Brian Winchester had to go through a year-long premarital program at Mrs. Winchester's church. These were conditions that Denise Williams insisted on before she married Brian Winchester."

The defense attorney then recounted the kidnapping incident between Brian and Denise—in more graphic detail than had Fuchs—attempting to persuade jurors that only one of the two was capable of such despicable conduct. "Now, Mr. Winchester is going to say that he only wanted to talk to Denise Williams," he said. "He only wanted to try to reconcile. But he had a handgun, and you should also know that he had a tarp and two containers of bleach in the cargo area. He put them there. They weren't in the Suburban. He put them there, but he says he only wanted to talk to her."

"Now, fortunately," the retried judge added, "she was able to calm him down with the promise, I guess that they were going to try to work things out. She had no intention of doing that—none whatsoever. She went straight to the police," he told jurors, without mentioning that her police officer brother-in-law had implored her to do so.

Padovano ended his 24-minute opening statement exactly where he started, telling the jury not to trust Brian or believe his testimony. "Mr. Winchester has a motive to lie to you … a motive to make up this accusation against Mrs. Williams. He didn't mention anything about her alleged participation in this murder until after he realized that he was facing a life sentence for kidnapping. He didn't mention it until after he realized that Mrs. Williams was going to go into court and ask for a life sentence, and at that point he made an agreement with the State for immunity."

That agreement, Padovano noted, ensured Brian wouldn't be sentenced to life for kidnapping and "guaranteed that anything he said about the disappearance of Mike Williams could never be used against him. So, that is what he gained by the agreement. In return, of course, he is going to give testimony, and the testimony he is going to give is going to be pretty much what Mr. Fuchs outlined about Denise Williams."

And by giving that testimony, Brian also derived another benefit, he asserted. Revenge. After Denise "threw him under the bus by turning him in for kidnapping," he would now "throw her under the bus."

There would be no credible evidence, he told the jury, that his client had participated in the murder. "On that point, you are going to have to rely entirely on the word of a murderer and a convicted felon." The case would end with "more than a reasonable doubt about the guilt of Denise Williams, and we are going to ask you then to find her not guilty. Thank you."

One witness Padovano didn't tell jurors they would be hearing from was his own client—Denise Williams. Though Ethan Way began his representation virtually guaranteeing Jennifer Portman the jury would hear from Denise, it now appeared the defense team was hedging its bets on that particular subject. With a jury now sitting just a few feet away from his client, the protection afforded by the Fifth Amendment was looking a bit more appealing than it had when Way had first touted his client's innocence.

••••

Though Judge Hankinson told jurors to expect the trial to last five days, the parade of witnesses streaming in and out of the courtroom that Tuesday made his prediction appear overly pessimistic. Between 11:00 a.m. and 4:45 p.m., six prosecution witnesses would complete their testimony and a seventh would begin his.

The State began its evidence with four witnesses who were part of the search for Mike at Lake Seminole. Greg Morris was the wildlife officer in charge of the initial search-and-rescue operation. Now retired after 27 years with the FWC, he testified he had met with Warren Merrell at Lake Seminole on December 16, 2000. Warren showed him Mike's Ford Bronco and empty boat trailer near a dirt landing. Morris testified about the events at the lake that afternoon and evening.

Next up was Scott Dungey, who had testified earlier at a videotaped deposition, which was now shown to the jury on a projection screen. Dungey noted that Mike, Denise, and Brian were all classmates of his at NFC, describing Mike as one of his closest friends. During the initial search, he testified, he was in one of the FWC helicopters looking down upon the lake, spotting numerous alligators swimming in the water from that vantage point.

In response to Andy Rogers' questions, Dungey said that on the first or second day of the search, while poling the deepest portion of the lakebed, he came across something suspicious "that seemed porous and gave back." He thought it might have been Mike's arm or leg. Though the spot was marked with bamboo shoots for further exploration, nothing of significance was found at the time.

"About six months later," he said, "I received a call that the waders had popped up basically at the exact same spot." The next day, he boated out to that location with his friend Kip Bembry and a diver named Lamar English, who quickly retrieved the camouflage hunting jacket and flashlight. Dungey was surprised to find the jacket in such "great shape." One of the sleeves was inside out, he testified, "like if somebody was trying to get it off." He was the one who pulled Mike's hunting license out of one of the pockets and first turned on the flashlight—which was in perfect working order.

Rogers asked him about the proximity between where those items were found and the spot he had marked with bamboo shoots in the initial days of the search. "Within five feet," Dungey answered.

Next to take the witness stand was Joe Sheffield, the fisherman who found the waders. He testified he actually first spotted them from afar a day before he fished them out of the water, initially believing that what he saw was nothing more than a tree stump.

On that first day, the object was about two feet below the water's surface, he testified. The next day when he was fishing, Sheffield recalled the mysterious object being even closer to the surface, only about six inches down. Able to see it more clearly this time, he realized it wasn't a tree stump after all. When he pulled the waders onto the side of his boat, he told jurors, they had some algae and sediment on them, as if they had been in the water for some time.

Sheffield also testified that inside the fanny pack was a name tag with Mike's name on it. Though that was his testimony on December 11, 2018, there was no documentation from June 2001 of such a finding. Moreover, not only were the waders and fanny pack not preserved, no pictures of them were taken either. Beyond Sheffield's testimony, therefore, the prosecution was unable to establish that the waders were actually covered in algae or sediment, or that Mike's name tag was inside the fanny pack.

Though the next witness to testify—former FWC Officer Alton Ranew—had a distinctly different recollection about the condition of the waders, neither Fuchs nor Way broached that particular topic with him. He testified he had retired in 2012, following 31 years as a wildlife officer.

He described in great detail the search efforts of officers, volunteers, cadaver dogs, cameras, boats, helicopters, and small planes. He also testified about his involvement after the waders, jacket, and flashlight were discovered. As Ranew testified, Fuchs clicked through images of the jacket and hunting license on the screen, as well as of Mike's boat against the reeds on the lake's western shoreline.

••••

A pair of law enforcement officers who had devoted

large chunks of their careers to the Mike Williams investigation would testify next—Tully Sparkman and Mike DeVaney. Though each had worked on the investigation for more than a decade, their testimony, collectively, lasted less than 50 minutes.

Sparkman told jurors he had been an investigator with the State Attorney's Office for 13 years, actually beginning his career with the FWC. He started working on the Mike Williams investigation in 2006 or 2007, he said. Though he made attempts to obtain phone records from the 2000 time period, none were available. Similarly, he testified, efforts to find the waders, hunting jacket, and Mike's boat also proved unsuccessful.

Fuchs showed the investigator Denise's June 29, 2001 petition for a presumptive death certificate and entered it into evidence. Incredibly, though, the prosecutor didn't ask a single question about its contents—such as Denise's contentions that Mike had gone hunting alone or that the Gibson Inn trip was a last-minute surprise. Based on the perfunctory reference to the petition, jurors had no reason to conclude it held any importance at all. And after showing Sparkman Denise and Brian's 2005 marriage certificate, Fuchs abruptly ended his questioning altogether.

During his cross-examination, Way asked the investigator if he had become aware of Denise's relationship with Charles Bunker prior to her marriage to Brian. Sparkman confirmed he had. Way asked him if that relationship had lasted for "several years," to which the prosecution witness responded he didn't know. He also acknowledged he had never interviewed Bunker as part of the investigation. And conceded he hadn't even started looking for phone records until 2008. Sparkman testified that he didn't even know who Denise's employer was and, for that reason, had never sought to obtain records about phone messages she might have received at work around the time of Mike's murder.

Under Fuchs's questioning, Mike DeVaney told jurors he had recently retired after 37 years with the FDLE. When he first became involved in the Mike Williams investigation, he testified, he considered it a "cold case." He and his fellow investigators were "handcuffed," the special agent noted, because evidence hadn't been gathered—and forensic examinations hadn't been undertaken—at the time Mike disappeared.

Reviewing the files, he determined that the missing-person case had, by 2004, become a "suspicious missing-person" investigation. "A lot of things didn't quite make sense," DeVaney told jurors, "too many things that were unanswered." Both Denise and Brian were identified as persons of interest early on, he noted. DeVaney said he became even more suspicious when he learned that it was Brian who had first begun asking what steps needed to be taken to have Mike declared dead. As well as by the fact that Brian had sold Mike a $1 million life insurance policy just before his death.

The retired agent testified that in early August 2016, he learned Officer Dave McCranie of the Tallahassee Police Department had tipped off one of his FDLE colleagues that Denise was on her way to the Sheriff's Office to report a kidnapping incident. DeVaney told jurors he watched Denise being interviewed from a video feed in another room. After McCranie completed his questioning, he testified, he entered the room and began questioning her.

"After talking to Denise for a few minutes, explaining who I was," he said, "I tried to talk to her about that there may be a connection between what happened that day and the disappearance of Mike. In other words, because of the activity with Brian that day, you know, there may be some culpability there. She did not agree to that. She told me that if she had any indication, any belief that Brian may have done something to her husband at the time, she certainly would not have married him."

"And when you asked her about his involvement in Mike Williams [death], she says, 'Certainly not?'" Fuchs asked.

"Correct."

"At any point, did she say, 'You know, all these years later, I never believed he would have, but given what happened today, maybe it was true?'"

"No, sir."

"Flat out denial?"

"Denial," DeVaney confirmed.

Fuchs then asked his witness to point out Denise at the defense counsel table—which he did—and abruptly ended his questioning. Surprisingly, he didn't ask Judge Hankinson for permission to show jurors the 20-minute video of DeVaney's August 5, 2016, interview of Denise, relying instead on just the few questions he had posed about their interactions that afternoon. The jury would never get to see her facial expressions or body language as she answered his questions—or factor them into their deliberations over Denise's guilt or innocence.

Even more puzzling, Phil Padovano started his cross-examination by focusing on that very interview, asking DeVaney if he had confronted Denise with his suspicion she had been involved in the murder. The State's witness denied he had, telling the jury he simply asked her if she knew where Mike had been buried. He also denied being rough on her in any way.

Shifting gears, the retired judge asked DeVaney if he was aware of a single overt action Denise had taken in furtherance of a plan to murder Mike. The former agent conceded he wasn't aware of any overt act. And further, that he wasn't aware of any physical or tangible evidence connecting Denise to the murder. He also acknowledged subpoenas hadn't been issued for credit card information which could have corroborated Brian's statement that he and Denise had been having an affair since 1997.

Unhappy with his witness's answers to those questions, on redirect examination Fuchs asked him whether credit card records are maintained indefinitely. The retired FDLE agent told the jury they aren't. Fuchs also had him confirm that law enforcement officers had tried to obtain those records, but learned they had been purged.

"The last question about no tangible evidence, no overt act, was done by Ms. Williams, Ms. Winchester," Fuchs asked, "fair to say if there had been an overt act or tangible evidence, she probably would have been arrested prior to the time she was, correct?"

"Correct."

"The nature of a conspiracy is to keep those secrets, is it not?"

"Correct," DeVaney agreed.

"And in fact, because it remained a secret for as long as it did—until [2017] when Brian Winchester confessed, they were pretty good at keeping that secret, were they not?"

"Very good," the retired special agent confirmed. With that answer, his testimony concluded.

DeVaney had devoted more than a decade to solving the mystery surrounding Mike's disappearance. Resulting in all of 23 minutes on the witness stand at the murder trial designed to bring one of his killers to justice. Puzzling to say the least.

The State would call just one additional witness that afternoon. He had been waiting nervously in a small cell—heavily guarded by armed sheriff's deputies—for his moment on the grand stage. The outcome of the entire case would hinge largely on his answers to questions and demeanor on the witness stand.

Hands cuffed, feet shackled, and dressed in a drab blue prison jumpsuit over a white T-shirt, Brian Scott Winchester was led by officers into Courtroom 3G. Eighteen years—nearly to the day—since his savage, cold-blooded killing of the best friend he ever had.

15

Star Witness

Every trial has its dramatic moments. In the case of *State of Florida v. Denise Williams*, there would be no more dramatic moment than Brian Winchester stepping up to the witness stand, swearing to tell the truth, and turning to face jurors to begin his testimony. With his ex-wife—whose fate depended almost entirely on what he had to say—glaring at him from her counsel table some 25 feet away. A moment that literally had been 18 years in the making.

The entire outcome of the trial would hinge on whether jurors believed what Brian had to say. For the prosecution team—considering its star witness was a confessed killer and convicted kidnapper—the task ahead would be daunting to say the least. For his part, Ethan Way sat at the defense table licking his proverbial chops, relishing the chance to tear from limb to limb the only witness standing between his client and freedom.

Though Tim Jansen's client wasn't the one on trial, the defense attorney did have a brief cameo appearance as Brian entered the courtroom at 2:45 p.m. Jansen informed Judge Hankinson that his client was invoking his Fifth Amendment right against self-incrimination. That statement, however, was simply designed to get the judge to order Brian to testify—which he promptly did—establishing that every word he uttered from the witness stand would be protected under a thick blanket of immunity.

With that choreographed dance complete, the stage was now set for the State's most important witness to begin his testimony. Though, unlike Denise, Brian wasn't permitted the luxury of shedding his prison garb, his handcuffs were removed so he could gesticulate as needed. His feet—hidden from view by the witness box—remained bound together by metal shackles. Armed deputies stood close by, just in case.

The former financial planner and insurance agent looked like a shell of his former self, his year as an inmate in a medium-security prison having taken a physical and telling toll. He appeared gaunt—almost malnourished—his eyes sunken deeply into his head. Though only 48 years of age, Brian looked like he had aged a decade rather than the one year he had been in prison.

From the very beginning of his testimony, Brian seemed to be gripped by three primary emotions, palpably evident in his quavering voice and strained facial expressions: grief, shame, and remorse. For what he had done to his best friend all those years ago. For throwing away an enviable life many of his NFC and Florida State classmates would have moved mountains to have. And for losing virtually everything that had ever mattered to him, most especially his son Stafford.

Standing at the podium wedged between the prosecution table and the jury box, Jon Fuchs readied himself for the most consequential direct examination of his career. He began by asking the witness to tell the jury how he knew Mike Williams.

Brian paused, biting his bottom lip in an attempt to keep his emotions from bubbling to the surface. "Mike and I went to high school together," he finally responded, voice crackling, "and got to know each other very well. We were very good friends. We continued to be friends all through college and … getting married. And we were very good friends." He told jurors Mike and Denise were high school sweethearts, as were he and Kathy, and that both couples had children roughly the same age.

Less than two minutes into his questioning, Fuchs asked if he and Denise had "become an item" prior to 2000.

Brian answered that they had indeed, dating their relationship to a Sister Hazel concert at Floyd's Music Store just off the Florida State campus—more than three years before Mike's death, even before Denise had become pregnant with Anslee. He and Denise used the October 13, 1997, concert date, Brian said, to mark the beginning of their relationship, clandestine though it was.

Just before then, he explained, he had found a note in Kathy's purse through which he learned she was having an affair of her own with a mutual friend. "After that happened, I began to look outside of my marriage," he told jurors. He had never been attracted to Denise previously, he said, during all the years they had known one another.

But one night, while out at a bar with Kathy, Mike, and Denise, he explained, "We started talking about sexual things and things that married couples shouldn't be talking about with each other. I think that's when the spark kind of started between the two of us."

That spark quickly ignited into a full-fledged romantic flame. He and Denise, Brian testified, had their first moment of passion shortly after entering Floyd's while Mike and Kathy parked the car. They "kissed each other and made out," he revealed. Later that night, he called Denise. The two ended up talking on the phone for hours. "And it was just like, I don't know. We just—we connected like nobody else. I mean, we just really connected. And we had a lot of sexual talk and had phone sex and that sort of thing."

The next day, the two met up during Denise's lunch break, Brian testified, intimating they had actual, in-person sex for the first time.

"It snowballed really fast," he told jurors, who were already hanging on his every word—as if they were watching an episode of the reality show *Big Brother*. "We started meeting in hotels. We started meeting during the workday. We started meeting whenever we had the opportunity."

He digressed to point out that Mike was a "workaholic," something Denise wasn't pleased about. But that gave them ample opportunities, he said, to get together frequently and have sex. Sometimes Denise would travel with Mike to his work conferences, he noted. Brian would occasionally make the trip as well—separately and secretly. He and Denise would enjoy their trysts while her husband listened to lectures in hotel ballrooms, blissfully unaware of what was going on behind his back. Unbeknownst to Mike, Brian and Denise also took their own trips to Destin, Panama City, South Beach, and New York.

They got more and more brazen very quickly, rendez-vousing at Denise and Mike's home, first on Starmount Drive near Meridian Road and later at Centennial Oaks Circle. These midday hookups often occurred during the lunch hour, the secret lovers placing their voracious sexual appetites above their gastrointestinal needs.

The two would meet up at a Home Depot parking lot or behind Keiser College, Brian testified, leave a vehicle there, and then head to Denise's house, sometimes his. If they were pinched for time, he told jurors, they would even take care of business in one of their vehicles and then go right back to work.

Fuchs asked the State's star witness to focus on the period of time Mike and Denise lived on Starmount Drive, prior to August 1999. Brian told jurors that, during that time, he would sometimes park at a church near Denise's home and walk down a drainage ditch for a short distance, through the woods, depositing him almost at her doorstep.

The prosecutor then pivoted to an affair within the affair—between Brian and Angela Stafford, Clay Ketcham's employee. The former financial planner told jurors he and Angela had a brief tryst one night, after Mike's death—but before his relationship with Denise had become public knowledge. On that particular evening, he said, he, Denise, and Angela were all supposed to go out together. But Denise wasn't able to get a babysitter and told the two to head out without her. He and Angela had a lot to drink, Brian recounted, and somehow wound up in bed together at his home.

"And it was dark and all of a sudden the light came on in my bedroom," he continued. "And I looked up and Denise was standing there. And she said something like—she said something sarcastic and said, 'I'm sorry' or something, and ran out. And I didn't want Angela to know it was Denise. I think she did know, but I didn't want her to know. And so I lied to Angela and told her that I thought it was my wife—my ex-wife at that point, Kathy."

Fuchs then shifted gears again—to the subject of life insurance. Brian told the jury that Mike's $1 million policy came about through "Denise and I talking about him having more coverage." They had several conversations with Mike about that subject, he said, with Denise encouraging him to get the policy. The plan all three agreed on was for Mike to drop his existing $500,000 policy with Cotton States in favor of the new $1 million policy.

With that background out of the way, it was time for the main event: the murder plot. Brian told the jury, "The more we were together, the more we wanted to be together. And the more we griped about Kathy and Mike, the more we wanted to be together. It just kind of—it just got worse and worse. I mean, it just snowballed."

Because of the way Denise was raised—and her pride—she made it clear she wouldn't divorce Mike. "But she still had a desire for us to be together, which narrowed the options … I mean, we wanted to be together and we weren't going to let anything stop that."

Denise decided it would be "better to be a rich widow than a poor divorcée," he added. "And her biggest concern with the divorce was she didn't want to share custody of Anslee with Mike—she was not going to have Anslee going back and forth to two different houses."

The pair hashed around "several options and alternatives of ways that we could be together," Brian told the jury. Because Mike worked late into the night at his office, one option they discussed was for him to be shot in some type of staged burglary. But they quickly scuttled that idea because it would have resulted in an investigation.

A second option was for the four of them—Denise, Mike, Brian, and Kathy—to be out on a boat on the Gulf of Mexico, with Kathy and Mike being pushed overboard and he and Denise finding a buoy to hang onto while the boat sank, in what they would call "an accident." Brian was the one to nix that option, he testified, because "I was never going to allow anything happen to my son's mom."

A third scenario they discussed was for Brian and Mike to go on a hunting trip in which Mike would end up in the water and drown. "Denise liked this idea," he said, because, "We could feel better about ourselves if there was a chance that he could make it out of it." They gravitated toward this scenario, concluding, "It will be up to God what happens and not us. It won't be a murder. It will be, you know, an accident. It's kind of screwed up thinking. But that was a scenario that she could live with, I guess."

"There were a lot of things that were kind of pressuring us for this to happen when it did," Brian testified. "One was, Mike had intended for that policy—the $500,000 policy—to lapse. He was not intending to continue it. And, so, behind his back, Denise paid one more—I can't remember if it was quarterly or semiannual premium. But we kept it going one more premium period. And we knew we weren't going to be able to keep it going perpetually"—because Mike would eventually figure out they were paying the premiums for him.

Also adding to the pressure, Brian said, was that Mike "was getting angrier and angrier about the fact that she wasn't having sex with him." He recounted how, on their trip to Arkansas that Thanksgiving—when they spent 20 hours in Brian's Suburban together—Mike shared "how unhappy he was, you know, with Denise. And he was not happy with not having—not having sex." Mike confided in Brian that Denise refused to have sex with him while she was pregnant with Anslee and ever since her birth as well—some 28 months of sustained abstinence.

Of course, Brian knew all too well why Denise had shut down her sexual relationship with Mike: that was his role in her life now, not her husband's. He told jurors he and Denise would actually check up on one another to make sure neither was cheating—*with their own spouses*. They considered themselves a monogamous couple—no matter what their marriage licenses said.

During their long trip to Arkansas, Mike also told Brian that he was having suspicions about Denise. "He thought she was using drugs," Brian told the jury. "He thought he had seen money disappearing. She had been taking cash withdrawals out of the ATM, which I knew was for travel for us when we would go out of town. But he kind of thought it might be for drugs or something. I think he even approached Denise's mom about it at some point, asking her about it." Mike's mounting suspicions, Brian testified, put pressure on them to accelerate their timeline.

At some point, Brian became aware of the anniversary trip to the Gibson Inn Mike had planned. The sex-starved husband "made it pretty clear," he testified, that the trip was "going to be their starting-over date. That it had been long enough since Anslee had been born. That it was time for them to start having sex again. I think he was kind of putting some pressure on Denise about that. And she did not want to go on that trip—did not want that trip to happen."

They accelerated their plan for Mike to drown while duck hunting. Brian initially scheduled their trip to Lake Seminole for Saturday, December 9, but that was thwarted when Mike called from his office close to midnight only hours before they were supposed to leave. Denise didn't want him to go, Mike had said. "And I was very surprised. Shocked kind of," Brian recalled. And "not happy."

He called Denise immediately after hanging up with Mike, telling her, "This isn't something you need to be wishy-washy about."

Denise told him she had gotten cold feet at the last minute. They had several additional conversations, he testified, Brian pressuring her to make up her mind. "Either we're going to go forward with this or we're not," he recalled telling her. "I mean, we're either going to be together or we're not. You know, like I said, the policy is ending. You've got that anniversary trip coming up next weekend. You know, duck season is going to be ending soon. Do you want this to happen or not?"

By this point in his testimony, Brian had already disclosed twice that Denise was fully aware of her husband's plan to take her to the Gibson Inn for their anniversary weekend—more than a week before they went hunting together on December 16. Indeed, that was one of the key reasons, he said, why Denise wanted Mike out of the picture before then. So she wouldn't have to have sex with him.

Apparently, the prosecutors didn't realize that Brian's testimony on this point directly contradicted Denise's June 2001 affidavit—in which she had stated, under oath, that Mike first told her about the anniversary trip on Friday, December 15, 2000, "as a surprise." That affidavit had been placed into evidence during Tully Sparkman's testimony as part of the petition for a presumptive death certificate. Fuchs could have easily placed that document in front of Brian to have him point out—based on his own personal knowledge—that Denise's sworn statement was false. A golden opportunity missed in the heat of battle.

Brian testified that he and Denise met up several times during the following week—after she had gotten cold feet—to discuss what to do next. During one of those meetings, he said, at a boat ramp on Lake Jackson, they decided to move forward with their plan the following Saturday, December 16.

"And in a sick sort of way," he added, "it was kind of like, 'You know, well, if God wants this to happen, this is what's going to happen.' Because the plan, again, was that it was going to be an accident. And, you know, there would be a chance that he could get out of it."

Brian wasn't asked, however, what he and Denise planned to do if Mike *did* get out of it—if God decided he *wasn't* going to drown. Was Mike just going to climb back into the boat, shake Brian's hand, and act as if his best friend's attempt to kill him was merely a good-natured prank? Did either of them think Mike was really that stupid? Or would an additional—more successful—attempt to eliminate the only witness to their attempted murder become imperative? Based on Brian's testimony, it appeared that neither he nor Denise had actually given these obvious questions even the slightest thought.

Fuchs then had the State's most crucial witness march through the events surrounding the murder. Brian choked back tears as he recalled scenes from Mike's last night on earth. Mike was ringing the Salvation Army bell, he said, utterly unaware of the fate awaiting him. He told jurors he and Kathy went to Floyd's, where he tried to get her "as drunk as possible" so she would sleep heavily and late into the next morning as he executed his diabolical plan.

The alibi he tried to establish, he told jurors, was to go hunting with his father-in-law, Jimmy Aldredge. Denise's alibi, Brian testified, was to be at home with Anslee. "And the plan was when Mike didn't come back home, that eventually she was going to start calling her sisters and her dad from her house phone so that she could establish she was at the house."

He told jurors he made sure Mike brought his waders, telling his friend, "We were going to a secret, special spot to go hunting." Choking back his emotions, he explained the "duck hunter's myth that if you fall overboard with your waders you're going to sink really quick and drown." In other words, his murder weapon was going to be Mike's own waders.

Before launching the boat, Brian recounted, he told Mike they were running short on time and needed to put on their waders. They both did so. "And because I knew where we were going hunting, I was in the back of the boat driving and he was in the front."

With the jury—indeed, the entire courtroom—completely mesmerized, Brian testified that "there was a deep area maybe a couple hundred yards from the landing that we put in at. And we got to that area that I knew was a deep area. And I don't remember exactly how I got him to stand up, but—I don't know if I pretended something was wrong with the motor or the weight in the boat was off or something. But I basically stopped the boat and got him to stand up. And when he did, I pushed him into the water."

When Fuchs asked what had happened next, Brian sighed deeply and paused for several seconds—as if he were hoping for some way not to reveal what he had done. He looked down, avoiding eye contact with both the prosecutor and the jury, gripped by anguish—and shame.

"So he was in the water," Brian finally got out in a strained voice. "And he was like, struggling. And the motor of the boat was still running. And I pulled off just a little bit to get, kind of, away from him so that he couldn't reach back into the boat. And I didn't know it at the time—I didn't know if he was trying to swim or—" he said, trailing off.

What he came to realize was that Mike "was taking the waders and the jacket off. And he got those off." Now openly weeping, Brian told jurors Mike had swum over to a tree stump and was holding on for dear life.

"And he was panicking. And I was panicking. And none of this was, like, going the way I thought it was going to go. And I didn't know what to do," he explained, his voice cracking with emotion. Though he didn't say it out loud, it was at that point that Brian obviously realized that letting "God decide" would likely mean Mike reporting to authorities that his best friend had tried to kill him. "I didn't know how to get out of that situation," he confessed remorsefully.

Brian lowered his head, eyes closed—in obvious shame—shrugged his shoulders, and told the jury that as Mike was screaming for help, he loaded his shotgun and "made one or two circles around, and I ended up circling closer towards him. And he was in the water." After pausing a few more seconds, almost under his breath, Brian was finally able to get out the words, "And as I passed by, I shot him."

"Where did you shoot him?" Fuchs asked, as the stunned jury absorbed Brian's confession.

"In the head," he answered with evident self-disgust, wiping his running nose with a tissue. "And I knew I couldn't leave him there being shot," he added. "So I was going to have to do something to cover this up." He recounted the sequence of events beginning with pulling Mike's corpse through the water to a dirt landing, backing his Suburban down to the edge of the lake, hoisting Mike's body up to the tailgate and stuffing it into a dog crate, and speeding back to Tallahassee in a fruitless effort to meet his father-in-law in time to establish his alibi.

"And I pushed the boat back out into the water," he told

jurors, "to make it look like, you know, his boat was out there and he had drowned or disappeared. Or, you know, I didn't give a lot of thought as to what was going to happen after that. I was just panicked as to getting out of that area and covering this up."

"How were you able to get a man that's 170 pounds dead-weight into the back of your Suburban by yourself?" the Assistant State Attorney wondered aloud.

"It was not easy and it was not pretty," Brian replied. "But I had to make it happen. I mean, I had no choice. And I can't even explain, like, how your body feels in that kind of a situation." He compared it to a wartime battle. "But, like, you have so such adrenaline pumping through your body. You're just— it's just crazy." He told jurors that as he loaded Mike's dead body into his truck, he "made a purposeful decision to never view him."

He left his phone off on the way back to Tallahassee, Brian said, to ensure there would be no record of where he had been. That also meant he couldn't call Kathy's dad to let him know he was running late, resulting in him no longer having Jimmy Aldredge to support his alibi.

"And I decided the best thing for me to do was to go back to my house and pretend that I had overslept," his narrative continued. "And then I could also make a phone call from my house to my father-in-law, which would kind of prove that I overslept and I was at my house."

He described being "freaked out" at a stoplight when he saw a State trooper and getting home and crawling into bed with his wife to try to establish another alibi.

He told jurors about washing the blood off the driveway, his trip to Walmart, and seeing his friend Mike Phillips, the FDLE agent. During the search at Lake Seminole a few days later, he testified, Phillips recalled seeing him at the store, telling him how panicked and hurried he seemed.

"And he was thinking I was in a hurry to go search for Mike," Brian added. "But I was actually in a hurry because I was trying to bury Mike."

Brian described in exquisite detail how he buried Mike

at Carr Lake. And how he had to make small talk with a deer hunter—whom he suspected was a wildlife officer—while Mike's tarp-wrapped corpse was lying in plain sight next to the makeshift grave he was in the midst of digging.

As he pulled away from Carr Lake—Mike's body now fully covered in the shallow grave—Brian realized that he needed to clean up the blood in the back of his truck. "And it was getting later and later in the day," he testified. "And I knew at some point people were going to start calling me. There was a family Christmas [gathering] with my wife's family up in Cairo that we were supposed to be going to that afternoon or that night. You know, I was just running out of time."

He first went to his parents' home at Lake McBride, he said, and used a garden hose to try to get rid of the blood. But that didn't work. He realized he needed to use a pressure washer and drove to a car wash and did his best to make the blood disappear. After going home, showering, and changing clothes, he finally drove to Georgia to join Kathy and her family for their Christmas celebration.

While driving back to Tallahassee that evening, he testified, his father called to let him know Mike was missing. The two then drove to Lake Seminole together with a borrowed boat in tow.

Brian and his dad waited out the torrential rainstorm that blew through and then went out onto the water after most everyone else had gone. They began to "search" for Mike, Brian told jurors—using his fingers to make air quotes, conveying that the search was actually a charade of his own making. "He was searching and I was just *lying*," he added, choking back tears once again.

"And my dad didn't want to give up," he testified, his emotions now overwhelming him. "*My dad loved Mike*," he sobbed, tormented by anguish. Brian's head dropped onto the desk in front of him, his ability to hold his composure together now clearly gone for good.

Recognizing the witness had reached the point of no return, Judge Hankinson abruptly announced a recess. As the bailiff led jurors from their seats, Brian's haunting, high-pitched wailing filled the courtroom for several minutes before deputies finally escorted him out of the room through a back doorway.

Though jurors, spectators, and journalists had clearly been captivated by Brian's raw, gut-wrenching testimony, one person listening to his account of his cold-blooded killing didn't seem bothered in the slightest: Mike's widow, the defendant.

For 70 solid minutes, Denise sat in her seat emitting an expression so vacant and distant, it was almost as if she were listening to a dull college lecture on ancient civilization. No tears. No emotion. No apparent concern. Ice water—rather than warm blood—seemed to be coursing through her veins.

Her utter lack of reaction wasn't lost on the prosecution team, the media, or—most especially—those who would soon be deciding her fate.

••••

By the time the courtroom reassembled fifteen minutes later, Brian had regained his composure. Fuchs asked him to describe the "discovery" of Mike's boat on the lake in the early morning hours of December 17, 2000. Brian explained that he didn't want to be the one to find it—for obvious reasons. "But my dad was just really determined" and eventually motored over to the very location where Brian had pushed Mike's hunting boat to just before leaving the lake the morning before. "So we found his boat" and then told wildlife officers where it was.

Brian told jurors the next two months were "kind of a blur" with him spending "lots of time at the lake during the search because I wanted to monitor what was going on. I wanted to put up a good, you know, front, to look like I was out there looking like everybody else."

Fuchs asked him about the camouflage hat Alton Ranew plucked out of the water on December 30. Brian admitted to planting it, telling jurors he and Denise had been getting concerned nothing had been found to confirm Mike had been in the water. "And I was hoping that his waders and jacket and all would be found to kind of confirm that he had drowned there."

After several days without the waders and jacket being found, he testified, he was on a boat with a friend. When his friend wasn't looking, Brian planted the hat very close to the spot where he had shot Mike.

Though Fuchs didn't ask him directly, if asked, Brian would have testified that the waders and jacket discovered in the very same location in June 2001 weren't planted, but had been submerged in the water the entire time. Which is precisely what he told investigators when he finally broke his silence about the events of December 16, 2000.

The veteran prosecutor then pivoted to Brian's interactions with Denise after Mike's murder. His witness told jurors, "Obviously, our communication needed to be minimal, both by phone and in person. Obviously, we weren't going to be meeting up in parking lots and having sex and doing all that was normal for us to be doing." Kathy had been going to Denise's house a lot right after Mike's disappearance, he testified, and he would learn from her what was going on with Denise.

Brian also explained that he never actually told Denise he ended up shooting Mike. At first, it was his choice not to tell her, he said. "But it was quite obvious from the circumstances that Mike was gone and, you know, she assumed that what we talked about, the plan that we had made, she assumed that that was what had happened. It wasn't until years later that I tried to and somewhat told her that that's not what ended up happening."

Eventually, he testified, Denise began to worry about how she could access Mike's life insurance without a body being found. He told jurors he wasn't in a hurry for her to claim the insurance proceeds, both so as not to arouse suspicion and because, by law, the proceeds were earning eight percent interest—a rate far higher than banks were giving. His father, however, began pushing the issue due to his concern for Denise "and he wanted her to get her money so she could pay her bills." Brian told jurors they hired Curtis Hunter, a probate attorney, who filed the petition for the presumptive death certificate.

Fuchs then shifted gears to the beginning of the criminal investigation into Mike's death. Brian told jurors he was questioned by two law enforcement officers in 2004. "And it became quite clear to me during that interview that they were suspicious of what happened," he testified. "And not only that, they were suspicious of me and Denise."

He and Denise had an "agreement," he said, "that she would never say anything about me and I would never say anything about her. Because we knew or we felt like that as long as neither one of us talked that nobody would ever, you know, find out what happened. So we called it our agreement, basically. And we were probably pretty arrogantly confident in that agreement, I guess."

But both he and Denise were shaken one day, Brian testified, while Anslee was visiting with Cheryl at her grandmother's home. "Denise found a notebook that Cheryl had and she had written her suspicions about Denise and me, and what had happened with Mike. And when Cheryl was in another room or something, Denise read that. And came back and told me what she had read and really freaked out about it." That discovery, he said, is what precipitated the abrupt halt to Cheryl's visits with her granddaughter.

He and Denise also became paranoid they were being watched by law enforcement, Brian recounted, explaining they believed the Centennial Oaks home was bugged and that law enforcement officers could somehow hear them through their phones—or track their location—even if they weren't using them.

So they began speaking to each other in code, Brian said, demonstrating a "C" hand signal they employed to denote Cheryl. On other occasions, one of the two would use both hands to grasp imaginary jail bars if they wanted to discuss the investigation. He told jurors they would go to a park off of Miccosukee Road if they needed to talk "and go way out in a field on a bench," leaving their phones behind. That explained the cryptic reference in the last line of the note Denise received from "Chuck" in the Doak Campbell Stadium parking lot the prior November.

Fuchs then transitioned to the demise of Brian's relationship with Kathy, asking him if he had tried to get back together with her as Phil Padovano suggested during his opening statement. Brian acknowledged making such an attempt. After Denise caught him having sex with Angela Stafford, he testified, she was "furious ... We had a briefcase full of mementos, cards, notes, letters, pictures, videos, all sorts of things." In a fit of anger, he told the jury, Denise burned them all that very evening.

Meanwhile, Brian learned he wasn't the only one having sex outside their relationship—that Denise had been hooking up with Chuck Bunker behind his back. "And, so, when she caught me with Angela, I think she decided at that point, 'Well, I'm going to drop Brian and pursue a relationship with Mr. Bunker.' And so things just, basically, like went to hell with me and Denise. And long story short, I mean, I just realized what a disaster my life was at that point."

Brian shared details about his confrontation with Denise and Bunker in Atlanta after learning about their trip from one of Denise's sisters. He was angry, he admitted. "Because we had been through a lot. Done a lot for each other. I mean, I gave up half of my son's life to be with her, you know, *killed her husband*. And we'd done a lot to be together. And then for her to turn around and go, you know, sleep with Chuck didn't make me happy."

"And Denise told me later," he said, "that the way that she got rid of Chuck was she told him that if he didn't leave that I could have her turned in for insurance fraud." He told jurors, "It blew my mind that she told him that. I couldn't believe that she admitted that to another party."

Not long after that, Brian recounted, he had a "spiritual reawakening" while listening to a sermon at church. "And over the next few months I decided that I wanted to try to reconcile with Kathy." But he still loved Denise, whose relationship with Chuck by then had "imploded" and involved "legal issues and whatnot."

And then Denise had her own "spiritual awakening," he added. "And I know this sounds all screwy. But we wanted to be together still but we both agreed that the right thing for me to do was to try to get with Kathy. And if Kathy decided that wasn't going to happen, then we were free to be together." And so, with Denise's blessing, he did try to reconcile with Kathy. But to no avail.

Fuchs asked whether sometime later Brian and Denise had gone "public" with their relationship. "We talked about it with a lot of people," he confirmed. "There were some people that took it well. There were some people—like her family and her dad—who took it horribly." Despite that, they got married in December 2005.

After Fuchs walked Brian through the August 2016 kidnapping incident, his confession during his proffer statement, and how he assisted law enforcement officers in locating Mike's remains, he had the State's chief witness identify Denise at the defense counsel table. And with that—content he had established what was necessary to prove Denise guilty of first-degree murder—the Assistant State Attorney ended his questioning. With the clock showing 4:45 p.m., Judge Hankinson decided to send the jury home for the evening. After an action-packed, riveting first day of trial.

••••

Ethan Way had been waiting for this very moment since the day he first laid eyes on the indictment against his client. Not only for the grand stage and media spectacle—which he of course relished—but for the opportunity to shred Brian Winchester to pieces as well.

He began his cross-examination focusing on Brian's proffer agreement. "You were granted immunity for killing Mike Williams, correct?"

"I wasn't granted immunity for killing him," Brian answered, quibbling with the defense lawyer's phrasing. "I was granted immunity for what I say in court."

"As a part of the proffer agreement in the kidnapping case where you held Denise Williams at gunpoint in her car, the State agreed not to seek a life sentence in that case. Isn't that true?"

"They agreed not to seek a life sentence," Brian acknowledged, "but asked in court for me to get 45 years. So, that's pretty much a life sentence, in my opinion."

"As you sit here today, you have not been charged in the murder of Mike Williams, have you?"

"No, sir."

"You are not in prison for the murder of Mike Williams, are you?

"No, sir."

"You're in prison today because you are a two-time convicted felon. Isn't that true?"

"Yes, sir. Three times, I believe."

Denise's lawyer spent considerable time discussing with Brian the August 5, 2016, kidnapping incident, asking him to agree that he had a loaded handgun, tarp, bottles of liquid, and a tool with him—all designed to dispose of Denise's body after he killed her. Brian told him that he had a sheet, not a tarp, that the liquid in the one bottle he had was water, and that the tool Denise thought he had was actually an empty clip for the gun. And further, that he had no intention of killing his estranged wife.

"And then, as she got in her vehicle to go to work, you crawled up over the back seat and shoved a gun into her ribs, didn't you?" Way asked accusingly.

"I didn't shove a gun in her ribs," Brian told the jury. "I didn't pull the gun out until later. I had it at her side for ten seconds tops." At Way's prompting, though, he conceded he had a loaded gun, not a bouquet of flowers. He told the defense lawyer that "at some point I calmed down and realized how ridiculous this whole situation was." But acknowledged it was also criminal.

At the ensuing bond hearing, Way asserted, Denise had vigorously opposed him being released. Brian agreed she had. "But after August 5th of 2016, up until the time you were sentenced, you were in jail and you were not getting out of jail," Way declared, setting up his next question. "And Ms. Williams had made her position clear that she wanted you to be—to remain incarcerated?"

Brian pushed back on that question, telling the jury that when Denise was interviewed by the FDLE that same day, she "realized that she had opened up a can of worms with the murder that *we committed together*. You're right. She changed her position and started asking for life in prison for me." Not exactly the answer Way had anticipated.

The bearded defense lawyer then had Brian acknowledge that, thanks to the deal he made with the State, he would be eligible for release from prison in 2036. "If I survive it," the witness added, making sure jurors knew his life in prison was no picnic.

Way shifted gears to Brian's affair with Denise. "You previously indicated that you and Ms. Williams would have sex up to 15 times a week. Do you recall ever telling me that?" he asked.

Brian agreed that 15 times would have been the top end of a range he had given the defense attorney at his pretrial deposition. He also acknowledged he and Denise had sex in public places, including at the top of the Capitol, raising eyebrows among many in the gallery—including Marcus Winchester and Denise's sisters.

"But in this three-year affair that you said included sex up to 15 times a week, you have no recollection of anyone ever discovering that?" Way asked, finally getting to his point. Brian corrected him, noting that their affair lasted eight years before they were married. And that several people did find out.

Having opened the door, Denise's attorney now had to endure Brian's long-winded answer, in which he told jurors a friend and local business owner named Randy Clutcher had run into him and Denise at a strip club in Panama City. And that a good friend of his named Lance Walker figured out one day that Denise was a romantic partner. "'That's not your cousin, bro,'" Brian testified Walker had told him after he tried to convince his friend otherwise. "I'm sure there's numerous times that I'm not even aware of that we were seen or observed by people," he added.

Way then made another unforced error, suggesting it

wasn't uncommon for a person to be seen in public "with someone you've known since they were three, is it?"

"When you're married to other people," Brian retorted, "and you're going into strip clubs together, I think that's a little odd."

"Well, the strip club trip, when was that?" the defense lawyer asked.

"Which one? We went to strip clubs regularly."

Recognizing he was now precariously close to opening the door to testimony about his own client's unique sexual proclivities, Way quickly shifted gears to a new topic. He didn't want the jury to hear what Brian had told investigators during his proffer statement—that Denise's sexual appetite was "off the charts," including sex with animals. Or what he had elicited from Brian during his pretrial deposition: that though his marriage with Denise disintegrated largely due to his infidelity with prostitutes, his wife actually had no qualms with him having sex with hookers—so long as she was included in the debauchery, as she often was.

Leaving the topic of sex behind altogether, Way asked Brian, "You previously testified that Denise Williams didn't want to be a divorcée?"

"Right," Brian responded.

"Except when it came to *you*," her lawyer stated derisively. "Is that fair to say?"

"Sure," Brian agreed, a touch of sarcasm hanging over his answer.

"You've testified—or you've indicated that part of the reason why you killed Mike Williams was because you wanted to be with Denise Williams. You wanted to be with her romantically."

"Yes, sir."

"But as it came to pass, after you murdered Mike Williams, you did not, in fact, come to be with Ms. Williams exclusively. You were still married to Kathy Thomas, weren't you?"

Brian agreed, admitting his divorce with Kathy wasn't final until 2003. And that Denise was in a relationship with Chuck Bunker by then. He also acknowledged feeling "very betrayed" when Denise had gone to Atlanta with Bunker.

"Because Mr. Bunker and Ms. Williams were in a physical, intimate relationship, weren't they?" Way pressed him.

"At the same time she was in a physical, intimate relationship with me—right," Brian shot back, telling jurors they were "equal cheaters. Actually, she was first," he added, staring directly at Denise at the defense table. "I forgot."

Curiously, Way then focused on Brian's hunting trip to Arkansas with Mike just before his murder, and how his best friend had confided in him that "he was unhappy with his marriage."

"And he wanted to move out west?" the defense attorney asked.

"That was one thing that he brought up," Brian replied.

"And you didn't just tell him to go ahead and file for divorce and move out west?"

"I should have," Brian answered.

"Because, according to your testimony, a month before you killed Mike Williams, he's giving you an indication that he's frustrated in his marriage and he wants to perhaps move away. Isn't that right?"

Sensing where Way was heading with this line of questioning, Brian clarified that Mike had no intention of heading out west alone. "He was talking about *all of them*," he told jurors. As a means of repairing his marriage.

"But you didn't encourage him to do that. Instead, you killed him," Way declared, not really asking a question.

"That's what *we* did. Yes," Brian agreed, making it clear that hideous act was the result of a conspiratorial plan, not a solo mission.

Unable to restrain himself, Way then asked one question too many: "Well, 'That's what we did.' When you shot Mike Williams at Lake Seminole with a 12-gauge shotgun, was Denise Williams standing there with you?"

"No, she wasn't," Brian replied. "*She was in my head. Behind me.*" That stinging answer would be quoted in Jennifer Portman's article in the *Democrat* the following morning and played on evening news broadcasts throughout the Panhandle.

To this point, the cross-examination wasn't proceeding anywhere near how Way had planned—not even close—the witness getting the better of him, rather than vice versa. He changed subjects yet again, hoping to regain some momentum, asking Brian if he had been "obsessed" with Denise for many years. Still on a roll, Brian responded: "Denise and I were best friends. We were Bonnie and Clyde. We were partners in crime."

Shifting gears again, Way intimated there was no way Brian could have seen Mike clinging to a tree stump in the pitch darkness. But Brian responded by telling jurors he had been wearing a headlamp and could see Mike with little difficulty—and was only three feet away when he shot him in the face. He acknowledged his best friend was "yelling for help" when he pulled the trigger.

"Denise Williams had no idea that you shot her husband in the face with a shotgun, did she?" Way asked.

"Correct," Brian agreed.

"She didn't learn or would not have been able to learn that you shot her husband in the face with a shotgun until after your proffer and testimony became public?"

"Actually, I tried to tell her about it one day," Brian said, plowing new ground. "And she did not want to know the details. She told me that she assumed that obviously, when his body was never found, that what we had planned did not happen. And that it never made sense to her that I was able to get to the shoreline, but he wasn't."

Having lost control of the witness again, Way stood at the podium in frustration as Brian told jurors that, during the same conversation, Denise told him, "We were forgiven. And we were like David and Bathsheba. And God was going to forgive us. And we didn't have to tell anybody about it. As long as we asked forgiveness from God, it was okay for us not to confess it to anybody else."

Trying to recover yet again, Denise's lawyer asked, "But to be clear, you never told Denise Williams that you shot her husband?"

"She didn't let me tell her that, no," Brian agreed. "And I didn't want to tell her that."

Pivoting again, Way asked, "You finally got divorced from Kathy on March 26, 2003. Do you recall that, that final hearing?"

"Yes, sir."

He contended Brian was seated in the courtroom that day crying, one row behind Kathy, trying to stop her from going through with the divorce—just as Padovano told jurors during his opening statement. "Do you remember that?"

"I cried, yes, sir," Brian agreed. "I don't know that that's trying to stop her. But, yes, I cried. I was not happy. I was upset about it."

"But you told her you didn't want to go through with the divorce that day, didn't you?"

Brian disagreed, telling jurors he didn't tell Kathy any such thing. Rather, it was long after the divorce was granted, he testified, when he told her he wanted to give their relationship another try. "And I went to church, like I said yesterday, kind of had a spiritual reawakening. And then over the next, maybe six months or so, became convinced that I needed to try to get back with Kathy." He felt it was "the right thing to do."

Seizing on the opening he sensed Brian was providing him, Way asked, "That 'spiritual reawakening' and 'the right thing to do,' that also may cover confessing one's sins, wouldn't it?"

"Yes sir, it should," Brian agreed.

As he had done earlier, though, the defense lawyer then asked one question too many: "You didn't confess the sin of murder to anyone, did you?"

"No, *we* haven't, Brian retorted, looking directly at Denise. "I have. But *we* haven't."

Way asked whether, after his August 2016 arrest, Brian had gone straight to law enforcement to "volunteer the details of the Mike Williams murder?"

"Absolutely not," Brian answered.

"In fact, while you were in jail awaiting the resolution of your kidnapping case, you decided you were going to take certain steps to try to frustrate the prosecution of the armed kidnapping case. Isn't that true?"

"Yes, sir," he admitted. "I was desperate to do anything that I possibly could to avoid going to prison."

"And that included obstructing justice, didn't it?"

"Yes, sir," Brian agreed, acknowledging his nefarious interactions with Wade Wilson.

"Was there ever any discussion about paying Wade Wilson to kill Denise Williams?" Way asked, finally plowing new terrain.

"Wade brought up the fact that he had been a hitman in his past," Brian replied. "I think he was lying. But he did offer to make Denise 'go away' and make other witnesses in the case 'go away,'" he testified—again using his fingers to signify quotation marks. "And I said, 'Don't ever speak to me of that again.'"

"So you were drawing the line at having witnesses eliminated?" Way asked, his voice filled with sarcasm.

"Yes, sir," Brian responded.

"But you were not drawing the line at having witness testimony and other evidence fabricated?"

"Correct," Brian agreed, letting Denise's lawyer finally score a point. He also admitted he had solicited help from others along similar lines, including a woman named Kimberly Adams and his own sister Jennifer.

"You didn't want to go to prison," Way asserted. "You didn't want to pay the consequences for what you had done, did you?"

"Just like Denise, right," Brian answered, getting the upper hand yet again.

Way did get him to concede that by the summer of 2017, his attempts to obstruct justice and fabricate evidence had become known to law enforcement. "Lying was just making things worse for me," the State's witness acknowledged.

"You had a very firm judge, didn't you?"

"*Hangman Hankinson*," Brian replied with a smirk, causing the judge to chuckle. "Yes, sir." Before Way could get his next question out, Brian swiveled his chair and looked up at the judge—almost affectionately—grinning at him as if they were kids playing a prank together. For just that moment, an air of levity finally broke the tension in the courtroom. But not for long.

The defense attorney then intimated that the proffer agreement came about solely to rescue Brian from the deep hole he had dug for himself. And that his secondary motive—apart from minimizing his time in prison—was to retaliate against Denise for reporting the kidnapping incident. "You got the benefit of seeing Denise Williams arrested, locked up, and brought to trial," Way sneered.

"That's not a benefit," Brian stated.

"You got the revenge for her putting you in the same situation you wanted to put her in," Way pushed back.

"No, sir," Brian disagreed. "I wouldn't want to put anybody in this situation. She got herself in this situation."

"Well, you would put your sister in the situation of tampering with witnesses?"

"I asked her for help, yes, sir," Brian acknowledged.

Reaching what he believed was a crescendo, Way then asked his final two questions: "Mr. Winchester, you're a murderer, isn't it true?"

"Yes, sir."

"Mr. Winchester, you're a liar, isn't it true?"

"Yes, sir."

"I have nothing else, Your Honor," the defense lawyer announced, vacating the podium for Jon Fuchs to begin his redirect examination. By any measure, Way's 45-minute cross-examination hadn't lived up to his pretrial boasts to the media intimating he would disembowel the State's star witness. Rather, anyone scoring his cross-examination objectively like a prizefight would have raised Brian's arm in the air, not his. Not necessarily a knockout. But a decisive win for the witness—and the State.

••••

Jon Fuchs had just a few more things to establish before

sending his key witness on his way. He had Brian point out that, following 20 years in the clink, he would then suffer through 15 years of GPS-monitored probation. Until his 80th birthday.

The Assistant State Attorney then approached Brian with some pieces of paper, which Brian identified as concert tickets. For shows in Tallahassee he and Denise attended together—just the two of them—before and after Mike's murder, including one in October 1999.

The prosecutor then let Judge Hankinson and the defense lawyers know he had some additional exhibits to discuss with Brian—of a more sensitive nature. The judge had the jury leave the courtroom so he could hash over the admissibility of the items with the lawyers before allowing the jury to hear about them.

The exhibits were photos—shocking photos. Of Denise and Kathy in bed together—topless and wearing only panties. Hugging and kissing one another. And grabbing each other's breasts from behind. Brian's reflection was visible in a mirror in one of them. Fuchs told the judge they were taken during a trip Brian, Denise, and Kathy had gone on to Panama City without Mike, before his disappearance.

Way strenuously objected, contending the photos weren't relevant and were highly prejudicial, telling the judge they were being introduced to "inflame the jury" and appeal to jurors' "prurient interest."

Fuchs told Judge Hankinson the salacious pictures were indeed relevant, to rebut the notion—pushed by Way on cross-examination—that there were no witnesses to Brian and Denise having sex together while Mike was still alive. Though he didn't quite explain how the photos demonstrated that Kathy witnessed Brian having sex with Denise—as Brian wasn't the one fondling her—the judge, having seen far worse during his time on the bench, concluded the pictures weren't unfairly prejudicial. He allowed the prosecutor to show the majority of them to the jury.

When the jury returned to the courtroom, Fuchs walked Brian through the photos one by one, having him identify who was in the pictures—though never having him describe *what* was actually happening when they were taken. Or how what was shown in the photos related to Brian's affair with Denise.

Further complicating this show and tell, Brian was unable to recall if the photos had been taken before or after Mike's death.

In the background of one of the photos, a business named Show-N-Tail was visible. Brian testified that the establishment was the same Panama City strip joint at which he and Denise—on another occasion—had unexpectedly run into Randy Clutcher. Though it was implied that he, Kathy, and Denise had gone to the strip club during their Panama City trip, Fuchs never asked him if that was actually so.

To buttress Brian's testimony that he and Denise had discussed his attempt to reconcile with Kathy—following their divorce—Fuchs handed the witness a 17-page handwritten letter he had saved for 15 years. From Denise. A letter she had written after they had discussed his decision to try, if possible, to get back together with his now ex-wife.

The Assistant State Attorney had him read some of the letter aloud, which began: "My dear sweet, adorable, beautiful Brian. Yes, this letter is going to be sappy. I'm sitting here on Day Two, still reeling from all of this. I feel every emotion a person can feel all at one time, all the time. There are so many things I wanted to say to you. So many things that I want you to know."

In the letter, Denise also told Brian, "There are no words that can describe to you how sad I will be on Christmas and New Year's Eve. I will know for sure that what we are doing is right. But I will still miss you and be so sad." She referenced the upcoming anniversaries of Mike's disappearance on December 16th and of their wedding date on the 17th, asking Brian to "please pray extra hard for me on those days and please have your parents call me. Most everyone will not even mention it to me so I know I will need someone to talk to."

Fuchs had Brian confirm Denise had signed the letter on the last page, after telling him, "I love you more than ever."

"And, again, that is in response to you trying to get back

with Kathy?" the prosecutor asked.

"Yes, sir," Brian answered.

Fuchs then asked him to identify the date of the letter on the top right-hand corner of the first page. But Brian was unable to do so as the page had been torn off in that spot. All he could make out was Wednesday, December 10, without the year. He agreed that whatever year it was, it was when he had been attempting to reconcile with Kathy.

Though he didn't publish the entire letter to the jury at the time, the veteran prosecutor knew there were several things in those 17 pages that jurors—during their deliberations following closing arguments—would find very interesting. And most revealing. He was content to let them discover those juicy tidbits for themselves later.

Ethan Way began his re-cross examination with the pictures of his client and Kathy in bed together. Making the obvious point, he asked Brian, "Those pictures don't show Ms. Williams kissing or hugging you, do they?"

Brian disagreed, telling Way that, in one of the photos, his face was pictured as well. But he acknowledged he and Denise "weren't being intimate in those pictures." He wasn't in most of the photos, Brian testified, because he was the one taking them.

Turning to his client's letter, the defense attorney asked Brian if it could have been written as late as December 2004. Brian responded he wasn't sure.

Apparently, neither Way nor Fuchs had noticed that, on page eight of the letter, Denise referred to an upcoming phone call she planned to make on December 15, 2003—some nine months after Kathy's request for a divorce was granted. And long before Brian and Denise had gone public with their relationship. The letter was therefore consistent with Brian's earlier testimony that his attempt to reconcile with Kathy postdated their divorce.

••••

In Florida, in addition to the lawyers, jurors themselves

are permitted to ask questions of the witnesses coming before them. They do so by writing them down and handing them to the bailiff when the lawyers' examinations are complete.

Judge Hankinson learned jurors had written out several questions for Brian. After hashing out with the lawyers at a sidebar which ones would be asked, the judge asked Brian whether he and Denise had any plan to divide the life insurance proceeds once they were paid out—a pretty obvious question neither of the experienced attorneys had thought to ask.

Brian responded that Denise was the sole beneficiary of about $2.25 million—including Mike's social security survivor benefits. And that he wasn't entitled to any of it. She kept all of that in her own name, he said. "But, of course, we knew—I knew, we knew, that eventually, when we ended up together, that I would secondhand benefit, I guess you could say."

Another question from the jury was whether the insurance money had been an incentive for their plot or simply a bonus. Brian characterized the proceeds as a bonus, telling jurors he and Denise had referred to the insurance as "the icing on the cake."

••••

Brian Scott Winchester stood up—a sheriff's deputy escorting him from the witness stand—likely sucking in his last breath of air in a public setting for more than 15 years. As it turned out, he was as good a witness as the prosecution team could possibly have hoped for. His testimony was compelling—both about his affair with Denise and the murderous plot they hatched, carried out, and then covered up. There was little doubt he had held the jury's attention during his hours of testimony—his credibility enhanced by his palpable emotional turmoil over what he had done, and the havoc he had wreaked on so many lives.

As Phil Padovano had made clear during his opening statement, Denise's defense hinged on establishing that Brian couldn't be trusted or believed. That he had fabricated his

story about having an affair with Denise as well as her participation in Mike's murder. With Brian's captivating testimony
now complete, however, the defense team had little reason
to believe any real headway had been made in those regards.
And if that were so, there was only one witness left who could
possibly convince jurors that Brian was lying. Perhaps Denise
Merrell (Winchester) Williams would testify after all.

16

Sprint to the Finish

No fewer than 13 additional prosecution witnesses would be called to the witness stand that Wednesday after the State's star witness was led out the back door in handcuffs and shackles—each one there to corroborate various aspects of Brian's testimony. The witnesses entered and exited the courtroom so quickly, it was a wonder they weren't wearing track shoes.

Dr. Stephen Mnookin told jurors about the desperate call he received from Brian on August 5, 2016, and their lunch following the kidnapping incident that led to the unraveling of Brian and Denise's pact of silence.

The anesthesiologist recounted his conversation with Brian in which his friend of 12 years told him the police had come by his home the day before to inform him they had been talking with Denise. The law enforcement officers suggested to Brian, Mnookin testified, that once his divorce from Denise became final, his ex-wife would surely spill her guts about what really happened to Mike Williams.

That interaction made Brian edgy and nervous, his friend said, prompting him to call Denise several times on August 4 to test what the investigators had asserted. But she wouldn't answer. "So he decided the best way to talk to her would be to kidnap her," the doctor told jurors.

Andy Rogers asked if Brian had told him Denise "was aware of something going on with the disappearance of Mike

Williams?"

"Yes," Mnookin replied, suggesting that was precisely what led to Brian kidnapping her, so that he could discuss with her that very issue. During cross-examination, however, he backtracked a bit, conceding that he didn't know whether Brian had actually been visited by the police at all.

Howard Drew, Mike's hunting mentor and Rachel Drew's dad, took the stand next. With his wire-rimmed glasses, bald head, and long, white bushy beard, Drew bore an uncanny resemblance to the Jolly Old Elf from the North Pole—making a public appearance a full two weeks ahead of schedule. His good humor and wit added a much-needed touch of levity to the proceedings.

Drew told jurors that a teenaged Mike had called him one summer afternoon excited about purchasing a pair of waders. He was concerned, however, that his pupil might have gotten in a little over his head, describing the situation as "very serious" because "many a good man and woman went to the bottom in a pair of waders." He explained how quickly waders can fill with water and, when that occurs, how most hunters panic, which can quickly lead to their demise.

He testified that he "rushed right on over" to Cheryl's home to teach Mike how to use the waders safely. He spent several hours at the backyard pool that afternoon showing Mike how to free himself from the waders should he ever happen to fall overboard with them on. He started the teenager out in the shallow end of the pool and eventually had him in the deep end, practicing over and over how to get the waders off without panicking.

Mike was an "easy learner," Drew testified, and quickly got the knack of performing the Houdini-like feat while underwater. His testimony corroborated Brian's testimony that Mike had freed himself of his waders at Lake Seminole—just before his best friend shot and killed him.

Lindsay (Ketcham) Lockhart—Clay and Patti Ketcham's daughter—and her friend Angela Stafford were each asked questions intended to corroborate Brian's testimony that his affair with Denise began some three years before Mike's murder. Both women testified they attended a Sister Hazel concert at Floyd's Music Store in the fall of 1997 with Mike, Denise and Brian—but not Kathy. It was unclear from their testimony if this was same night Brian testified his romantic relationship with Denise began—as his testimony was that Kathy attended the Sister Hazel concert on that particular evening.

Lockhart testified that she, Mike, and Angela were at the bar "and I looked over and saw Brian and Denise together. And Brian was standing behind Denise with his arms around her waist. And it struck me as very odd because Mike was married to Denise." She said it "seemed like a new love. Like a boyfriend-girlfriend type position they were in." The following day, when her parents asked her how the concert went, she told them, "'If I didn't know any better, I would have thought Brian was married to Denise and not Mike.'"

She also noticed Mike drinking at the concert a lot more than he had in the past, so much so that he asked her not to mention it to her father—his boss.

"How long did it take for Mike to get over there and punch Brian in the face?" Way asked her, somewhat sarcastically, after the podium was passed to him for cross-examination.

Lockhart responded that Mike neither punched Brian in the face nor confronted him in any way.

Stafford recalled Brian and Denise being "very touchy, very hands on with each other, arms around each other," and that their overly friendly behavior occurred right in front of Mike, who was drinking mixed drinks—something she had never seen him do before.

She also testified about her 2004 sexual liaison with Brian at his home—following his divorce from Kathy—after the two went out for drinks at a gay bar. "In the middle of the intimacy," she told the jury, "Denise walked into the bedroom."

When Denise saw the two of them in the throes of passion, she "ran out. Brian got up and put a pair of pants on and ran out after her." Though Brian tried to persuade her the woman who interrupted their festivities wasn't Denise, she was certain it was. And Brian later admitted she was correct.

••••

After the lunch break, the State called a trio of witnesses intended to corroborate Brian's testimony about how he had killed and buried Mike. Jason Newlin, an investigator with the State Attorney's Office, told the jury how Brian—immediately after giving his second proffer statement in October 2017—led investigators to the spot at Carr Lake where he buried Mike.

William Schwoob, the FDLE crime lab supervisor, described the joint efforts between his agency and Leon County Public Works to drain and clear the part of the lakebed where Mike's remains were ultimately found. He told jurors about the laborious, six-day process through which what was left of Mike's body was finally unearthed.

It was through Schwoob that the prosecution team was able to introduce one of its most powerful pieces of evidence—Mike's gold wedding band, still in a plastic evidence bag, which Fuchs had the bailiff pass to each juror for a closer look.

Through Lisa Flannagan, the Medical Examiner, Andy Rogers showed jurors X-rays of Mike's bullet-ridden skull, forearms, and hands, a photo of the shotgun pellets and plastic shot cup pulled from his skull, and grisly images of his jaw-bone, teeth, and skull fragments. Flannagan testified that she concluded the cause of death was a shotgun blast to Mike's face from close range.

Next up was a pair of witnesses covering the subject of life insurance. Timothy Langland, associate general counsel of Kansas City Life, walked jurors through Mike's April 15, 2000 application for a $1 million KCL policy—signed by Brian as "writing agent"—and Denise's January 4, 2001, claim form seeking payment on both that policy and an earlier $250,000 policy, signed by both Denise and Brian. Rogers projected onto the screen images of the two checks KCL issued to Denise in 2001, totaling over $1.3 million.

Chad Carpenter, a claims manager at Country Life—the company that acquired Cotton States in 2004—testified about Mike's $500,000 Cotton States policy, Denise's claim form, and the check issued to Denise. Between the payout on the two

KCL policies and Cotton States policy, the jury learned, Mike's widow had been paid a total of $1,831,477.86.

Jon Fuchs then called a pair of law enforcement witnesses—first FDLE Special Agent Will Mickler and then Florida State Police Sergeant Richard Wooten.

Mickler described the "bump" in the Florida State parking lot between an undercover FDLE agent and Denise. The incident, he told jurors, was coordinated with Sergeant Wooten. After Wooten informed Denise the FDLE had taken over the investigation, Mickler testified, he called Denise repeatedly, but she never returned his calls. He also told jurors Kathy Thomas had become a "confidential source" for the FDLE and described the instructions and equipment she had been supplied to attempt to obtain incriminating information from Denise.

Surprisingly, despite the FDLE agent's significant involvement in the case, Fuchs completed his questioning in just 12 minutes without asking the officer a single question about his interaction with Denise on her front doorstep the morning of December 20, 2017—when he informed her that her long-lost husband's remains had been found. Jurors wouldn't get to learn about Denise's odd reaction to that news.

During his cross-examination, Ethan Way did his level best to dirty up Mickler—and the FDLE. He got the special agent to agree that Sergeant Wooten was the "lead investigator into a nonexistent crime" which was "basically a lie" to his client.

The defense attorney questioned Mickler about the note placed on Denise's vehicle. "It was a setup," Way declared. "It was a fictitious letter that was written with the efforts to try to facilitate something out of this bump, wasn't it?"

"Yes, sir," Mickler agreed.

"Did anyone give any thought to the idea that approaching a woman who'd been kidnapped at gunpoint less than a year before, approaching her in a menacing manner at her place of employment, was a pretty cruel thing to try to do?"

"I don't believe the approach was menacing," the agent pushed back. "But that was not considered," he acknowledged. "No, sir."

"Just didn't think about how she would react to what you were doing," Way pressed.

"No, sir," Mickler conceded.

In his brief redirect examination, Fuchs asked his witness if Denise had maintained constant communications with the Florida State Police during its fictitious investigation of the parking lot incident.

"That's my understanding, yes sir," Mickler replied.

"And as soon as she found out the Florida Department of Law Enforcement was assuming the investigation, she stopped communication, did she not?"

"With me, yes."

As Mickler was stepping down from the witness stand, Sergeant Wooten came barreling through the courtroom door which, based on the speed with which witnesses were coming and going, could easily have been mistaken for a revolving door.

The campus police officer explained to jurors that he became involved in the "investigation" of the Doak Campbell Stadium parking lot "incident" as part of a coordinated plan with the FDLE. Denise reached out to him on a near-daily basis, he testified, "asking what we've done and that sort of thing," noting she wanted his office to identify the "perpetrator" as quickly as possible.

He ultimately told Denise the case was being reassigned to the FDLE's "cyber-crimes people" and that Agent Will Mickler would be contacting her. Wooten testified that, during the course of the fictitious investigation, he never had any trouble communicating with Denise.

Upon cross-examination, Way had the officer confirm that Denise seemed "genuinely scared and concerned about what happened to her" even though what happened was "a lie," nothing more than an "investigative setup by the FDLE." Even his description of Special Agent Mickler being with the FDLE's cyber-crimes unit, Wooten acknowledged, was untruthful.

And just like that, a mere seven minutes after taking his seat at the witness stand, the campus police officer was on his way out the door.

The final law enforcement witness to testify was Joni Chase, a retired Tallahassee Police officer who spent 24 years with the TPD prior to her 2013 retirement. Fuchs asked her about an evening she had been on patrol in December 1999, when she spotted a large SUV at the Grace Lutheran Church parking lot off Miccosukee Road — a couple of miles from Mike and Denise's Centennial Oaks home. Chase testified the vehicle was the only one in the parking lot and that she noticed a baby car seat in the back seat.

Because she suspected the vehicle might be stolen, Chase explained, she asked TPD dispatch officers to run the license plate. They were able to give her a phone number for its owner. She dialed that number and spoke with a female. While on the phone, the woman identified the vehicle and license plate number.

The woman told her the truck belonged to her husband, who she said was out of state on a hunting trip — or at least believed he was — telling the officer, "It shouldn't be there." Later that evening, the retired officer told jurors, she was visited at the police station by someone who claimed to be the father of the vehicle's owner, who said he had gone to the church to look for the SUV, but found it was no longer there.

Due to the passage of time and purging of records, Chase testified she couldn't recall the names of anyone involved with the incident — though it seemed clear enough that the owner of the vehicle in question was Brian Winchester, the woman she spoke with that evening was his wife Kathy, and the man who came to the police station was his father Marcus.

When Way declined to cross-examine Officer Chase, she raced off the witness stand. Her testimony was so brief, just four minutes, that its significance — corroborating Brian's testimony that he sometimes parked in church parking lots to avoid detection during his secret trysts with Denise — was likely missed by all but the most attentive jurors.

••••

The jury would hear next from Mike's older brother Nick. During his brief direct examination, Fuchs had him describe the two incidents in which Denise had threatened to withhold Anslee from him and Cheryl if she didn't halt her pursuit of a criminal investigation. Nick told jurors the second incident—in his mother's kitchen in January 2005—occurred in the midst of the FDLE's investigation into Mike's disappearance. Indeed, Derrick Wester had interviewed Brian in November 2004 and Denise in late December—less than three weeks before the January 2005 confrontation. The jury, unfortunately, would never learn those important details.

Nick recalled Denise being angry as she sat across the kitchen table from Cheryl, saying, "'Why are you lying about this? Why are you telling all these lies about us all over town? And we want it to stop.'" With Brian looking on, he testified, Denise told them, "'Anslee and I love you, but, you know, you're not going to see her anymore if you don't get this investigation stopped.'"

Way tried to change the subject in his cross-examination, asking Nick, "Your brother loved Denise, didn't he?"

"He did," the witness replied.

"Worshiped her?"

"Yes," Nick agreed. "From everything he told us, he did."

"Absolutely. There was nothing that ever suggested to you that there was any trouble or any worries between Denise and Mike?"

"Not that he told us."

"And Mike loved his little girl?"

"Yeah. He did worship her."

Way asked him if the February 2001 memorial service for his brother was an opportunity for those who loved him to have a certain type of closure. Nick agreed. He also agreed that many of the people who knew and loved Mike, by then, believed he was no longer alive. And that Denise needed to move on with the task of raising Anslee as a single mother.

"Would it be fair to say that your mother believed, up until as recently as December of 2017, that your brother was going to come home one day, didn't she?"

"She held out every hope that he was alive somehow," Nick confirmed.

"And she was not shy about expressing her belief that your brother was going to walk in the door one day?"

"Correct."

Way questioned him about whether he believed Anslee was too young to be told by her grandmother that her dad would someday walk back through the front door of their home. "Isn't it also fair to think that Anslee needs to be protected, perhaps, from the thought that her father could walk through that door when almost everyone else has thought he died?" he asked.

"I'm not sure," Nick answered. "We just wanted the truth."

"But since there's no set way to grieve with something," Way probed, "wouldn't it be also fair from the facts that Ms. Williams had an obligation to protect her daughter?"

"She did what she thought was right," Nick agreed.

Content with that answer, Way abruptly ended his questioning.

Fuchs, however, wasn't about to allow him to end Nick's examination on that note. "You and your mom never saw her in 2005, did you?" he asked his witness, the "her" referring to Anslee.

"We did not," Nick responded. "We were never allowed another visit after 2005." He also explained that Denise didn't complain to them about Cheryl filling Anslee's head with the idea her father was still alive and would return.

"No conversation like we're having right now," Fuchs asked, "of, 'Ms. Cheryl, I can't have you saying that around her. It's hard on her. If you want to believe it, that's fine?'"

Nick told the jury that Denise never said any such thing. Rather, her position was to "stop the investigation or else." And the "or else" was that he and his mom would never get to see Mike's daughter again.

Fuchs closed on an even stronger note, asking Nick, "Whenever it was determined that Mike had been murdered in December 2017, did she reach out to you and try to facilitate a conversation between y'all and Anslee?"

"No."

"Never said 'I'm sorry?'"

"No," Nick answered, making clear his view that his sister-in-law's decision to withhold Anslee from them had nothing at all to do with protecting his niece and everything to do with protecting *Denise*.

••••

With Nick's testimony complete, the stage was finally set for Cheryl Ann Williams to take the stand. It had been nearly 18 years since she had begun her relentless crusade to find her son. It was her tenacity and persistence—when virtually everyone around her believed she was crazy—that had led inexorably to this very moment.

But as she came through the courtroom door that Wednesday afternoon, Cheryl was nowhere near content she had fulfilled her mission. That wouldn't come until justice was finally served. As the next-to-last witness for the prosecution, she was just about close enough to touch that elusive, amorphous ideal. And prayed with every ounce of her slight, fragile body the jury would soon deliver it.

Too frail to walk on her own power, the 74-year-old grandmother was wheeled into the courtroom and up to the witness stand. She had her gray hair pulled into her trademark pigtails with black hair ties wrapped around them. Her wheelchair sat so low in the witness box, her head barely protruded above the walls of the wooden structure, framed on either side by the red handles of her wheelchair.

As she introduced herself, Cheryl told the jury she had been running her home daycare service for 50 years. Fuchs quickly turned to the subject of her missing son, asking if she had taken steps to initiate an investigation into Mike's disappearance, including putting up posters and billboards and writing to the Governor. Cheryl agreed she had. She also told jurors about the August 2001 confrontation in Denise's front yard about the missing-person article published in the *Tallahas-*

see Democrat.

"She was screaming at me," Cheryl recounted. "She was mad about the article. And she said, screaming at me, 'I don't *ever* want to hear Mike's name again. I don't *ever* want to see Mike's picture in the paper again. I don't *ever* want to know anything you're doing about Mike again. I have to get on with my life.'" That was the first occasion, she testified, when Denise had threatened to withhold Anslee from her.

The second occasion was on January 8, 2005. She recalled the date because it was the day before her birthday. She sincerely believed Denise was coming over with Anslee as a birthday surprise, rather than to tell her she would never see her granddaughter again. Cheryl explained that she hadn't seen Anslee since Halloween.

Her description of the incident was consistent with Nick's account, but she added that Brian played an active role and even screamed at her to "shut your mouth." Denise was crying, she told jurors, when she said, "'Cheryl, if you will just stop this investigation, you can see Anslee again." Not only did Cheryl tell her she wouldn't stop the investigation—even if she could—she recounted for jurors that Nick accused Denise and Brian of having done something to Mike. It was at that point, she testified, the two stormed out the door.

"Did you ever see Anslee again?" Fuchs asked.

"Never seen her since," Cheryl replied sadly. "Not in my house."

At that point, Fuchs handed her an eight-by-ten photo of Mike—the same one that for years had been plastered on missing-person posters, billboards, and Cheryl's picket signs, as well as on the poster board at the FDLE press conference the day Mark Perez announced that Mike had been murdered. The veteran prosecutor projected Mike's image onto the screen, the only picture of Mike's face—while alive—that jurors would ever see. And the closest the prosecution team would come to informing them of his compelling biography.

Phil Padovano drew the unenviable task of handling Cheryl's cross-examination. He wisely treated Mike's mom gingerly, not wanting to create the specter of the defense team beating up on a 74-year-old woman who had fought for justice so tirelessly. He had her confirm that, by the time Denise confronted her in August 2001, a circuit judge had already declared Mike dead and that a memorial service had already been held. Cheryl agreed with the retired judge that Denise would have had to explain to Anslee that her dad wouldn't be coming home.

As for the second confrontation in January 2005, he asked Cheryl if Denise had been innocent "and thought that you were accusing her of doing something to your son, do you think it would be logical for her to be upset with you?"

"If she were innocent, yes," Cheryl agreed, leaving the unmistakable impression she believed no such thing.

Under Padovano's questioning, the pigtailed grandmother confirmed that her son Mike was "a good father, a good husband, and a good provider." She told jurors she thought his relationship with his wife was "good" and agreed they "got along." She even told jurors she loved Denise.

Fuchs again took advantage of his opportunity to ask a few questions on redirect, having Cheryl confirm she became aware the FDLE had located Mike's remains and concluded he had been murdered before the information was shared with the news media.

"How long did it take before Denise called you and said, 'I'm sorry, I was wrong all these years?'" he asked.

"She never did."

"How long did it take before she called you and said, 'Hey, I'm sorry, maybe I need to help you see your granddaughter again?'"

"She never did," Cheryl repeated.

"So from the day that she threatened you to stop the investigation—the day before your birthday—you've never seen your granddaughter?"

"No," Cheryl replied with a slight shake of her head, her painful answer hanging uncomfortably in the air as Fuchs told Judge Hankinson, "No further questions."

For 18 solid years, Cheryl Ann Williams had fought for justice. With all her might. Shockingly, in the end, her tireless crusade would translate into all of 15 minutes on the witness stand—less than one minute per year.

Perhaps even more shockingly, for some reason, Fuchs didn't ask either Cheryl or Nick about the last time they had seen Mike alive—the Thursday evening they had been with Denise, Mike, and Anslee watching *Friends*. Because on that occasion, Denise and Mike both made clear he was going hunting that Saturday morning *with Brian*—contrary to what Denise told her father that Saturday afternoon when Mike hadn't come home, to what she swore under penalty of perjury in her petition to have Mike declared dead, and to what she had told insurers as she sought payment on his life insurance policies.

Nor was Cheryl asked about her discussion with Denise that Sunday—after Mike went missing—when her daughter-in-law told her Mike had awakened her very early that Saturday morning to let her know that Brian had cancelled on him and that he was forging ahead alone. To prove Denise had been complicit with Brian, those two facts seemed of critical importance. Yet as Cheryl was wheeled out of the courtroom, any chance the jury would ever hear about them rolled out the door as well.

••••

The prosecution team saved its second most significant witness for last: Brian's first wife Kathy Thomas, who flew into Tallahassee from her new home in the North Carolina mountains, the first witness to testify that Thursday morning.

Apart from Cheryl Williams and Jennifer Portman, no other person had provided more valuable assistance toward the efforts to discover what had happened to Mike. For nearly four years, despite Brian's incessant threats about embarrassing pictures and videos—and his efforts to intimidate her about what would happen to their son Stafford if he were charged with Mike's murder—Kathy had cooperated fully with the FDLE, helping investigators learn that Brian had no alibi for the morning of the murder and wanted his ex-wife to fabricate one for him.

Following Brian's arrest, proffer statements, and sentencing, once again, it was Kathy who would become the FDLE's critical confidential source whose phone call with Denise in February 2018 tipped the scales sufficiently for murder charges to be brought against her lifelong friend. And now, days away from the 18th anniversary of Mike's disappearance, Brian's first wife sat at the witness stand, there for one singular purpose—to convince the jury to convict his second wife of murder.

From the outset of her testimony, it was evident Kathy was nervous and uncomfortable—the gravity of the moment, and everything that had transpired over the past three decades, weighing on her heavily. She told jurors that she had known Mike since the fifth grade at NFC and met both Denise and Brian when they enrolled there for high school. Her romantic relationship with Brian began when they were juniors, she testified. The foursome did lots of "couple things" together, she said. She told the jury she and Brian separated on September 11, 2001 and were finally divorced in April 2003.

"Did you suspect that Brian Winchester, your husband, was having an affair with Denise Williams?" Andy Rogers asked.

"I did suspect that," she answered.

The Assistant State Attorney asked her about the December 1999 parking lot incident Officer Chase described during her testimony. Kathy told jurors the Tallahassee Police officer was standing next to Brian's truck when she called, telling her the vehicle was in the Grace Church parking lot. Chase even described the bumper stickers on it. Kathy confirmed to the officer it was their vehicle. She told the jury she was confused "because I had been told by Brian that he was in Arkansas with the truck hunting."

At Rogers' prompting, Kathy confirmed that Grace Church was very close to Mike and Denise's Centennial Oaks home. Which implied strongly that Brian was with Denise that evening, not shooting prey in Arkansas.

The prosecutor then shifted to a new line of questioning, about the Panama City trip Brian had described in his testimony. Kathy told the jury the entire foursome was supposed to go on that trip to celebrate Denise's 30th birthday—in either March or April of 2000. Mike and Denise, she said, were going to meet her and Brian at their home and all four planned to drive together to Panama City.

But Denise showed up without Mike, she testified. At that point, Kathy told Denise and Brian, "'If Mike doesn't have to go, I don't have to go either.' I didn't want to go. And I had, I guess, sort of a little tantrum and I ran inside and I locked myself in the bathroom and I said, 'I'm not going.'" She told the jury she didn't want to go with Denise and Brian "because at that point in our lives, whenever it was just me with Brian and Denise, it was uncomfortable. I felt like a third wheel. I felt like I was on a date with the two of them." Somehow, though, Brian and Denise persuaded her to go.

She told jurors, clearly embarrassed, that the three of them went to a strip club and that photographs were taken of her she recalled seeing only much later. Rogers didn't show her the photos, however, letting jurors conclude on their own they were the same ones that had been passed through the jury box during Brian's testimony.

Kathy testified that she saw movie tickets in Brian's wallet for *The Virgin Suicides*, which made her believe he had taken Denise to see the movie. She also testified about a receipt from the Gold Center she had found in Brian's office for a necklace that included a charm with the name "Meridian"—which she told jurors was Denise's "party-girl" nickname. The receipt was dated July 28, 2001.

The junior prosecutor then fast-forwarded to August 2016, after Brian had been arrested for kidnapping Denise. He asked her, "About a week after that incident, that kidnapping, did Denise ask you to do something?"

"Yes," she replied.

"What did she ask you to do?"

Kathy responded that Denise "wanted me to tell Marcus to tell Brian that she wasn't talking."

Rogers then had Kathy confirm that she was cooperating with FDLE Agents Mickler and DeVaney and used audio equipment they supplied to record calls with Denise. For the next 25 minutes, the jury—and everyone in the courtroom—listened to the entirety of her emotional February 2018 conversation with Denise, the one in which she accused her lifelong friend of having had an affair with Brian while Mike was still alive and of having been involved in his murder.

When the audio recording ended, the Assistant State Attorney had her confirm that the other voice on the recording belonged to Denise and had her point to the defendant at the defense counsel table. He then passed the witness to Way for cross-examination.

The defense lawyer had Kathy admit that she lied to Denise when she told her she had received a subpoena to come to the State Attorney's Office—as part of a script she was given by the FDLE. He then asked if she actually knew that Denise and Brian had been having an affair.

"I never caught them kissing or—I never saw with my own eyes them specifically in a physical embrace," she agreed. "No, sir. I never caught them."

"You don't know if they were having an affair as a fact?"

"I never caught them in the act. That is correct," she acknowledged.

Way also tried to get her to admit she had no idea whether Brian had taken Denise to see *The Virgin Suicides*. To which she responded, "Brian told me that he took Denise to the movie." She told the jury she had no idea Brian had taken her until she found the tickets and confronted him.

Denise's lawyer then pivoted to the Panama City trip. He plopped the photographs Brian had testified about down in front of her and had her go through them one by one. Though embarrassed, Kathy confirmed the photos were of her and Denise having a good time together.

When Kathy completed her testimony, Judge Hankinson announced that several jurors had questions. The first was whether anything stuck in her memory about either Denise's or Brian's behavior the day Mike disappeared.

Kathy replied that she never saw Denise that day, but spoke to her on the phone around lunchtime, when Denise told her that Mike hadn't come home yet and that she was "looking for him." As for Brian, she testified "the plan was that he would get back from hunting and we would leave and go together to my family Christmas party in Cairo, Georgia." When he hadn't returned by 2:00 p.m., she told jurors, she couldn't wait any longer and headed to Georgia without him.

Another question from the jury was whether Denise appeared "emotionally distraught" about Mike's disappearance in late 2000 or early 2001. Kathy responded that she "did not seem distraught. In those days after Mike was gone, I could remember saying to Brian—"

Before she could utter another word, the judge cut her off, saying, "I think you answered the question."

Kathy's facial expressions and body language suggested she was about to testify that she recalled telling Brian that something about Denise's behavior seemed suspicious. But when Judge Hankinson offered Andy Rogers a chance to ask more questions, he didn't have his witness complete her thought. Instead, before Kathy could rise up from her seat, Fuchs announced that the State was resting its case—less than 48 hours after calling its first witness.

••••

In their haste to present their case, the prosecutors had omitted key pieces of evidence that could have added significantly to their narrative of Denise's involvement in Mike's murder and that could have destroyed two important defense themes.

For instance, Kathy could have been asked about her and Deanna Lamb's unsuccessful search at Mike and Denise's home for any sign of packed bags the day after Mike disappeared. That evidence was nearly as incriminating as her February 2018 telephone conversation with Denise. And would have been all the more incriminating once the jury learned that a suitcase mysteriously appeared at the bottom of the staircase that Sunday evening. Both Clay and Patti Ketcham would have been glad to tell jurors about the mysterious piece of luggage—had the prosecution team called either to testify.

Perhaps even more surprisingly, the State didn't call Derrick Wester as a witness, even though he had been the first law enforcement officer to speak with Denise following Mike's disappearance—nearly 12 years before Agent Mike DeVaney. Denise had admitted to Wester that her romantic relationship with Brian had begun in April or May of 2001—a mere four to five *months* after her husband had vanished.

That fact alone would have would have obliterated the defense team's contention that the romance between the two began *years* after Mike's disappearance. And would have established quite convincingly that there *had* been an illicit affair between Denise and Brian—as he was still married to Kathy at the time. From there, it wouldn't have been a significant leap for the jury to conclude that Denise had been cheating on Mike every bit as much as Brian was cheating on Kathy.

Another witness the State didn't call was Tallahassee Police Officer Dave McCranie, Denise's brother-in-law. That was particularly surprising because Fuchs referred to McCranie by name during his opening statement, telling jurors Denise had reported the kidnapping incident to law enforcement only because McCranie had implored her to do so.

By not calling McCranie as a witness, the prosecution team had no comeback to what Ethan Way was sure to argue during his closing—why would Denise report Brian to law enforcement if she had been hiding a dark secret about her own involvement in Mike's murder? That would have made no sense, Way would inevitably tell jurors. Yet without any testimony from McCranie, the State wouldn't be able to respond to that argument and explain that Denise wouldn't have gone to law enforcement had it not been for the intervention of her brother-in-law.

Finally, during Brian's direct examination, he was never asked specifically what Denise had actually done to further the commission of Mike's murder. Because she had been charged as a "principal" to a premeditated murder, it wasn't enough for the State to establish that Denise knew of and agreed with the plan for Mike to be killed. The law required her to do something active to be charged as a principal. And during cross-examination, Mike DeVaney told Ethan Way he wasn't aware of anything Denise had done in that realm.

Yet Brian had told investigators in his October 12, 2017, proffer statement that Denise *had* done something active which led directly to her husband being killed. Mike needed "extra permission" from Denise, he told them, to go hunting that morning because the two were leaving for their anniversary trip that afternoon. "And so Denise and I had discussed and planned that she was going to have to make him feel like he was not going to be in trouble for going on that particular day," Brian had said in that statement. "So she specifically had to encourage him that, 'hey, it's okay, it's fine. You go ahead and go, uh, you know, I'm good with it.'"

But no such words came out of Brian's mouth during his testimony before the jury—when it really mattered. Indeed, he wasn't specifically asked whether Denise played an active role to ensure that Mike went on the hunting trip. The lack of any trial testimony on that point provided the defense team a golden opportunity to contend during closing arguments—and if necessary, on appeal—that no evidence had been offered which could establish Denise's guilt for being a principal actor in Mike's murder.

For whatever reason, at the time Jon Fuchs announced that the State's evidence was complete, these particular witnesses and facts didn't make the cut. Time would tell whether their omission would prove significant enough to allow Denise to walk out of the courtroom a free woman.

••••

As it turned out, the blazing speed of the State's case would pale in comparison to the rocket-like burst of the defense's evidence. Indeed, if jurors hadn't been paying close attention, they would have missed that evidence altogether—as the defense team's witnesses were on and off the witness stand in just 18 minutes.

Probate attorney Curtis Hunter testified about the process

through which he had assembled the June 2001 petition to have Mike declared dead. During cross-examination, he agreed that in Florida presumptive death certificates are very rare and even more unusual if the person involved is still missing. He acknowledged that he knew nothing at all about the existence of the Cotton States life insurance policy because Denise had never told him about it. He also conceded he was never told that Denise had tried to collect on the Kansas City Life policy prior to her initial contact with him.

Jimmy Martin, who Denise dated in 2003 prior to Chuck Bunker, testified next. He told jurors that he had been friends with Mike since kindergarten and had become particularly close to Brian just before his 2016 arrest. The two fished and rode mountain bikes together, he testified. His last contact with Brian had been in July 2016, just weeks before he was taken into custody for kidnapping Denise. Brian seemed to be in good spirits then, he said. He also testified that he believed Mike and Denise "had a very happy marriage" and that Mike seemed "absolutely thrilled" to be married to her.

The defense then called FDLE Agent Mike Phillips. He told jurors that he had no recollection of seeing Brian at the Walmart the day Mike went missing—the defense's attempt to tear a hole in Brian's story. He went to Lake Seminole the following Monday, he said, to join in the search and recalled bumping into Brian then. At that time, as best as he could remember, Brian hadn't mentioned to him that the two had seen each other at the Walmart just a few days before. Phillips also testified that seeing Brian at Lake Seminole didn't jog his memory about any encounter at the Walmart. Yet during cross-examination, he acknowledged that he couldn't recall anything of significance from December 16, 2000.

••••

Phil Padovano had forecast during his opening statement that the jury would be hearing from a financial advisor named Dick Gainey, who had been pushing Mike to get life insurance. Gainey, however, never walked through the courtroom door.

The retired jurist had also told jurors they would be hearing from Chuck Bunker—whose name they had heard referenced repeatedly by other witnesses. Yet Bunker would never enter the courtroom either. Why neither of these gentlemen were called as witnesses wasn't clear.

That left just one question everyone in the courtroom—and throughout Tallahassee—was dying to know the answer to: would the defendant testify in her own defense? Would she walk up to the witness stand, place her hand on the Bible, face the jury, and answer questions about her marriage to Mike, her relationship with Brian, and about the events surrounding her husband's disappearance? Only one person alive had knowledge of whether Brian's testimony about those subjects was true or false.

It stood to reason that Denise Merrell (Winchester) Williams had every incentive to take the stand and forcefully deny that she had any knowledge Brian was going to kill her husband. But would she?

17

Curtain Down

In his very first interview with the *Democrat*'s Jennifer Portman, Ethan Way had all but guaranteed that his client would take the witness stand in her own defense, telling the journalist, "I'm certain when a jury hears from Denise Williams, and the facts come out, the inescapable conclusion is that Brian Winchester killed Mike Williams." Alone. Yet as the clock neared 11:30 that Thursday morning, it was beginning to look far less likely the defendant would be placing her hand on the Bible after all.

Under the Fifth Amendment to the Constitution, Denise had the absolute right not to testify—the privilege against self-incrimination the bedrock foundation of the American criminal justice system. And she certainly wouldn't have been the first murder defendant to take advantage of that protection. Not hardly. Indeed, murder defendants rarely take the stand, knowing that if they do, they will surely face a withering cross-examination about the very worst aspects of their lives with questions that box them into corner after corner—even if they are truly innocent. The risk of taking the stand is typically greater than any potential reward.

Yet this was hardly a typical murder case—Denise a most atypical murder defendant. The prosecution's evidence against her wasn't circumstantial in the least. Rather, it was based almost exclusively on Brian Winchester's testimony that

Denise had plotted the murder with him so they could continue their affair without Mike in the way. And also, so they could
reap the reward of nearly $2 million in life insurance—most of
which he had procured.

What's more, Brian's testimony had been compelling, jurors hanging on his every word, his raw emotion making virtually everything he said seem believable. In many ways, what
he told jurors was corroborated by other witnesses—especially
Lindsay Lockhart, Angela Stafford, Officer Chase, and Kathy
Thomas. Moreover, Cheryl and Nick Williams' testimony
about Denise's threats, and her withholding Anslee from them
as retribution for not pulling the plug on the investigation, left
jurors with little reason to doubt her guilty mind—or cruel
heart.

Had Way destroyed Brian's credibility during his cross-
examination—and made clear to jurors he was lying—there
would have been little need for Denise to take the risk inher-
ent in testifying. But that simply wasn't the case. Though the
seasoned defense lawyer did his level best to disembowel the
State's star witness, it was actually Brian who had gotten the
better of him, rather than the other way around. And not a single defense witness had cast any real doubt on Brian's central
testimony about Denise helping him plot and then cover up
Mike's murder.

Thus, the entire case largely boiled down to a classic "he
said-she said" battle over the truth. Without there being a "she
said" component to that battle, the jury would literally be left
with only one side of the story. To have any real chance of
walking out of the courtroom a free woman, Denise had to
swallow hard, gird herself for whatever would come her way,
and do the best she could to persuade the jury that Brian's testimony had been unadulterated fiction.

••••

The moment of truth finally arrived. Judge Hankinson
asked Way, outside the presence of the jury, if the defense had
further evidence to present. To the disappointment of virtu-

ally everyone assembled—in particular the media—Denise's attorney announced that, after consulting with their client, the defense team had determined she wouldn't be testifying after all. Brian's testimony about her involvement in Mike's murder would go unchallenged by the woman he claimed to be his accomplice.

The defendant—wearing a long, open-front light gray sweater—moved forward with Way into the well of the courtroom. The two stood just a few feet from the judge, who marched through a litany of standard questions intended to confirm her knowing and voluntary waiver of the right to testify.

"Ms. Williams, Mr. Way had indicated that you do not desire to testify. Is that correct?" Judge Hankinson asked.

"Yes," Denise confirmed, her voice firm and resolute.

The judge asked whether anyone had told her that she couldn't testify or pressured her not to. Denise replied that the decision not to testify was hers and hers alone. Judge Hankinson made clear she had the absolute right to testify, but if she decided not to, that he would instruct jurors they couldn't hold that decision against her. Yet whether jurors would actually heed that admonition was something over which he had no control.

"Do you wish to testify?" he asked once more.

"No," Denise repeated, shaking her head for emphasis.

With that exercise now complete, Way informed the judge that the defense would be resting its case. And at only 11:35 a.m., the prosecutors, defense lawyers, and judge mutually decided to let the jury go home for the day. Friday would begin with Judge Hankinson's instructions to the jury, followed by closing arguments, and then jury deliberations. And with any luck, an end to the 18-year saga surrounding the disappearance of Jerry Michael Williams.

After a lunch break, however, the lawyers, Denise, and judge came back to the courtroom to hammer out the instructions the jury would hear before closing arguments. As they neared the completion of their work, Ethan Way informed Judge Hankinson the defense wouldn't be seeking an instruction for the jury to consider any lesser-included offenses, such as second-degree murder. "Is that correct Ms. Williams?" the judge asked Denise directly. She answered affirmatively.

He explained to her that her lawyers' preference not to have the jury instructed on lesser-included offenses "is a relatively radical decision that's not made in many cases. Do you understand it's a little bit out of the ordinary?"

"Yes," Denise answered.

"I guess for want of a better word, it's a little bit of a gamble. If convicted as charged on first-degree murder and probably, to some extent, the other charges, my hands are going to be tied to a large extent on sentencing. Do you understand that?"

"Yes," the defendant replied. The judge explained that if the jury found her guilty of first-degree murder, he would have to impose a life sentence. "Do you understand that's the result of it?"

Once again, Denise answered affirmatively and indicated that she understood she was legally entitled to an instruction on lesser-included offenses. And that she wouldn't be able to come back later saying she actually did want such an instruction.

"That is your request—that you waive the lesser-included offenses?" the judge asked one final time.

"Yes," Denise responded, the very last word she would utter before the jury delivered its verdict.

••••

Once again, a packed courtroom sat in rapt attention the morning of Friday, December 14, 2018—two days shy of the 18th anniversary of what everyone now knew was Mike's savage, brutal killing. A nervous tension hung uncomfortably in the air, the uncertainty of the outcome combining with the final crescendo of the trial to create a palpable, omnipresent mix of emotions for virtually everyone in attendance.

Denise sat at the far end of the defense counsel table beside her lawyers, wearing a pale, pink cardigan. Would this be the very last day of her life in civilian clothing before being sent off to prison forever? Or would she walk out of the courtroom that evening a free woman, sleep in her own bed in the comfort of her spacious home, and be able to resume her life just as it was before May 8, 2018?

The gallery was filled with spectators who were rooting hard for one result or the other—including Denise's sisters and friends on one side of the courtroom and Clay and Patti Ketcham and Kathy Thomas on the other. Denise's sisters were so convinced she would be acquitted, they had planned a big celebration for her, including a trip to Las Vegas.

After Judge Hankinson completed his brief instructions to the jury, Jon Fuchs took center stage behind the podium, his PowerPoint presentation queued up on the screen behind him. He spoke in a calm, matter-of-fact tone—his argument workmanlike, no more passionate than a college professor delivering a lecture on earth science. Which was surprising considering the stakes and the emotions that had gripped the courtroom the prior two and a half days.

He began by telling jurors that, initially, the case had been classified as a "missing person" case rather than a homicide investigation. "But we know now," he continued, projecting Brian's mugshot onto the screen, "that man murdered him."

He reminded jurors about the three life insurance policies totaling $1.75 million, "all of which Denise Williams was the sole beneficiary of," the final one placed by Brian "the summer before he murdered Mike Williams."

Fuchs then flashed Denise's mugshot onto the screen with an enlarged red question mark obscuring her face. "The question you have," he told jurors, "is how does *she* fit into the picture? How does she fit into the murder, the conspiracy for murder, and helping him after the murder?" He started with the accessory-after-the-fact charge.

The veteran prosecutor reminded jurors that Dr. Mnookin had testified Brian told him—before he was arrested—that he was "worried that Denise was going to go to law enforcement and that she's going to tell them about a murder that happened and what she knows from many years ago. The murder of Mike Williams. Prior to the arrest."

The next slide, in giant lettering, included Denise's words to Kathy within the week of Brian's arrest and her being interviewed by the FDLE: "Tell Marcus to tell Brian that I didn't say anything." Fuchs then played the portion of the telephone call in which Kathy told Denise: "I know you know something Denise. Because whenever I was going out to see Marcus, you're like, 'Tell Marcus to tell Brian I'm not talking.'"

On the recording, jurors could hear Denise responding, "Yeah," followed by Kathy saying, "And I knew what that meant."

"So we know," Fuchs picked back up as he stopped the audio, "that she has knowledge of the homicide because Brian has told Dr. Mnookin already. And now she's sending a message to Brian to let him know that she didn't say anything."

He reminded jurors of Brian's testimony that he and Denise "had a pact, an agreement, that nobody would say anything to another person. Nobody would say anything to law enforcement. And that's what she's saying. She was continuing that pact, and letting him know that she didn't say anything to law enforcement that day."

And she wanted him to know that, Fuchs added, "… so that way he doesn't then turn around and confess and dime her out, in accord with the agreement they had." Those facts, he argued, met the required elements for being an accessory after the fact.

"So let's turn to the elements of conspiracy," he transitioned, as a new slide bearing that title was displayed, with Denise's and Brian's mugshots side-by-side. He acknowledged that for the conspiracy charge, the jury would need to rely on Brian's testimony—specifically, that his affair with Denise started in 1997 and had been going on for three years.

That testimony, the Assistant State Attorney reminded jurors, was corroborated by Lindsay Lockhart, who saw him and Denise at "a different concert, but another concert at Floyd's … And she sees Brian Winchester and Denise acting in a manner that is not just friendly. It's above friendly. As if they were dating. Arms around each other. Brian standing behind her. Three years prior to Mike's death. Just like Brian said."

His first wife Kathy also corroborated Brian's testimony, the veteran prosecutor said, reminding the jury of the movie tickets, Meridian necklace, and her statement that "she always knew that they were in love with each other." And then there were the concert tickets Brian kept "from 1998, more from 2001, 2002, before they 'came out.' They were kept because those are things that they did together and dates they went on to concerts."

He also focused on Denise's handwritten letter to Brian. "You have it in evidence if you want to take a look at it," he said. "But in that she talks about her love and she professes love for him. How she's going to miss him. That didn't happen overnight."

Though he told jurors Brian was still married to Kathy at the time Denise had written the letter, he apparently didn't realize she wrote it in December 2003—eight months after their divorce.

"The letter confirms that this is an ongoing relationship between Brian Winchester and Denise Williams," he argued. "At one point she says, 'I love you more than ever.' You don't love someone more than ever if you didn't love them before."

He reminded jurors that Officer Chase had found Brian's truck in the church parking lot in 1999—a year before Mike was killed—at a time he supposedly was hunting. "But he wasn't. Because he was there … with Denise. Just like he said. Just like Brian told you." He asked jurors to bear in mind that "affairs and conspiracies are secretive by their very nature. And they were good at it. They kept the secret of his murder for 17 years."

Finally, Fuchs pivoted to Brian's testimony about the conspiracy—how he and Denise had plotted Mike's death for a year. "That insurance was a motive," he said, "but it wasn't the sole motive. It was to be together, as far as he was concerned." Brian had testified, he reminded the jury, that Denise had "major concerns—given her upbringing—with being a divorcée. Didn't want to be a divorcée. Was concerned about custody of her child. Didn't want to share custody of her child. Balancing act being a divorcée or a widow? A widow with $1.75 million? The sympathy of the community because your husband is missing in a hunting accident? A lot better than a divorcée."

"The plan was," Fuchs continued, "to get him onto a boat, push him over, so he would drown in the waders. Because of the myth that if you go into the water with waders, you're going to in fact drown. You can't escape. They drag you down." Brian knew the water wasn't very deep in that area, he added, except for the 12-foot hole where he eventually pushed him over.

"And somehow he's able to get out of those waders," Fuchs recounted. "And we know that's corroborated because Joe Sheffield, who's the man that found the waders six months later, he says whenever he found the waders they were pulled halfway down, inside out, down the waist area."

Once again, despite law enforcement officers' belief *for years* that the waders had been planted, Fuchs wanted jurors to conclude they had been there all along—though offered no explanation for why they hadn't been found during the months-long, intense search in that very spot. Indeed, he pointed out how Howard Drew's testimony about his training with Mike to ensure he could pull the waders off if he ever fell overboard matched Sheffield's testimony of how he found them.

Fuchs told jurors he wasn't going to delve into the details of how Brian shot Mike "because it was brutal. Brian Winchester is not a good person. He's a murderer. Just like he told you. But that doesn't mean his testimony isn't accurate." In fact, the prosecutor continued, his testimony was corroborated by Mike's remains being found exactly where he said they'd be and by the determination he had been "shot in the face, just like Brian Winchester told you."

Brian's testimony that he had "pulled the shirt over his head because he didn't want to have to look at his friend's face," Fuchs continued, was also corroborated because "that's how the body was found." Apparently, however, he didn't realize Brian had never testified that he pulled the shirt over Mike's head—not even in his proffer statements or pretrial deposition. On this point, Fuchs was obviously confused.

As to Denise's motive, the prosecutor asked jurors to "follow the money." He reiterated that she was the beneficiary of $1.75 million in life insurance. "Not Brian Winchester. She is. And when you add all that up, each and every element of that conspiracy has been met."

In his final four minutes before the jury, the Assistant State Attorney focused on the charge of Denise being a principal in her husband's murder. He reminded jurors of Judge Hankinson's instruction that "if the defendant helped another person or persons commit the crime of first-degree murder, the defendant is treated as a principal and must be treated as if she had done all the things the other person did if she had the conscious intent that the crime be done."

"Did she have a conscious intent that he go on that hunting trip and die and never come home?" Fuchs asked rhetorically. "And the answer, of course, is 'yes.' Did she do an act, word, or other thing that encouraged, assisted Brian to commit the crime?" Though the prosecutor answered that question with a resolute "absolutely," he failed to tell jurors what she had actually done that assisted Brian in committing the crime, telling them instead the law didn't require her to be physically present when the murder occurred. Though the prosecution theory was that Denise had provided assistance to Brian by encouraging Mike to go duck hunting that morning, Fuchs never articulated that theory out loud.

Summing up, the State's lead counsel told the jury that when it considered and evaluated all of the evidence, "I am confident that you will, in fact, find her guilty of conspiracy to commit murder, first-degree murder, and accessory after the fact." As he spoke those words, a slide of Denise's mugshot reappeared with the heading "Guilty" in large red letters and all three charges, in red, scrawled across her face.

Though his 25-minute argument was now complete, Fuchs would get to take his place behind the podium one final time—following the defense closing—as the prosecution enjoyed the privilege of having both the first and last word.

••••

After a brief recess, Ethan Way stepped up to the podium to address the jury one final time. Though he had no Power-Point, Denise's lawyer was far more passionate than his adversary had been, gesticulating forcefully and using his voice for emphasis like a finely tuned instrument. He grew more and more animated as his argument progressed, his tone becoming increasingly sharp and biting—dripping with sarcasm and derision at times. Denise Williams had paid good money for a full-throated defense lawyer. Ethan Way more than lived up to that billing, putting on a theatrical performance like a Broadway actor, the well of the courtroom his stage.

"This is not—this is not a case about feeling sorry for anyone," he began. "This is not a case about trying to get 'justice for Mike.'" He told jurors it also wasn't a case about how they felt about Denise or felt about Cheryl Williams—oddly, Way being the first attorney to reference Mike's tenacious mom.

"It's not a case about how people mourn," he continued. "It's not a case about how people grieve. It's not a case about whether people smile. It's not a case about whether people sit there and stare," he said, apparently referring to Denise's vacant expressions throughout the trial. "This is a murder case."

He asked the jury to consider the evidence the State had presented without "any taint of Brian Winchester. Take the evidence that has been presented to you and take Brian Winchester out of it."

"If you take Brian Winchester out of the things that have been shown to you," he asserted, "you have nothing." Indeed, Agent DeVaney, he reminded jurors, had testified there was no physical or "tangible evidence that implicates Denise Williams in the murder of Mike Williams."

Way contended the insurance was "a red herring" amounting to no proof of anything. "Mike Williams was insured," he said. "Mike Williams passed away. The insurance paid out." To him, it was no more significant than that. He noted the State hadn't bothered to present any evidence at all about what had happened to the money after it was paid or how it had been spent. "Because it's a throw-away line," he argued.

He again asked the question, "If you take out Brian Winchester, what do you have? You have a couple of concert tickets to some marginal bands. Maybe they were in '98. Maybe they were in 2000. Maybe they were in 2001."

Referring to Officer Chase's testimony about Brian's truck, the defense attorney argued, "That wasn't Denise Williams' truck. It was Brian's truck. And we already know, in 1999, that's after Brian had already started fooling around with Ms. Stafford. We heard that testimony from her own mouth."

Way intimated Stafford had been staying overnight with Denise on that particular night and that Brian had parked his truck at the church to be with her, not Denise. Yet the defense lawyer was badly mistaken on this point, as Stafford had testified the first time she had sex with Brian was in 2004 — long after Mike's murder.

"All of the things that have been presented to you by the State Attorney to suggest corroboration," Way argued, his left hand pointing at the blank projection screen for emphasis, "standing on their own, do not prove anything. They never have. They never did. And they never will." Removing Brian Winchester's testimony, he repeated, "There is nothing about any of this evidence ... that supports any of the three charges against Denise Williams."

He then highlighted Denise's push to get divorced from Brian, noting that his client had no "philosophical, religious, or moral objections to divorce against Mr. Winchester," implying she wouldn't have had any qualms getting divorced from Mike had she been unhappy in their marriage. Which also suggested that she hadn't chosen being a grieving widow over being a divorcée.

Way then introduced a theme he would return to repeatedly — that Brian was "a controlling man ... the type of man who did not like to have someone tell him what to do. Because what was he? He was a financial planner. He sold insurance. He planned. And he sold."

He shifted gears to the events of August 5, 2016, reminding jurors how Brian had crawled into the back of Denise's SUV and waited for hours. And how, when Denise got into the truck, he "crawled over two rows of seats, scared her, put a gun to her ribs."

"He kidnapped her at gunpoint," Way said emphatically, feigning anger. But Denise was able to calm him down "enough to get him to let her go. This man who supposedly knows the deepest, darkest, most heinous secret, that Denise Williams plotted and planned for the murder of Mike Williams."

He then got to his central point—one that wouldn't have been possible had the State called Denise's brother-in-law, Dave McCranie, to explain that he was the one who had urged Denise to report the kidnapping to law enforcement. Instead, the crafty defense attorney asked jurors, if it had been true that she had been involved in Mike's murder, "Why does Denise Williams go to the police? The man with a secret that could lock her up—*she* goes to the police. *She* turns him in. Because he kidnapped her at gunpoint."

And then Agent DeVaney walks in and decides "he's going to *confront* Denise Williams," Way stated derisively, his hands gesticulating forcefully. "He's going to confront her while she is in the Sheriff's Office preparing reports and giving evidence related to being kidnapped by Brian Winchester. And Agent DeVaney is mean to her. He doesn't treat her well." She wanted to talk about being kidnapped, he said, and the FDLE agent just wanted "to pester her and needle her" about Mike's disappearance.

"Denise Williams didn't have a hard time talking to law enforcement, ladies and gentlemen, because *she went to them*," Way argued. "She drove to the Sheriff's Office. Now if a woman doesn't want to talk to law enforcement … driving to their office is a bad way to go about it," he said sarcastically. He reminded jurors that Denise also hadn't had any difficulty talking to Sergeant Wooten about the parking lot incident. He then pointed toward his client, telling jurors, "She's willing to talk to these people even though, supposedly, Brian Winchester has this deep, dark secret over her because they planned it together." As he finished that sentence, Way was shaking his head, smirking, openly mocking the State's position.

The veteran defense lawyer then began a slow transition

to the subject of Brian's proffer agreement, his tone becoming more caustic as he progressed. "He was facing felony charges," Way said. "He happened to have the misfortune, or luck, depending on how one looks at it, to have his case assigned to a division presided over by Hangman Hankinson." He reminded jurors Brian had testified that he didn't like being in jail and didn't want to go to prison.

"So what does Mr. Winchester decide to do? Well, what do we know about Mr. Winchester up to this point? He's a planner. He's a salesman." And admitted to planting evidence—the hat found weeks into the search at Lake Seminole. But just like Fuchs, for some reason Way didn't even intimate Brian had planted the waders, hunting jacket, or flashlight.

He then reminded jurors how Brian had tried to get Wade Wilson, the confessed hitman, to help him out "with some witness tampering. Some obstruction of justice." Kimberly Adams and his own sister as well. "He was in jail from August 5, 2016, and he was in jail in 2017. He had never had any epiphany," Way said, again in a mocking tone. "He had never gone to law enforcement to say, 'Oh, by the way, I killed Mike Williams and I want to be forgiven.'" But he knew how much law enforcement officers wanted to solve Mike's case.

According to Way, that's when Brian hatched his plan. Now roleplaying as if he were Brian himself, the defense lawyer said, "I have tried witness tampering. [I'm] sitting in jail. I got nothing else to do. And I'm a planner. I'm a salesman. And I'll obstruct justice. So what do I have to do? Hmm." At that point in his mock Brian soliloquy, Way began rubbing his beard with his left hand, as if he were Brian cogitating over his dilemma.

With a twinkle in his eye, he again channeled Brian, suggesting that the State's star witness finally had his epiphany: "I will come up with—not a life insurance policy. I am going to come up with a Brian Life Policy ... I'm going to give the State something *so good* they're going to give me a free pass to murder. They're going to let me get away with it," Way continued, smirking. "And as icing on the cake, I get revenge on Denise for turning me into the police on August 5, 2016."

The bombastic defense lawyer then walked over to a desk near the judge, grabbing hold of a piece of paper, asking, "So what does Mr. Winchester, the salesman, planner, the liar, the murderer—what does he come up with?" He placed the document—Brian's proffer agreement—on the projection screen, pointing out to the jury that Fuchs hadn't mentioned the agreement a single time in his closing. He told jurors, sarcastically, it wasn't titled the "Brian Winchester Life Policy" because that "probably would have been a little too obvious."

Way then grabbed a yardstick and started twirling it around in his hand—a curious choice considering Cheryl Williams' own use of a yardstick to hold the picket sign she had carried relentlessly for years. As he fiddled with the three-foot ruler, he told jurors that, through the proffer agreement, the State had given Brian immunity "for anything you tell us." All at a time that law enforcement had been stymied by the Mike Williams investigation with no evidence beyond a "few little suspicions" and "a few little things that look funny."

He pointed to Denise's marriage to Brian, suggesting law enforcement officers had concluded, "Well, she married him. She must know something." Yet Denise, he said, had known Brian "since she was three. She didn't know he was a murderer. Did find out ultimately that he was a bad husband."

"But up until October of 2017, there's no evidence," he continued. "Nothing's going to happen on this case. So Mr. Winchester sells the Brian Winchester Life Policy to the State Attorney's Office. And what does he get? He gets never arrested with Mike Williams' murder." He told the jury Brian would never be sentenced for killing Mike, would do no time at all for it, not even probation or a fine. "He will never have to write a letter of apology for that murder. *Nothing*," Way said, his hands parting in front of his face to underscore his point. "He got everything he could ever hope for for himself. And all he had to do was tell a little story and take them to where he had buried Mike."

Way then pivoted to the murder itself, reminding jurors of Brian's testimony that he pushed his best friend out of his own boat. He suggested that his testimony about wanting him to drown in his waders made no sense at all. "There was no reason to believe," he said, in view of how long and how often Mike and Brian had been hunting together, "that Brian Winchester would not have known that Mike Williams had had that wader training," adding, "when you're a hunter, you learn these things."

Brian was circling Mike in the boat, he said, beginning to recount the murder itself. "And he gets up close to him. He pumps his shotgun. Mike's yelling. He's bringing the boat. He gets up to three feet," Way said, now holding the yardstick in front of him to emphasize the short distance, "and he shoots him in the face. Looked him in the eyes, probably one last time, before he took away the front of his head," he said in disgust, reminding the jury that Brian then shoved Mike's lifeless body into a dog crate and later pulled him out of that crate, "rolled him up, put him in a tarp, put him in a hole. That's what he did."

Way rightly pointed out that none of this testimony from Brian was corroboration. "That's called a confession. If I tell you where I buried the body, I'm not corroborating another fact. I am confessing to you what I have done." Brian was happy to share all of this with law enforcement, he said—even to have a "field trip" out to Carr Lake.

Again, channeling Brian's inner thoughts, he said, "I can feel relieved because I have the Brian Winchester Life Policy. It does not matter how bad this looks. It does not matter how bad it sounds. I am going free on the murder. *Scot-free.*"

And then, Judge Hankinson—who was unaware of the proffer agreement, Way said—sentenced Brian to only 20 years in prison. "And it's only for kidnapping Denise. It's only for sticking a gun in her ribs. It is not for shooting his best friend in the face with a 12-gauge shotgun."

At that point, no one had been held accountable for Mike's murder, he told the jury. The defense lawyer then began channeling the Assistant State Attorneys seated at the prosecution table just to his right, saying sarcastically, "But we're prosecutors and so we're kind of in the somebody's-got-to-pay business. Brian Winchester is over there saying, 'Hey, Denise helped me. Hey, *why not*?'" Way said in a squeaky, high-pitched voice—like a character from *The Chipmunks*.

"So what does law enforcement do?" he asked with mounting sarcasm, pounding his two index fingers on the podium to simulate a drum roll. Now channeling Agents Mickler and DeVaney, he said, "'Let's do some lying. We're FDLE.' As if they take a page out of the Brian Winchester playbook. 'Let's not be truthful. Let's tape this phone call.'"

Denise's lawyer pleaded with jurors to listen carefully to the recording of his client's call with Kathy, telling them that nowhere in the audio did Denise say, "'Tell Marcus to tell Brian I'm not going to talk.' That's not in that audio. What it is, it's Kathy Thomas, who has been scripted by the Florida Department of Law Enforcement, who is putting on a semi-Oscar-worthy performance with the snot and sniffling talking about her marriage."

Nearing the end of his 45-minute closing—semi-Oscar-worthy itself—Way mocked the prosecution. "So, ladies and gentlemen of the jury, it's always the wife. Follow the money. Do the easiest thing you can do. Just throw it up there and hope something sticks. Let's help Brian get the revenge he needs. Let's go after Denise. Because that's the story everybody wants to hear. That's the easy story."

He told jurors, sarcastically, it wasn't their place "to feel sorry for the State Attorney's Office for the horrible decision they made to give a murderer a free pass. But you certainly don't have to try to help them undo that horrible decision. This case is only about Brian Winchester. It is only about him killing Mike Williams. It is only about him doing the most heinous thing that can be done to another human being. He took his life. He took away Denise's husband. He took away Anslee's father. He took away Cheryl's son. He took away Nick's brother. He took away all of the friends and family. Brian Winchester did that. Not Denise Williams."

"There is no evidence that supports any of the allegations against my client," Way concluded. "Not accessory. Not principal. Not conspiracy." He asked jurors not to deliver a "miscarriage of justice. We are counting on you to return a verdict that speaks the truth and that verdict is not guilty ... Denise Williams is not guilty." With those final words, he strode confidently to his seat, hopeful the jury would set his client free.

••••

Standing before the jury a second time was the same Jon Fuchs who had made the State's initial passive, low-energy closing argument. As the Assistant State Attorney prepared to deliver his final argument, his demeanor was noticeably different. It was as if he had been transformed into an entirely different lawyer—full of energy and passion. Outraged by the way he and his colleagues in the State Attorney's Office and FDLE had been openly mocked and derided in his opponent's presentation. Ethan Way had clearly laid down the gauntlet. The veteran prosecutor was fired up and ready to explode right through it.

"Mr. Way said, 'Let's take Brian out of the equation,'" he began. "'Without Brian there's nothing. Brian's a liar. Brian's a murderer.' Yeah, he is," the prosecutor acknowledged. He accepted Way's challenge of "taking Brian out of the equation." He told jurors they would listen, once again, to Denise's own words, queuing up the audio recording of her telephone call with Kathy.

Before hitting "play," Fuchs advanced his PowerPoint to a slide containing a question Phil Padovano had asked Cheryl Williams about why Denise began withholding Anslee from her. The silver-haired defense lawyer had asked, "If she was innocent and accused of murdering Mike, you would expect her to react in anger, wouldn't you?"

The State's lead attorney then hit "play" on the audio, asking jurors to pay special attention to the part where Kathy "accuses Denise Williams of planning and plotting and her involvement in the murder."

The recording began to play. "Brian told me that y'all planned it," Kathy said. "Planned what?" Denise responded. "Oh my God." Kathy told her that Marcus had come by her parents' printing business telling her how she would have to "take this to my grave."

"Wait, wait. So Marcus knew?" Denise asked bewildered. "When you said Brian, said y'all, you're talking about me and Brian? Or Marcus? Or who?"

"You and Brian," Kathy responded.

"And that Marcus is involved?" Denise asked. "I mean, obviously, if he came and talked to you." A moment later, she added, "Yeah, you know, that's pretty major. Especially with Marcus involved."

Fuchs stopped the recording. "She is just accused of murdering her ex-husband by her friend and her concern is that Marcus is involved? *That's her issue*?" he asked incredulously. "'Brian told me that y'all conspired, planned, and killed Mike Williams,'" he quoted Kathy as saying. "'Wait. Marcus is involved?'" he said, now role-playing Denise. "This is the same person who cut off the grandmother from the granddaughter because she made accusations against her?"

Though Way's theatrical closing argument may have been effective, he had failed to address this one crucial point—his client's decision to yank Anslee away from Mike's mother if she continued pursuing an investigation. Fuchs was now making him—and Denise—pay for that critical omission.

"She's just accused of murder," Fuchs continued, his passion evident, "and the only thing she wants to know is if Marcus is involved. Why? Because the pact that she had with Brian Winchester was that *nobody* else would know." His right arm slashed downward forcefully with those words. "Just them. And that's how they kept it a secret for that 17, 18 years. That's why she's concerned about 'maybe Marcus is involved.' It's not the fact that, 'Oh, by the way, I've been told that you killed your husband.' Her concern is Marcus is involved."

"It's not even what she says. It's what she doesn't say," the Assistant State Attorney added. "In this recording, she's just accused by one of her best friends of plotting to murder her husband, who was in fact murdered, and she never says, 'Oh no I didn't.' What she says is, 'Wait, Marcus is involved?'"

Fuchs urged jurors to listen to the entire audio recording between Denise and Kathy because "it lays out this entire case *without Brian*. Accuses her of the homicide. We've already heard that part. Two times … When she accuses a second time, she says, 'Why couldn't y'all have just gotten a divorce.' She asked if Mike knew … And Mike didn't find out about anything. That he didn't suspect anything. Didn't suspect the affair. That recording goes beyond just the statement that implicates her for the accessory after the fact. That recording," he argued, "without Brian, lays out the whole thing. Listen to it."

The veteran prosecutor then shifted gears, flashing a giant photo of Mike onto the screen, his energy and passion escalating. "Mr. Way says this is not about justice for Mike," he reminded jurors. "This absolutely is about justice for Mike. This is about holding *that person*," he said, pointing stridently at Denise, "accountable for it in what her role is. That's what you are here to decide, what her role was in all of this. That is solely what you are here for."

Fuchs then addressed the proffer agreement head on, Brian's mugshot now on the screen. "My signature is on that proffer agreement. I had to make a decision to solve a 17-year-old homicide case. Was it a good decision? I don't know. Time will tell. That is a cross that I must bear." He told jurors it turned his stomach to listen to Brian describe how he killed Mike. "But he is a part of this case, like it or not."

The proffer agreement was never intended, he said, to gin up a case against Denise. Rather, it had been intended "to get closure for the family and to find Mike Williams." From there, investigators and prosecutors merely followed the evidence to where it led, he noted. Which was directly to Denise Williams.

"Brian Winchester is not going free," he assured jurors. "He has 20 years in the Department of Corrections followed by 15 years of probation. While he's sitting there in the prison cell—as he wakes up every day on that bed and stares at those bars—at no point, I assure you, does he say, 'I'm glad I'm here on this and not that.' He is in prison. A prison cell looks the same whether you're there for murder or whether you're there for kidnapping.

Fuchs then referred to a paragraph in the proffer agreement Way had conveniently omitted from his impassioned speech. "If at any time he lies or perjures himself about any-thing contained in any of his statements," he pointed out, "the entire statement can be used against him and he can be prosecuted for murder." "That man," he argued, pointing to Brian's photo on the screen, "has absolutely every reason to tell you the truth. Because if he lies in any way, shape or form, that immunity agreement gets shredded and he goes down for murder by his own confession."

The next slide in Fuchs's PowerPoint had the notorious mugshot of Al Capone side-by-side with Brian's. To drive home the point that the government was only able to bring Al Capone to justice with a case for tax evasion, rather than mur-der. "Just like Brian Winchester, he was a murderer as well. They got him for what they could get him for. And that's why the immunity agreement exists. And the only thing the immu-nity agreement says is I couldn't ask for life imprisonment. I asked for 45 years. I got 20."

A giant image of Denise's mugshot then flashed on the screen, the Assistant State Attorney reiterating, "This is about justice for Mike and what her role was in all of this." He asked rhetorically why Denise had to send that message—through Kathy—that she wasn't talking to law enforcement. Because, "She knew a very real possibility in this situation was that Bri-an was going to turn around and dime her out," he argued. "And she wanted to make sure that she's told him, 'Hey, I want you to know I didn't say anything.' Say anything about what? 'Tell Marcus to tell Brian I didn't say anything.' *Say anything about what*?" Fuchs, indignant, asked a second time.

The only reason Denise had to send that message, he told jurors, was because Brian had told them the truth. That they had a pact. An agreement. Not to talk to law enforcement. That neither would dime the other out. Denise wanted Brian to know she was keeping her end of the bargain, Fuchs argued, to ensure that he kept his. Which protected *her*. "It's the only logical reason for sending that particular message within the week of his arrest," he insisted, gesticulating forcefully with his right arm.

At that point, Fuchs finally revealed the prosecution theory about why Denise was a principal to Mike's murder. He laid the foundation by reminding the jury how controlling Denise was—how she could get Mike to meet her at the gas station to pump her gas. Or to leave his office to bring her food when she needed it. He posited that Mike and Denise would clearly have had a conversation about him going hunting with Brian the morning of December 16, 2000. "On the day of their anniversary when they're going to Apalachicola, how is it that he doesn't ask her for permission to go?"

Now showing off *his* thespian side, Fuchs played out their likely conversation, first Mike asking, "'Is it all right if I go hunting Saturday morning before we go to Apalachicola?'" Then Denise responding, "'Sure. Who are you going hunting with?' 'Brian.' 'All right. What time you going to be back?' 'What time are we leaving? OK. That works.' So use your common sense," he urged jurors. "Use your skills, experience, life skills. This conversation occurs."

Since she knew Mike was going hunting with Brian, if she had no idea he was going to kill her husband—as Way had argued—"what's the first thing she says to law enforcement, or anybody for that matter … when Mike doesn't come back from hunting? 'Call Brian, he's the one that was with him.' That's the first thing you would do," Fuchs insisted, his massive frame twitching to help emphasize the point.

That's what would have happened, he argued, "… *unless* they have a plan and a pact to set up alibis and not dime each other out. And she's involved in the homicide." So what she told law enforcement when Mike didn't come home that day wasn't that he was with Brian, but rather, "'I don't know,'" the prosecutor said, almost under his breath. "'He went hunting and he just didn't come back.'"

He transitioned to Way's point about how cooperative Denise supposedly had been with law enforcement, particularly Sergeant Wooten, pointing out that cooperation had come to a screeching halt when she learned the FDLE was involved. Because she knew from Mike DeVaney that the FDLE was investigating Mike's murder. And that's why, he argued, Denise wouldn't return Will Mickler's calls.

Fuchs then returned to Denise's threats to withhold Anslee from Cheryl—making Way and the defense team pay the price, yet again, for not addressing that important topic. "If Brian's lying to you," the Assistant State Attorney asked—his passion now reaching a crescendo—"why, *why* are you threatening the grandmother to stop the investigation on two occasions? And, 'You'll never see your granddaughter again.' Brian didn't make that threat. *She* did," he reminded jurors through gritted teeth while pointing at Denise.

He highlighted the second confrontation, noting it was the day before Cheryl's birthday. "Ladies and gentlemen, that's not the actions of an innocent person. That's the actions of someone who was in a plan to commit a murder … And was afraid of an investigation and all the hubbub that Mrs. Cheryl was making. She was afraid Cheryl would succeed," Fuchs argued. "And she did."

He returned briefly to the insurance, reminding jurors that Brian wasn't a beneficiary. The insurance therefore wasn't a motive for him—only for Denise. "And what did *she* do?" he asked as the claim form to Kansas City Life appeared on the screen. "She wasted no time. Kansas City Life, $1 million policy, $250,000, $1.25 million submitted for. Her signature. Look at the date," he said, using the laser pointer to point it out on the screen. "January 4th of 2001. Ladies and gentlemen, the search didn't even end until February." Doing the math, he told jurors that was "19 days later she's filing for an insurance payment of $1.25 million. Nineteen whole days. *That's a cold individual.* That's a person that's involved in a homicide."

The State's lead attorney then asked jurors to think back to Brian Winchester's testimony about how he had "shot his best friend. How he circled around the stump. Approached, three feet away," he continued, now holding the yardstick in front of the jury for emphasis. "Shot him in the face. Everybody in this entire room was moved by that and the sheer horror of that situation. *Except for one person*," he said, holding up his right index finger. "That one person," he continued, pointing with his right thumb over his shoulder, toward Denise, "sat here and listened to Brian Winchester describe … how he had shot and killed her husband, the man she supposedly loved and cherished, *absolute stoned-faced. Didn't bat an eye. Didn't shed a tear*," Fuchs said, unable to contain his scorn and derision.

As he began wrapping up, Denise's mugshot appeared once again on the projection screen. Fuchs responded to Ethan Way's point about Denise having no problem getting a divorce from Brian. "She could get a divorce from Brian," he told jurors, "because Anslee wasn't involved. That's why she couldn't get the divorce from Mike. She didn't want to have to share custody with her father. Doesn't that make sense for the same person that took Mike Williams' daughter away from the grandmother? Who 19 days later filed for an insurance claim? Who sat here stone-faced?"

"Ladies and gentlemen, Mike Williams was a devoted father," Fuchs reminded jurors, as he prepared to make his most theatrical gesture yet. "He was a devoted husband. Mike Williams died with his ring on—with that devotion." The Power-Point slide then advanced, Denise's mugshot now side-by-side with the X-ray of Mike's forearms and hands—his wedding ring clearly visible on his left hand.

Slowly walking toward the jury box, the veteran prosecutor continued, "The only part of that that Denise Williams took to heart," he said, now reaching into his pocket and pulling out Mike's gold wedding band, "is 'till death do us part.'"

As he said those words, he carefully laid Mike's ring on the wooden bar at the front of the jury box—the sound of the metal coming to rest reverberating throughout the otherwise silent courtroom.

"And she took it to the extreme," the Assistant State Attorney added, his contempt for Denise now bubbling to the surface. "And she, along with Brian Winchester, made sure that death did him part. She helped plan it. She held up her end of the bargain by helping with alibis. She [kept] her bargain by helping him afterwards. By making sure that even though she had him arrested, that she didn't say anything."

"And when you take all that into account, that lady right there," Fuchs stated resolutely, pointing stridently at the defendant, "Ms. Denise Williams, is guilty of conspiracy to commit murder, first-degree murder, and accessory after the fact. Thank you."

Though his opening argument may have been lackluster and mechanical, Jon Fuchs delivered the goods in his second. His performance came with every bit as much passion and gusto as Ethan Way's. And Fuchs was able to knit together an argument with many more supporting facts than his theatrical opposing counsel.

Having done his job, he was content to leave the rest of the work to the jury. Who promptly retired to the jury room to deliberate on its verdict. Which would finally bring an end to Cheryl Williams' 18-year march toward justice. Whether that march actually ended in justice, however, remained to be seen.

18

Case Closed

The door latched shut behind the bailiff. Six men and six women of assorted ages sat around a government-issued, wooden table. All strangers when the week began, they now knew one another by name. They had eaten lunch together, learned about jobs and family members, even formed friendships. The American jury system at its finest.

They were about to embark on an experience nothing in their lives could possibly have prepared them for. A job for which they had been provided virtually no training at all. A 48-year-old mother's life literally hung in the balance. They and they alone would determine whether she lived the rest of her days behind bars or as a free woman—a monstrously heavy burden. To a one, the jurors felt the enormity of the task weighing down upon them.

Their first decision was someone to lead them—a foreperson. When four or five raised their hands to express interest, their names were placed into a bag and one was chosen. As it turned out, the youngest of the twelve was selected to lead the group, an 18-year-old woman named Kierra Idlett. Perhaps the choice was fitting, as Idlett's life had begun in 2000, the year in which the most critical events they had seen play out in the courtroom had occurred. The year that ended with Brian Winchester viciously snuffing out Mike Williams' life.

From their vantage point in the jury box, the twelve decision-makers had a birds-eye view of all of the evidence the lawyers had presented. They saw up close and listened intently to Brian's emotional and compelling testimony about his affair with Denise and their murderous plot. They heard recollections from Lindsay Lockhart and Angela Stafford about Brian's seemingly inappropriate behavior with Denise at Floyd's Music Store in 1997 — when he had his hands all over her — and of Mike drowning his apparent sorrows with booze.

The jurors had heard for themselves Denise's odd reactions when Kathy suggested she was having an affair with Brian, that "Mike knew" about it, and when Kathy accused her of being involved in his murder. They had learned about Denise instructing Kathy to tell Marcus to let her jailed estranged husband know that she wasn't going to say anything. As Jon Fuchs asked them rhetorically during his closing argument, "Say anything about what?" Was the message she asked Kathy to convey connected to a 16-year pact between Denise and Brian, one which to that point had kept a tight lid on what they each knew about the other's involvement in Mike's disappearance?

They also had seen and heard evidence about how quickly Denise sought the nearly $2 million in life insurance. They saw her signature on the January 4, 2001 claim to Kansas City Life projected onto the screen — a mere 19 days after her husband went missing — right in the thick of the intense search to find him. Brian wasn't the beneficiary of that life insurance payout, they were reminded during the closing arguments. Only Denise.

Finally, there were the two confrontations with Cheryl, in which Denise had used Anslee as a pawn to pressure her mother-in-law to back off her push for a criminal investigation. If someone had harmed her husband, wouldn't Denise have been the most logical person to be pushing for an investigation? Instead, she took an innocent child away from her grandmother. Forever. Merely because Cheryl had the temerity to try to get to the bottom of what had happened to her son.

Was all that enough? Did they see and hear enough evidence to conclude beyond a reasonable doubt that Denise had conspired with Brian to kill Mike so they could be together?

Did they know enough to determine that Denise had deliberately, with premeditation, sent her high school sweet-heart—and the devoted father of their beautiful girl—on a death march the very day they were supposed to leave town to celebrate their sixth wedding anniversary? Did they have enough to conclusively determine that she knew he was never coming back—and that she didn't want him to?

••••

Within minutes, the group took its initial vote by a show of hands. Nine votes for guilty and three for not guilty. For them to accomplish their mission of unanimity, the nine would need to convince the other three of Denise's guilt. Or the three would need to persuade the other nine the evidence just wasn't sufficient.

As they discussed their recollections of the testimony, one thing became apparent. No matter how much Denise's law-yers had tried to cast doubt on Brian Winchester's credibility, it hadn't worked. As they focused on Brian's testimony, jurors were unfazed by the fact that he had been wearing prison garb while testifying or their knowledge that he had killed Mike in cold blood. Though they were revolted by his actions, not a single one bought into the "Brian Winchester Life Policy" Ethan Way tried to sell them during his closing argument. Rather, all twelve jurors were convinced Brian had told them the truth.

Two of the holdouts, though, were struggling over not having heard directly from Denise. How could they vote to convict, they quizzed the other jurors, without any physical evidence directly connecting Denise to the murder?

Those favoring a conviction reasoned with the holdouts, pointing out how Denise, not Brian, was the one who had ben-efited from the life insurance. Like Jon Fuchs had toward the end of his second argument, they also pointed to Denise's de-tached demeanor and complete lack of emotion as Brian de-scribed how he shot Mike in the face and then buried him in a hole.

"How can you not show any emotion?" one of the jurors favoring conviction asked rhetorically. "There should have been at least a tear." If Denise were truly hearing about these events for the first time, others chimed in, she would have conveyed at least some emotion. Instead, her demeanor was flat-lined.

Eventually, they started looking at the exhibits. The most persuasive document, it turned out, was one that had received only scant attention in the courtroom—Denise's December 10, 2003 letter to Brian. But there it was now, sitting on the table, beckoning them to read it. Seventeen pages in Denise's neat, cursive handwriting. They passed the letter around the table, each taking their time to review it carefully.

The dominant theme running through Denise's letter was what God had intended for her and Brian's lives—and their relationship. The letter referred to God or Jesus no fewer than 32 times and quoted verses from the New Testament. Denise repeatedly referenced "40 days"—the "40 days of purpose" at the heart of evangelical Christian Pastor Rick Warren's *The Purpose Driven Life*. The letter made clear that Denise and Brian had agreed to 40 days of separation from each other in the tradition of a religious fast.

"There are no words that can describe to you how sad I will be on Christmas and New Years [sic] Eve," she told Brian, referring to the upcoming holidays they would be apart. "I will know for sure that what we are doing is right—but I will still miss you and be so sad. Also on the anniversary's 16th and 17th—will you please pray extra hard for me on those days?" she asked, referring to what would have been the ninth anniversary of her marriage to Mike and the third anniversary of his disappearance.

Denise congratulated herself and Brian on the progress in their spiritual journeys, noting how thankful to God she was "for you and your new life. I am so proud of you following God like this. It is so incredible to me that you have come so far in such a short amount of time. We both have. Our hearts are completely different and I am so thankful to God for that."

Denise reflected on "how in the past I was always telling you I was not happy and that something was wrong with me. I tried (we tried) to come up with hobbies for me—and I felt so bad that I did not have a passion for hobbies the way you did. I would also tell you how I wanted to volunteer and do 'good deeds'—of course I never did—but in my mind I thought it would make me be happy. I was <u>so</u> <u>so</u> lost. This *Purpose Driven Life* stuff has brought me focus in my new Christian life which I needed so badly and by doing these purposes that God created for me I will (and do) have joy and peace (not just being happy but <u>real</u> joy)."

Ironically, Denise stated, "The first time in my life I got to feel real joy [was] in that prison," a reference to her weekend ministry at the federal women's prison in Tallahassee. She described her "addictive feeling" being amongst the prisoners and noted, "I want to feel it again. I pray I will during this 40 days be used by God to bring someone to Him. Pray that for me to [sic]. It is a passion that I have—isn't that great?!? I finally found <u>peace</u> (living <u>one</u> life following God daily) <u>joy</u> (sharing Jesus with unbelievers) <u>passion</u> (inmates and other lost people). <u>Everything</u> I ever wanted was right in front of my face the whole time."

"I believe God put the 40 days in our laps," Denise wrote. "I do not believe it was an accident—and it is pretty exciting to see Him work like that isn't it?!?" She told Brian, "God is real and He is working in our lives and I am so thankful!!"

Denise said she would be keeping a journal of her experiences during the 40 days. "If at the end of the 40 days we can be in a relationship I want you to have full knowledge of the important things I went through—problems/solutions/temptations/failures/successes/situations/Devil/God/etc."

She asked Brian to keep his own journal so she would know what he "went through good and bad in order to move ahead with you if we are allowed to." From their journals, she told Brian, she hoped to "see progress in your spiritual life like I hope you will see in mine."

"The last commitment to you and God is to not waste these 40 days and to live for God every one of them," her letter continued. She noted she would likely get depressed during the time ahead and would be turning to Ron Rickner—the same therapist who would later become Brian's sex addiction counselor—for help to get through her sadness.

Denise also told Brian she planned to have Patti Ketcham take her to Lake Seminole. "This whole time I will be trying to grow spiritually—Purpose book/video, lake, my parents, witnessing, giving, serving—basically I am commiting [sic] to putting into action my purposes (which I try to do every day any way [sic])."

She mentioned the temptations she hoped to avoid during the upcoming holiday period, telling Brian, "I will not go to secular Christmas parties or singles groups or be looking for a man. I will be following God through this time and hope you will also—I hope you will not go to parties, singles groups or be meeting women."

"When I think of you," she said, "which is constantly and I am only on Day 2—I pray. It helps and reminds me why we are doing this—so try it. God is the only way we are going to get through this."

Toward the end of her letter, Denise paraphrased what Jesus said in Matthew 19:29, making clear Brian's central role in her life: "You have been my life and in this verse you have been my family and my most valuable possession. I know you understand this and feel the same—and we are doing the right thing and will be blessed. I am so proud of us and when I am the saddest and so lonely—I am going to try to remember these verses." She reiterated she would miss Brian terribly over the 40 days they would be apart.

"I know one thing for sure," Denise said, wrapping up. "'It's not about me!' and I will ask God to help me not to focus on myself. Brian, there are about 100+ more things I want to say, but I know I can't write forever. Thank You for loving me the right way and for caring about me and listening to me and for forgiving me. Words cannot describe how thankful I am to you for all of these things and to God for allowing us to see these miraculous changes in each other!!! I hope in the end God wants us to be together and we can love each other the right way forever—but in the meantime I will be praying for God's will because He knows best."

She signed her letter: "I love you more than ever—Denise."

Considering the despicable crime Brian had confessed to committing just three years before Denise had written these words—and what Denise was now on trial for herself—her lengthy missive was stunning. How could two people who participated in the most heinous atrocity known to humankind at the same time be leading a "purpose-driven life" fully devoted to God? The juxtaposition between the thrust of Denise's letter and the brutal murder of Mike Williams—her devoted husband and Brian's best friend—couldn't have been more stark. It was almost as if Denise and Brian, in some sick way, had decided they could wash away their God-awful sins by fully committing themselves to God. "I'm sorry," her letter seemed to be saying. "I'll do better now. The next 40 days of devotion and spiritual focus will fix everything."

Though none of Denise's words were in and of themselves incriminating, they were illuminating nonetheless. Her letter provided an open window into her psyche, a glimpse through her own telling that jurors hadn't gotten to see in any other piece of evidence during the three-day trial.

By the time they each had their turn with Denise's letter, the vote in favor of guilt had grown to 11-1. The lone holdout was Jim Karabasz, a retired executive, who at 76 was by far the oldest member of the jury. Indeed, whereas Kierra Idlett, the foreperson, was a year younger than Anslee Williams, Karabasz was two years older than Cheryl, her grandmother.

Unlike most of the other jurors, having just recently moved to Tallahassee before receiving his jury summons, Karabasz hadn't learned anything about the case at all. With a business degree from the University of Miami, he was one of the more well-educated members of the jury and by far the most successful, having risen in his career to the position of vice president of Midas International. At one time, he also owned six Midas franchises, four in southwest Florida.

Despite the others' readiness to convict—and get home

for the weekend—Karabasz dug in. Something Brian had said during his testimony had given him pause—that when he and Denise planned out the murder, Denise had said, "If he drowns, it's God's will. If he lives, it's also God's will."

Though Karabasz believed Brian's testimony that he and Denise had plotted together to kill Mike, something about Brian pulling out a shotgun and blasting a hole in Mike's face, in his view, diminished Denise's culpability. That wasn't what she had ever intended, Karabasz told his fellow jurors. Brian's decision to point his 12-gauge shotgun at Mike's head and pull the trigger, he argued to the others, was one Brian alone made without Denise's input or approval. She had only agreed to Brian pushing Mike overboard with his waders on.

By the time Mike extricated himself from his waders and clung to safety at the tree stump, Karabasz believed, Brian had become a free agent—his decisions from that point his and his alone. He doubted that Denise could be guilty for Brian's actions from that point forward.

But his efforts to budge his fellow jurors on this line of thinking was going absolutely nowhere. The stalemate seemed intractable, the other 11 jurors becoming increasingly frustrated with each passing hour. Karabasz kept arguing with them. Yet he was no more successful bringing any of them into his camp than they were getting him to side with them.

It was beginning to look as if the trial would conclude with a hung jury, meaning everyone's efforts would have been little more than a rehearsal for a new trial. Even worse, the key participants, witnesses, and family members would have to relive their intensely emotional experiences all over again.

At a deadlock for nearly seven hours, one of the jurors suggested getting ahold of Brian's testimony so they could review together the portion that seemed to be twisting Karabasz into knots. Perhaps that would break the impasse, several thought. The foreperson Kierra Idlett dashed off a quick note to the judge: "Can we have Brian's testimony? Is it possible?" She knocked on the door and handed the note to the bailiff.

Moments later, at 6:35 p.m., the jurors were seated in their familiar seats in the jury box. Much to their chagrin, Judge

Hankinson explained that it wouldn't be possible for them to have a transcript of Brian's testimony. The court reporter could read his testimony to them, he explained, but doing so would take somewhere between three and a half and four hours.

The judge told the jurors that if they could narrow down what they wanted to hear from Brian's testimony to a very specific segment, that might be possible. But because of the late hour, if they really wanted to hear again all of Brian's testimony, they would have to come back on Saturday morning. He asked them to step back into the jury room to decide how they wanted to proceed.

Just a few minutes later, Idlett sent out another note to the judge letting him know they were "trying to overcome a request for portions of Brian Winchester's testimony and would like to deliberate without it." They would make one final attempt to reach a verdict before calling it a day. A very long day at that.

••••

Suddenly, there was another knock on the jury room door. Though the betting odds were that jurors would give up for the day and come back in the morning, the note the bailiff delivered to Judge Hankinson had an entirely different message. They had reached a verdict. After eight solid hours of deliberations.

Denise was led into the courtroom, taking her seat beside Phil Padovano and Ethan Way. Jon Fuchs and Andy Rogers nervously awaited the news from the prosecution table.

The gallery filled in quickly, Denise's sisters and friends clustered together in anxious anticipation behind the defense table.

Jennifer Winchester, Brian's sister, sat a few rows behind them.

Cheryl's closest friends and kids from her daycare, Denise Brogdon—Mike's first Denise—and Clay and Patti Ketcham took their places in the rows behind the prosecution table.

Jennifer Portman sat up front banging away on her laptop.

Nick, his wife Jeanne, and Cheryl were among the last to enter the courtroom. Cheryl was wheeled into the aisle between the two sets of wooden pews, her wheelchair parked toward the front of the gallery. She was wearing a white coat, black dress, and a long necklace. Attached to the bottom of her necklace were two rings—gold wedding bands—the ones she and her husband Jerry slipped on the day they were married. Nick took a seat directly behind his mother, his hand resting on her shoulder for comfort.

"All right. Let's have the jury please," the judge instructed the bailiff. The 12 jurors walked back in slowly and took their seats, weary expressions on many of their faces. The tension in the courtroom was palpable, almost unbearable.

"Has the jury arrived at a verdict?" Judge Hankinson asked.

"Yes," Idlett replied.

"Would you hand it to the bailiff please?" the judge asked.

Glancing at the piece of paper in front of him, Judge Hankinson began to read the jury's verdict, his voice devoid of any emotion at all: "We the jury find as follows as to Count 1 of the indictment: the defendant is *guilty* of conspiracy to commit first-degree murder. As to Count 2, we the jury find the defendant is *guilty* of first-degree murder. We the jury find as follows as to Count 3 of the indictment: the defendant is *guilty* of accessory after the fact of first-degree murder."

As she had throughout the entire trial, Denise stared straight ahead, without flinching, wincing, or shedding a tear. No emotional reaction whatsoever. Consistent from beginning to end.

Ethan Way asked that jurors be polled individually to ensure that the verdict as read was truly the verdict of each and every juror. The judge then asked each juror if the verdict he had just read accurately reflected his or her own verdict. One by one, the six men and six women comprising the jury—including Jim Karabasz—confirmed that it did.

"The jury has unanimously confirmed the verdict," the judge announced. "It appears to be in order. It will be filed."

Behind the defense counsel table, Denise's three sisters sat in stunned silence. Jennifer Winchester began weeping loudly. Nearly everyone filling the pews behind the prosecution table broke out in tears, including Cheryl Williams, whose relentless 18-year crusade to learn the truth, and then to bring those responsible for Mike's death to justice, was finally over.

Within minutes, Denise was led out of the courtroom by armed sheriff's deputies—her hands already cuffed in front of her, her ankles shackled together with a metal chain. She would soon be exchanging her pretty pink sweater for a drab blue jumpsuit, her civilian clothing minutes away from being a thing of the past.

Moments after hearing the word "guilty" announced three times, Jon Fuchs raced back to the gallery to give Cheryl Williams a bear hug, feeling the intense emotions of the entire week reach a fever pitch as he wrapped his huge arms around her.

"We got justice for Michael," Cheryl told him, thick tears rolling down her cheeks.

In the hallway outside the courtroom, Jennifer Portman found herself in a most unusual situation. TV cameras were pointed at her and a microphone stuck in her face, reporters asking for her reaction. "There's no good that comes out of this for anyone at all," she lamented through a steady stream of tears. "I just feel so sorry for everyone involved. Like after 18 years, you know, to get a resolution like this, that's something."

A reporter asked if she had any words for Cheryl. "Oh my God," she responded. "Cheryl knows I love her. She's more deserving of some kind of justice and some sort of peace than any person I know."

Clay Ketcham, upon seeing Portman out of the corner of his eye as he and Patti walked out of the courtroom—drained from the long day's emotional roller coaster—rushed up to the journalist and hugged her tightly.

"You did it!" Clay told her through his tears.

"No, I didn't," Portman replied through her own, refusing to take credit for her tireless devotion to Mike's cause for more than 12 years.

"You did," he insisted. "You gave Cheryl a voice."

There were many more hugs that evening and a lot more tears. Mike Williams' life and death had now come full circle. From the hugs and tears born of anguish, despair, and sorrow in December 2000 to the hugs and tears of closure, finality, and justice in December 2018. Just one final step remained for Cheryl Ann Williams to add peace to that list.

••••

Denise's sentencing took place the morning of February 6, 2019. Unlike the last time the defendant, her lawyers, the prosecutors, and Judge Hankinson had all been assembled together in a courtroom, there would be little suspense that morning, the day's proceedings a mere formality, lasting all of 14 minutes. Florida law provided only one possible sentence for a defendant convicted of first-degree murder where the State hadn't sought the death penalty—life in prison without the possibility of parole.

Denise sat at her counsel table sandwiched between Ethan Way and Phil Padovano—this time wearing a blue jumpsuit with the words "Leon County Jail" stitched in white lettering across the back. Though Jennifer Portman and the media writ large were back in the courtroom, the lack of suspense made the morning's hearing somewhat anticlimactic. With one exception, however. The time had finally come for Cheryl Ann Williams to take center stage.

Nick pushed his mother's wheelchair into the well of the courtroom, where she sat directly in front of—but far below—Judge Hankinson. The 75-year-old grandmother held her prepared, typewritten remarks in her trembling hands. Nick stood to her right, her victim's advocate to her left, as she read her victim impact statement. Her words were crisp, resolute, and heartfelt—nearly 20 years of raw emotion making it difficult at times for her to get them to leave her mouth.

"On the morning of December 16, 2000," she began, "the world as I knew it changed forever. Denise, my daughter-in-law, called to tell Nick and me that Mike was late returning from a duck hunting trip to Lake Seminole in Sneads, Florida. Her father and a friend had been to the lake and found Mike's truck and trailer. There was no sign of Mike."

She recounted her first trip to the lake, when "God told me Mike was not in Lake Seminole. He didn't drown. He didn't get eaten by alligators. I had to find him and bring him home," she said, her voice cracking, tears already cascading down the faces of spectators filling the gallery.

She described her personal crusade over the next 17 years to find him, making telephone calls, putting up missing-person signs, compiling her copious notes, having people post on social media, paying for billboards and ads in the *Democrat*.

"I stood on street corners waving my picket signs with pictures of Mike on them," she said. "I was cussed out by ministers for being too close to their church."

Cheryl told the judge how state and local officials had failed her time and time again. "I wrote 2,600 letters to the Governor of Florida asking for help in finding my son. I begged Fish and Game to do a criminal investigation. They told me Mike drowned and got eaten by alligators and there was no need for an investigation. They laughed at me and called me crazy."

She then directed her comments at her daughter-in-law—the one sitting just a few feet away in a blue jumpsuit. "Nine months after Mike disappeared," she said, "his wife Denise told me if I continued to seek a criminal investigation, I would lose Anslee, my granddaughter, Mike's only child. Denise might as well have waved a red flag in front of a bull. I knew that she knew where Mike was or what happened to him."

"Judge Hankinson, I am a fighter, not a victim," Cheryl continued. "I love Anslee, but Mike was my son." After Denise's ultimatum, she said, "I became even more determined to find the truth. If I had not done what I did for 17 years, Mike's disappearance would have never been solved." No one seated in the courtroom that morning could have doubted those words in the slightest.

"It took me three and a half years to get FDLE to open

an investigation into Mike's disappearance," she lamented, "because the Winchester and Merrell families pushed the theory that alligators had eaten Mike. Fish and Game and FDLE should have known that alligators are ectothermic. They don't eat in cold water."

"Instead of investigating, they chose to ridicule and call me crazy and tell me that I didn't do things the right way," she told the judge, her voice breaking up as she recounted that heartbreaking fact. "There is no manual to tell a mother what to do when her child goes missing. I just did what God put on my heart to do."

Cheryl then got to the most difficult, gut-wrenching portion of her remarks, telling the judge that "not only did Denise kill my son, she stole my granddaughter Anslee, Mike's only child. For her entire life, Anslee was raised in the house with the murderers of her father, while being denied the love of her father's family. She was told that Grand Mama Ms. Cheryl was crazy and would hurt her. I have had no relationship with her since she was five and a half years old."

Stating the obvious, she told Judge Hankinson that no amount of prison time "will bring Mike back to me. I don't know if I will ever have Anslee in my life again because of the damage her mother has done. I am asking you to lock Denise Merrell Williams Winchester up for the rest of her life with no chance of parole. She has already lived 18 years longer than my son. She got to watch Mike's daughter grow up. Nick, Mike, and I didn't," she said, tears now flowing steadily down her cheeks.

She implored Judge Hankinson: "Please don't allow Denise to ever be around any of her future grandchildren because one generation of Williams children growing up around murderers is enough."

Her words now crackling with intense emotion, Cheryl painted the horrific image she told Judge Hankinson she would be seeing "for the rest of my life as I try to sleep at night. I will see my son clinging to a tree stump in Lake Seminole in the dark, knowing that his best friend is trying to kill him. I hear his voice screaming for help," she said, almost shrieking as if she were standing on the banks of Lake Seminole watching helplessly as Brian pointed his shotgun at her son's face. "I wasn't there to help him. It will haunt me forever."

"In conclusion, Judge Hankinson, we are in this courtroom today because of God, not Cheryl Williams. I am Mike's mother and I did what God told me to do. My son's horrific death demands justice. With today's sentencing of Denise Merrell Williams Winchester, I believe justice will have been served. Thank you."

Nick wheeled his courageous mother away from Judge Hankinson as she dabbed at her cheeks with a crumpled tissue. As if that might slow the steady stream of tears let loose by her emotionally charged statement.

Cheryl had set off a chain reaction. Virtually everyone in the gallery was now bawling. Her words were moving and powerful, grabbing anyone whose blood ran warm by the heart. In five short minutes, she had encapsulated the deeply emotional journey on which she and she alone had been for more than 18 years.

Just one final act remained and it would all be over. Denise and her lawyers stood up for the judge to issue his sentence on the conspiracy and first-degree murder charges. The accessory charge had been dropped after the verdict because it was redundant.

Judge Hankinson meted out the maximum punishment on the conspiracy charge—30 years—and the only punishment reserved for first-degree murder in a non-capital case: life in prison.

His sentence pronounced, the judge passed on the opportunity to make his own statement—about the trial, the verdict, or the conduct that had led Denise Merrell Williams down her path to prison. He simply wished her luck and adjourned court.

Denise was whisked out of the courtroom one final time, ultimately destined for the Women's Reception Center in Ocala, Florida—a correctional facility located two and a half hours from Tallahassee. Where a small, dank prison cell awaited her.

19

Upon Further Reflection

Though trials often bring pieces of a vexing puzzle together in a much clearer picture, it isn't uncommon for them to conclude with key pieces missing or seemingly out of place. That can result in a tumble of questions, some of which can be answered only upon deep reflection and analysis, long after the dust settles. Others may go forever unanswered and haunt those in search of ultimate closure. Alternate theories about Mike Williams' murder—and profound but unanswerable questions—abound to this day.

Despite the jury's verdict, and Brian's compelling testimony that he shot Mike in the face while his best friend was clinging to a tree stump, some have been unable to let go of their belief that Mike was never even at Lake Seminole that December morning and posit instead that Mike was murdered in Tallahassee, possibly even inside his own home.

Mike's burial at Carr Lake, these disbelievers contend, suggests that his murder occurred much closer to home than at Lake Seminole—some 50 miles away. Those in this camp explain the presence of Mike's truck, trailer, and boat near Stump Field as elaborate staging designed to throw law enforcement off track as well as to lend credence to the drowning theory that ultimately took hold.

There are even some who consider it more likely that Denise had been the one to pull the trigger and that Brian merely helped her cover it all up after the fact. The thinking along those lines is that Mike either caught Brian and Denise in the act or finally figured out they were having an affair. Once the jig was up, either in the heat of passion or with some level of premeditation, Denise was left with no other choice than to off her husband, so the theory goes.

However interesting these theories might be to ponder, the evidence makes them highly improbable. Mike arrived at Ketcham Appraisal at about 4:00 the morning of December 16, 2000. That is when the Sonitrol alarm system indicated someone had entered the building. That fact just happens to perfectly coincide with Brian's testimony that he met Mike on Thomasville Road—nearby Mike's office—at about that time to begin their drive to Lake Seminole.

Mike's autopsy locks in another undeniable fact: he was shot in the face from very close range—which also matches Brian's description of the murder. Accepting that fact, it's highly implausible that he was murdered indoors. A shotgun blast to the head would have sent blood splattering on walls, flooring, and furniture—too many places for his killer or killers to have concealed. Sooner or later, that blood would have been discovered. That makes it difficult to make a case that Mike's murder happened anywhere other than outdoors.

For those who believe that Denise or Brian could have been in some remote outdoor location closer to Tallahassee and lured Mike to his death there after 4:00 a.m., the ticking clock and distance to Lake Seminole make any such theory highly improbable. It would have taken two people to move the Ford Bronco and Gheenoe motorboat to Lake Seminole and then coordinate a return to Tallahassee. And if Denise made that trip, where was Anslee? At home by herself? Not likely. Meanwhile, someone had to be at Carr Lake to dig Mike's grave and push him in. Who did that?

Brian's deeply emotional narrative is far more likely the accurate story of how Mike's life came to an end. Not only are there key pieces of tangible evidence that match his testimony, Brian's recounting of the murder didn't vary in the slightest details in the *five* different statements he gave: three to investigators between October 2017 and February 2018, his pretrial deposition conducted by Ethan Way, and his testimony at trial.

Some of those details he described so vividly—including how he panicked when Mike got the waders off, his close calls with law enforcement officers, and the ants swarming his legs as he dug Mike's grave—it seems far more likely his testimony was truthful rather than a contrived collection of lies.

••••

Zooming out further from the evidence presented at trial, other aspects of the case come into sharper focus, allowing additional glimpses into the psyches of both Denise and Brian.

When Mike and Denise moved into their new home at Centennial Oaks Circle in August 1999, they decorated the walls of the master bedroom with large framed pictures of their wedding. Those pictures of a smiling Mike in his tux and a seemingly happy Denise in her wedding gown greeted them every morning when they arose from their sacred, marital bed.

Yet during the last 16 months of Mike's life, the only person who would make love to his wife in that bed wasn't the man smiling in those pictures. Rather, it was the man Mike believed was his best friend. As Mike had confided in a coworker and even in Brian, he and Denise didn't have sex a single time after she gave birth to Anslee in May 1999. Yet she and Brian were having sex as many as 15 times a week, sometimes in that very bed.

It is downright creepy to think about Denise and Brian having sex in that bed with her wedding pictures with Mike hanging on the walls all around them. And even more chilling to ponder the discussions they were having as their sweaty bodies cooled after their lovemaking. About how they would eliminate Mike from the picture so they could be together whenever they wanted, not just when Mike was at work and the coast was clear.

Once Mike was gone, Denise and Brian presumably began using that bed even more frequently, as their time constraints no longer existed. Only now, the smiling pictures of

Mike staring at them from the walls was of the man they had murdered—and taken away from his only child.

How on earth could a man and woman who had brutally and selfishly snuffed out another life stomach the thought of their victim's smiling face staring at them every time they made love—*in his bed*?

If those mind-blowing thoughts aren't sufficiently disturbing, it's worth considering how Denise and Brian moved on with their lives in the years that followed. The very same man who had blasted a spray of tiny pellets into Mike's brain and hidden his lifeless body in a shallow hole quickly assumed the role of Anslee's father. What mom would welcome the killer of her child's father into her home, much less allow him to become her new dad? Denise Merrell Williams didn't bat an eye at that very notion. She actually embraced it.

Consider how Denise and Brian presented themselves to society at large once they were married. Month after month, year after year, they would take Anslee to North Florida Christian School in the morning, watch her middle school volleyball and softball games—where she wore the same number 25 Mike sported on his football jersey decades before—and act as if their marriage and parenting were perfectly normal and wholesome.

They would take Anslee and her friends waterskiing and wakeboarding, presenting themselves as upstanding parents sharing their good fortunes with their daughter's friends. They would attend church services together as a family as if they were God-fearing Christians living virtuous lives.

Yet it was all a mirage. A charade. Denise and Brian weren't upstanding parents and certainly weren't God-fearing Christians. No, they actually were the killers of Anslee's father, who year after year literally continued to get away with murder.

••••

Another question many continue to wonder about is whether Anslee actually is Mike's child, rather than Brian's.

Since Brian and Denise started hooking up in October 1997—months before Anslee was conceived—that possibility certainly exists. Though it wasn't terribly relevant to the homicide case, Ethan Way couldn't resist putting this very question to Brian during his pretrial deposition. Brian told the defense attorney that he was 99% sure he isn't Anslee's dad.

When asked why he believed that, Brian explained, "Because her appearance looks too much like Mike." That is exactly what Cheryl, Nick, and Clay and Patti Ketcham believe as well. The uncanny resemblance between Mike and Anslee—both blessed with piercing blue eyes—would seem to foreclose any possibility that Brian could be her real father. Yet until a DNA test is done, no one will ever know for sure.

••••

Jon Fuchs gave jurors a small window into Denise's psyche during his final closing argument, telling them, "That's a cold individual." He made that remark in reference to Denise signing a claim form to collect on Mike's life insurance policies a mere 19 days after he went missing. He also reminded jurors how she didn't "bat an eye" or "shed a tear" as Brian described his brutal assassination of her husband. Rather, she listened to that testimony "absolute[ly] stone-faced," the Assistant State Attorney had said.

Once again, zooming out just a bit from the evidence presented at trial, it doesn't take very much to open that window into Denise's psyche a good bit wider. Just think about life from her vantage point the final week of Mike's life—the week she knew would be his last. It was Christmastime, after all, with vibrant decorations displayed throughout their Centennial Oaks home, most of which were her handiwork. Presents for Anslee were piled under the tree, awaiting her tiny hands on Christmas morning.

That Thursday, Deanna was over to snap their annual portrait in front of the Christmas tree—Denise, Mike, and Anslee all smiling as if they were the featured family in the holiday issue of *Better Homes & Gardens*. What's hidden, though, was the darkness lurking behind Denise's smile—and the evil thoughts cascading around in her mind the moment the camera flashed.

That same evening, they sat and watched *Friends* in the living room as an extended family. Denise was the one who told Cheryl and Nick that she and Mike were planning to have have another baby, implying she was still very much in love with her husband and anxious to deepen their relationship. All the while knowing full well he would be dead and gone in less than two days—long before Christmas arrived. Now *that* is a cold individual.

••••

It's difficult to bring this story to a close without pondering two questions for which there are no real answers. First, what thoughts likely flashed through Mike's mind in the final moments of his life?

Mike's best friend since the ninth grade had just pushed him out of his own boat into the freezing cold water. As he got his waders off and clung to safety at the tree stump, what was Mike thinking as he saw Brian pick up his shotgun and pump it full of ammunition? As his eyes met Brian's for the very last time and saw the steel barrel of Brian's weapon aimed at his face?

Was that the moment it clicked that Brian was the one who had been having an affair with his wife? Did he finally realize that Brian wasn't actually his best friend—but rather his worst enemy? Did it dawn on him that Brian was merely doing what Denise asked him to do, no different from the many times Mike himself had rushed to the gas station to pump her gas? Did he have a chance to think about his beautiful baby girl he would never get to raise—or his devoted mother and brother he would leave behind—before the 70-plus shotgun pellets penetrated through his skull?

Second, what kind of life would Jerry Michael Williams have led had it not ended in a senseless act of selfishness, brutality, and cowardice that early December morning? What if

Denise had shown the human decency to simply divorce him, rather than execute him?

It seems obvious that Mike would have relished his time with Anslee on his custodial days and raised her with his loving, guiding hand, just as his own father J.J. had raised him. His success as a real estate appraiser portended partnership with Clay Ketcham or Mike establishing his own successful firm, and possibly a run for political office as well.

At only 31, Mike would have had ample time to meet another woman, hopefully one who—unlike Denise—would appreciate all of his special qualities. He desperately wanted more children. Anslee could have grown up with a half-brother or half-sister, or maybe one of each.

Without doubt, Mike would have continued to play an important role in Cheryl's life as she grew older instead of leaving the gargantuan void in her heart she has never been able to fill. Surely, he would have been the best man at Nick's wedding in 2004 and a fun-loving uncle to his brother's daughter Phoebe, now 13.

Although Denise wouldn't have supported—much less encouraged—her daughter's relationship with Cheryl and Nick, Mike would have made sure that Anslee was as much a part of their lives as any grandmother or uncle could have hoped for. Now a 21-year-old getting ready to begin her senior year at Florida State, Anslee would likely be proud to tell her classmates and Alpha Phi sorority sisters about her smart, gritty grandmother.

After having been raised for nearly her entire childhood by her father's killers, there's no telling what Anslee currently thinks or believes about her Grand Mama Cheryl. Her thoughts are almost certainly tarnished by the poisonous lies she heard repeatedly over the years. Yet, maybe one day she will be able to extend her hand to Cheryl again as she did as a five-year-old when the two walked down the aisle together at Nick's wedding as flower girl and flower grandma.

For Cheryl, now 76, hope springs eternal for such a reconnection. Her own mother still lives independently at 94 so she's hoping the years won't run out before Anslee is ready to extend that hand. She's not giving up. Anyone who knows Cheryl Ann Williams would be quick to say that the tenacious, pigtailed grandmother *never* gives up. No matter the odds stacked against her.

••••

The Mike Williams saga no doubt reveals the deep flaws permeating the human condition: the narcissism, hedonism, and pure, unadulterated greed that unfortunately exists all around us. But just as importantly, this story also poignantly illustrates what separates humans from the rest of the animal kingdom: our insatiable hunger and unquenchable thirst for justice. For every Denise there is a Cheryl Williams. For every Brian, a Jennifer Portman. There truly is good in this world. It doesn't always prevail, but when it does, it is oh so sweet.

A shotgun blast that foggy December morning near Sneads may have ended the life of the 31-year-old Tallahassee native and Florida State graduate who is the subject of this story. It may have abruptly halted the career of an accomplished real-estate appraiser whose future was shining brightly. It may have cruelly extinguished the boundless love of a doting father, beloved son, and loyal brother. But make no mistake. The legacy of this special man will endure. His life truly did have meaning and purpose far beyond his brief time on earth. Those whom he touched will never, ever forget him.

Rest in peace Jerry Michael Williams.

**A very bad day: Brian's mugshot
following the August 5, 2016
kidnapping incident.**

**Denise had no desire to discuss
Mike's disappearance with Mike
DeVaney.**

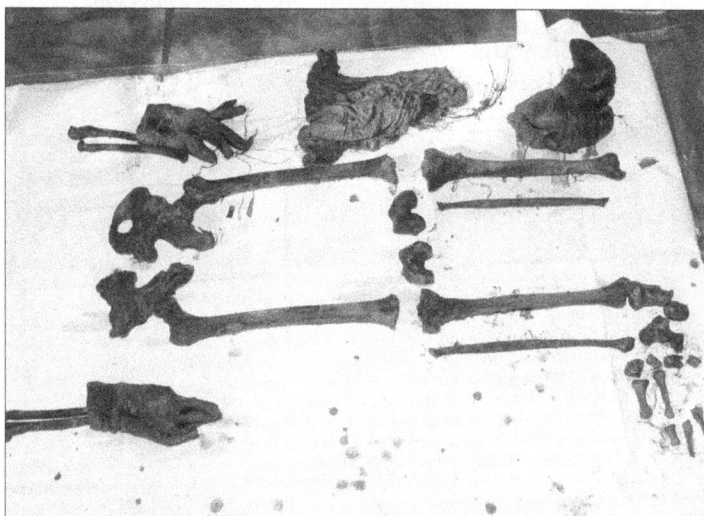

**The grisly carnage unearthed at Carr Lake, including even clearly
recognizable articles of Mike's clothing (top).**

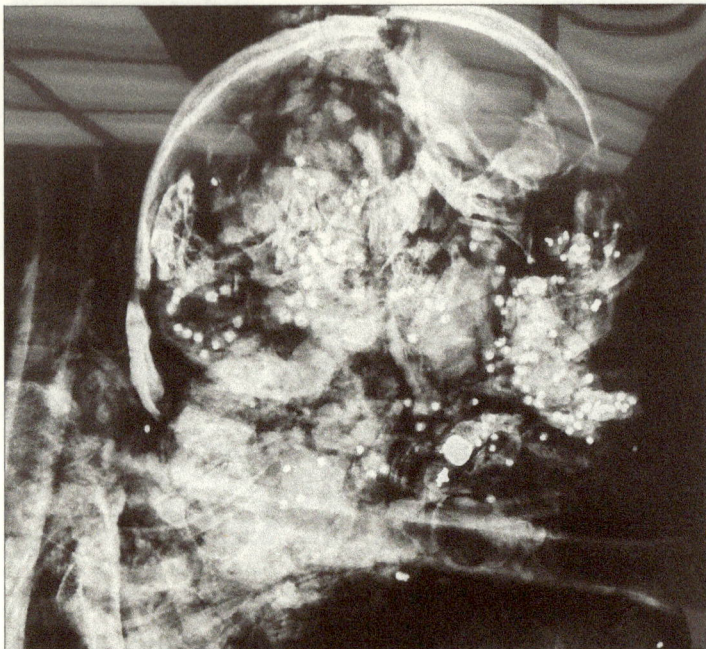

Photo courtesy of the Florida Second Circuit State Attorney's Office.

X-ray of Mike's skull riddled with birdshot from Brian's shotgun.

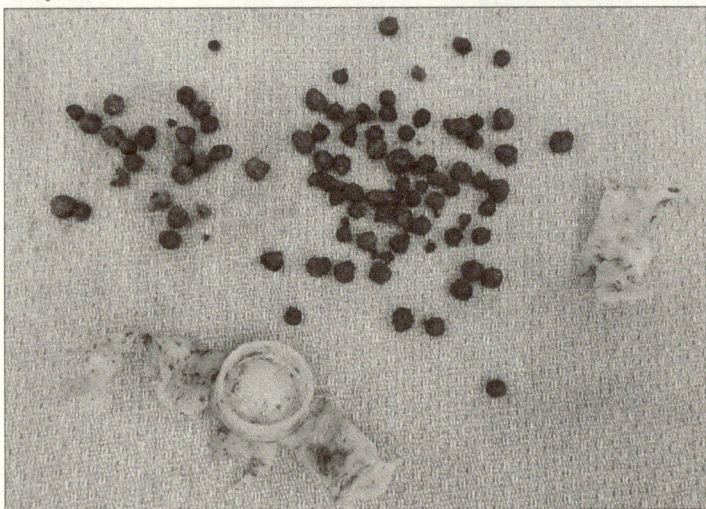

Photo courtesy of the Florida Second Circuit State Attorney's Office.

Over 70 birdshot pellets and the shell's plastic cup that blasted from Brian's shotgun and lodged in Mike's skull.

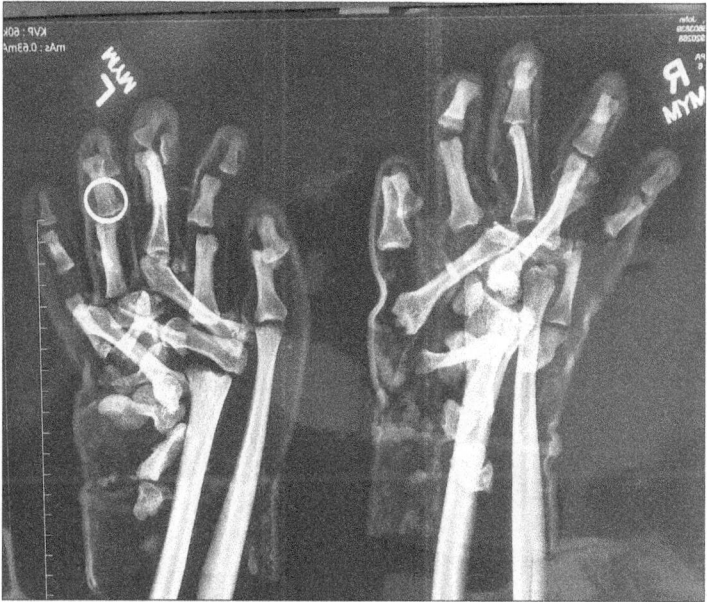

Photo courtesy of the Florida Second Circuit State Attorney's Office.

Mike's wedding ring still on his finger, 17 years after his murder.

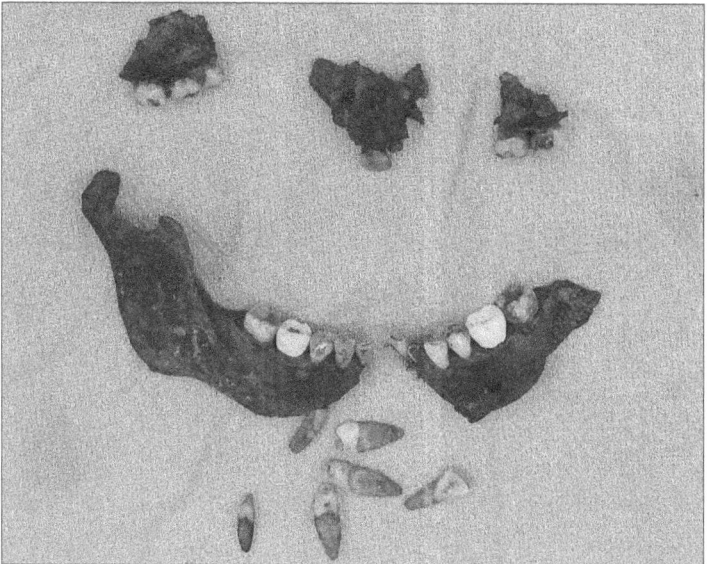

Photo courtesy of the Florida Second Circuit State Attorney's Office.

Mike's jaw and teeth, incredibly well-preserved after 17 years.

*Photo used with permission. © Joe Rondone / Tallahassee Democrat—
USA TODAY Network via Imagn Content Services, LLC.*

The long-awaited walk of shame. Not exactly dressed for the evening news, Denise is paraded across the Florida State campus.

Photo courtesy of the Leon County Detention Center.

The eyes of a killer? Denise's first mugshot.

Photo courtesy of the Leon County Detention Center.

Sans makeup and blowdryer: mugshot #2.

Photo courtesy of the Law & Crime Network.

Judge James Hankinson ran a tight ship during the trial.

Photo courtesy of the Law & Crime Network.

Assistant State Attorney Jon Fuchs implores the jury to find Denise guilty.

Photo courtesy of Patti Ketcham,

Assistant State Attorney Andy Rogers awaits the jury's verdict.

Defense lawyer Ethan Way argues with gusto for Denise's acquittal.

Retired judge and defense lawyer Phil Padovano tells jurors the evidence doesn't add up.

Denise, moments before passing on the chance to testify in her own defense.

Photo courtesy of the Law & Crime Network.

The State's star witness (and cold-blooded killer): Brian Winchester.

Photo courtesy of the Law & Crime Network.

The third woman who joined the fight for justice: Kathy (Winchester) Thomas.

Photo courtesy of the Law & Crime Network.

Cheryl finally gets to speak after 18 years of anguish.

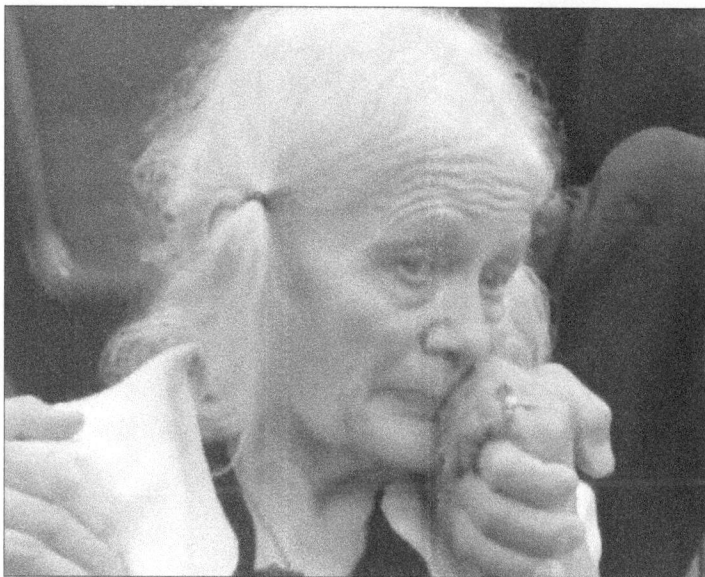

Hearing the word "guilty" three times wouldn't bring Mike back to her.

Happy day: Clay Ketcham with daughter Lindsay and Angela Stafford.

Photo courtesy of Patti Ketcham.

Lindsay (Ketcham) Lockhart elated with the jury's decision.

Photo courtesy of the Law & Crime Network.

Her last breath of public air: Denise leaving the courtroom after being sentenced to life in prison.

Acknowledgements

The foregoing pages wouldn't have been possible without the contributions of numerous people whose lives were profoundly affected by Mike Williams, both while he was alive and after he went missing. I was very fortunate they were willing to share with me their stories about Mike and how the mystery surrounding his disappearance impacted them.

In December 2019, I made my own pilgrimage to Tallahassee and to Lake Seminole, to see for myself many of the sites I describe. I am proud to say the picture of Stump Field adorning the front cover—snapped amid a stunningly beautiful sunrise—was taken by yours truly (with an iPhone), while standing in the very spot where Mike's boat was likely launched that fateful morning 19 years earlier.

I'm grateful to Alton Ranew for allowing me to climb aboard his boat and survey Stump Field for myself. And even more thankful for his quick reflexes. When his boat unexpectedly collided with an underwater stump, my body lurched forward violently. I was saved at the last second by Alton's strong grip on the back of my life jacket just as I was about to tumble into the water—not more than a few yards from where Mike and Brian had been when the horrific events described in Chapter 10 transpired.

Alton, David Arnette, and Jeff Jackson were also kind enough to sit with me as I read them an early version of Chapter 1, helping me fact-check each and every detail of the months-long search for Mike. Even after returning to Raleigh,

Alton continued to assist me in fact-checking intricate details surrounding Lake Seminole and the search for Mike. Derrick Wester helped me fact-check several details from the early days of the criminal investigation.

Clay and Patti Ketcham, who I was lucky enough to meet during my Tallahassee trip, were very generous with their time, support, and encouragement. They spoke with me about Mike numerous times and for many hours and also put me in touch with others who could help me tell this story. Patti was also kind enough to read the finished manuscript and provide insightful comments. I'm grateful to them both.

I'm also thankful to Clay and Patti's daughter Lindsay Lockhart and son Brett Ketcham, who shared with me their own fond remembrances of Mike and, in Brett's case, his recollections of Brian's behavior during the initial days of the search at Lake Seminole. Mike's coworker at Ketcham Appraisal, Damon Japer, also provided helpful insights.

While in Tallahassee, I had three amazing tour guides shuttling me to nearly every venue described in the book: Mary Denmark, her daughter Marya—who was a six-year-old in Cheryl's care at the time of Mike's death—and Denise (Pate) Brogdon, Mike's first Denise (and the one Cheryl rejected). Marya air-dropped onto my iPhone hundreds of photos of Mike, several of which I included in the photo inserts. And Denise shared with me her heartfelt recollections of Mike as they grew up together on Jeffrey Road, briefly as boyfriend and girlfriend. She also read the completed manuscript and offered helpful thoughts.

Mike's NFC classmates and other kids who grew up under Cheryl's care provided background and texture that enriched my descriptions of his formative years, most notably Rachel Drew, to whom Mike was like a big brother. Rachel shared with me several stories that found their way into Chapters 2 and 3, not only depicting Mike's strengths, but his weaknesses as well. Her father Howard—Mike's hunting mentor—also provided insightful thoughts and comments about his pupil and the search to find him.

Amazingly, Jason Fykes, one of Cheryl's kids who befriended Mike while still in elementary school, was able to impart vivid recollections of Mike as a mischievous boy all these years later.

Scott Dungey and Jennifer Stinson, Mike's classmates at NFC, provided valuable insights not only about Mike, but about Denise, Brian, and Kathy as well. Jennifer was also kind enough to cull through her NFC yearbooks, sending me screenshots of the numerous pages on which Mike, Denise, Brian, and Kathy appeared in the various roles they played in high school.

For background information on the legal characters—Judge Hankinson, Tim Jansen, Ethan Way, Phil Padovano, Jon Fuchs, and Andy Rogers—I'm thankful to Don Pumphrey and John Leace, two excellent Tallahassee lawyers.

When I began this project in August 2019, I needed quick access to information and documents and turned to an energetic, free-spirited private investigator, Burt Hodge, for help. Though Burt charged me for his time, he got back to me promptly each time I needed something and helped get me out of the starting blocks very quickly.

Thanks to Jim Karabasz's willingness to share with me his experience as a juror—for which I am grateful—I was able to provide the reader a rare window into the jury room as 12 men and women from completely disparate walks of life worked together as citizens to deliberate over Denise's guilt or innocence.

I'm especially thankful for the able assistance and encouragement I received from Anne Blythe, a long-time newspaper reporter in Raleigh who thoroughly reviewed and commented on the manuscript. Anne has an amazing knack for words and "visual writing," helping me tell this story more vividly than I could have on my own. She deserves credit for some of the most colorful, descriptive passages in the book.

I'm equally grateful to Kerry McQuisten and Black Lyon Publishing, who took a huge gamble on an unknown wannabe author in January 2019, accepting *Murder on Birchleaf Drive* as BLP's very first true crime publication. I couldn't be happier to be on this second journey with Kerry and her wonderful company—very proud to have authored its second work in that genre.

I owe a tremendous debt of gratitude to two incredible women, without whom this book would have read like a missing-person story, rather than one ending with answers and justice: Jennifer Portman and Cheryl Williams.

As the foregoing pages hopefully make clear, without Jennifer's persistence and beautifully written stories in the *Tallahassee Democrat*, very few people would have known about Mike Williams and his killers likely would never have been brought to justice. For my purposes, her dozens of articles and columns provided the foundation upon which I was able to construct the larger narrative told in this book.

I'm enormously grateful to Cheryl Ann Williams for allowing me to tell her son's story—indeed, *her* story. Though her son's tragic death and her heartbreaking loss make the word "heroine" seem misplaced, Cheryl truly is just that: a heroine. As Jennifer Portman made clear in article after article, were it not for Cheryl's tenacity, grit, and perseverance, no one would ever have been able to tell (or write) the true story about what happened to Mike. And no one would have been brought to justice for killing him.

When I first wrote Cheryl in September 2019, I had no expectation or belief she would even respond. Yet within just a few days, as I answered my office phone for what I expected to be a routine business call, I heard the words, "This is Cheryl Williams" for the first time. She told me she wanted the entire world to know her son's story, and was pleased I had committed to writing it.

One of the most gratifying parts of this journey was getting to know this amazing woman. I will never meet anyone else like Cheryl Williams as long as I live. I so appreciate her insights, support, and encouragement and hope with all my might she likes the finished product.

Last, but certainly not least, is my family: my beautiful and talented wife Aletia and amazing children Benjamin, Madeline, Enzo, Tucker, and Thomas. Unlike my last project, my children—to whom this book is dedicated—were fully aware of this one in real time. And very supportive. My wife Aletia deserves a medal for putting up with me during the many hours I would go dark—despite being in her midst—and others where my mind would wander to Lake Seminole or Tallahassee even while seated next to her on the couch in our living room.

Aletia was my sounding board as many of the chapters of this book took shape and, as in everything else I do, her support made this process so much more rewarding. Thanks for being there for me and for your never-ending love and support, Sweetheart. Yes, we can now take that much-needed vacation.

❧